BLOODY PARALYSER

BLOODY PARALYSER

THE GIANT HANDLEY PAGE BOMBERS
OF THE FIRST WORLD WAR

ROB LANGHAM

FONTHILL

Dedicated to my friends and family for their support, particularly Cocoa who has served as a suitable good luck mascot—like his kin were for the Handley Pages and crew of 7 Squadron Royal Naval Air Service and 207 Squadron Royal Air Force in 1917–18.

Fonthill Media Language Policy

Fonthill Media publishes in the international English language market. One language edition is published worldwide. As there are minor differences in spelling and presentation, especially with regard to American English and British English, a policy is necessary to define which form of English to use. The Fonthill Policy is to use the form of English native to the author. Rob Langham was born and educated in Britain and therefore British English has been adopted in this publication.

Fonthill Media Limited
Fonthill Media LLC
www.fonthillmedia.com
office@fonthillmedia.com

First published in the United Kingdom and the United States of America 2016

British Library Cataloguing in Publication Data:
A catalogue record for this book is available from the British Library

Copyright © Rob Langham 2016

ISBN 978-1-78155-080-9

Typeset in 10.5pt on 13pt Sabon
Printed and bound in Great Britain by CPI Group (UK) Ltd, Croydon, CR0 4YY

Contents

Acknowledgements

First of all it would only be right to thank those who built the Handley Pages and served on the Handley Page squadrons, particularly those who recorded details of their service either in writing or through sound recordings. It was their experiences that interested and inspired me to write this book—as we come to a century since they served, their words bring what happened all that time ago back to life. Unfortunately, all of those involved with the Handley Pages of the First World War have long since passed away.

My thanks also go to those who have helped me in various ways, providing me with additional information, aiding the research I was undertaking, or leading me down new paths—or just helping with my writing. There are many who have helped, some without realising; however, I would particularly like to thank Peter Hart and Jim Grundy who have provided additional research material and aided me in using it, as well as James Kightly for his guidance. Thanks also go to Barbara Gilbert of the Fleet Air Arm Museum and Bryan Bowen of the Paralyser Group who aim to build a replica Handley Page O/400. John H. Watson provided very valuable information regarding the RNAS Redcar-based Handley Pages on U-boat patrols. I would also like to thank John McKenzie whose incredible work on recreating the FE2b night bomber (now on display in the RAF Museum at Hendon) helped, on several occasions, to inspire me to continue my research on First World War night bombers.

Finally I would like to thank my publishers for their patience.

Introduction

There are two stories as to where the nickname of 'Bloody Paralyser' for the Handley Page heavy twin-engine bombers originated; one came from a meeting between the Director of the Air Department of the Admiralty, Captain Murray F. Sueter, Frederick Handley Page and his chief designer, George R. Volkert, who were discussing the Admiralty's specification for a bomber with a 114-foot wingspan, powered by two 150-hp engines, and capable of carrying six 100-lb bombs. Sueter, exasperated with Handley Page's relatively small designs, declared, 'Look, Mr Handley Page, what I want is a bloody paralyser not a toy'.[1] The other suggestion is that it came about from Commander Charles Rumney Samson (who commanded Eastchurch Squadron's fleet of aeroplanes and armoured vehicles in Belgium in 1914) supposedly sending a message to Captain Sueter for a 'bloody paralyser of an aeroplane to stop the Hun in his tracks'.[2]

Whatever the real background to the nickname 'Bloody Paralyser' (and it is entirely possible both are accurate), it was an apt description for the aircraft that emerged from a factory in Kingsbury, North London, on the night of 9 December 1915. This aircraft was the prototype Handley Page Type O, serial number 1455—it had an upper wing span of 100 feet, with the wings folding backwards outboard of the 250-hp Rolls-Royce Eagle II engines, one fitted each side of the fuselage. The aircraft was covered in undyed Irish linen, as other aeroplanes at the time were, and would have been in a natural off-white/cream colour.

On arrival it spent a week being prepared for its first flight until the day finally came on 17 December 1915, when the largest aeroplane to date in Britain took to the skies. Like most, if not all, prototypes it was far from perfect and modifications were soon made to improve it—unsurprisingly, the large enclosed cockpit did not last long. HP 1455 was later modified with a plywood open cockpit with an extension forward for what would become the gunner's position, and by the third prototype the Handley Page O/100's shape was defined.

The first Handley Pages flew to France at the end of 1916 and first saw action in early 1917. After initial doubts within the Royal Naval Air Service as to the function of the aircraft, by late 1917 it was being used as a strategic night bomber that targeted industrial towns, important railway junctions, and the U-boat bases at Zeebrugge, Ostend, and Bruges. The U-boat bases were of particular interest to the Royal Navy as the submarines were, by 1917, causing severe losses to merchant shipping in an attempt to starve Britain into submission. Together with the smaller Royal Aircraft Factory FE2b night bombers, used by the Royal Flying Corps, the use of night bombers increased as more aircraft and trained crews became available. With the formation of the Royal Air Force on 1 April 1918 the Royal Naval Air Service and Royal Flying Corps became one force and the night bombers were used to best effect, including the formation in June 1918 of Independent Force, which in conjunction with day bombers and their scout escorts intended to do as much damage as possible to the enemy from the air. The Handley Page O/400 (a version with the more powerful Rolls-Royce Eagle VIII engine as well as other minor changes to the original O/100 design) gave an improved performance, allowing the Handley Pages to fly higher, faster, and carry a heavier load including the enormous SN 1,650-lb bomb. A shortage of Rolls-Royce Eagle engines meant there were never as many Handley Pages available as desired, which held back the number of squadrons sent across to France. Although other types of engines were put to sample, none were found to be truly satisfactory. Towards the end of 1918 an even bigger aircraft emerged from Handley Page's Cricklewood works—the V/1500. This enlarged version of the Type O had four engines and was built with the aim of being able to fly even longer raids and with a heavier bomb load—with Berlin as the intended target, striking back at Germany's capital as the Germans had done to Britain with the Zeppelin airships and Gotha bombers.

The sight of the Handley Pages must have been incredible; no aeroplane anywhere near as big had been seen in Britain up until that point. The last of the Type O's and Type V's were scrapped in the 1920s. Now, the only way to try and understand the sheer presence these aircraft would have had is by looking at old photographs and the limited film footage that exists of them. The only aircraft of the period that comes close in scale is the Vickers Vimy. Although this was also a large twin-engined bomber from the end of the First World War, it was still only two-thirds the size of the Handley Page O/100 and O/400. A few parts of the giant Handley Pages do still remain, which gives some idea of their immense size—the RAF Museum holds sections of wing from O/400s, including those from the 2013 discovery of a number of 25-foot wing sections that had been used to support a garage roof in Flintshire, Wales. With no surviving

'Bloody Paralyser' for people to see, this may be part of the reason that these aircraft, and their crews, seem to have been largely forgotten. Hopefully this book will go some way to making people more aware of the men involved with these extraordinary aeroplanes, and also be a fitting tribute to their bravery and sacrifice.

Rob Langham
Bowburn, County Durham
November 2015

1

Beginnings

Frederick Handley Page, a name that would eventually become linked to large multi-engined aeroplanes, was born in Cheltenham, Gloucestershire on 15 November 1885. He left school in 1902 at the age of sixteen and started a three-year course studying electric engineering at Finsbury Technical College, London. Handley Page developed an interest in powered flight during his studies, initially designing and attempting to fly flapping-wing model aeroplanes before finding this a dead end. After completing his course in 1906, Handley Page landed a job as chief designer at the electrical machinery manufacturers of Johnson & Phillips Ltd in Charlton, South East London. He was successful in his work and in May 1907 gave a lecture to the Institution of Electrical Engineers. In the same year he joined the Aeronautical Society of Great Britain and became aware of, and interested in, the work of Jose Weiss who had experimented with different wing types. In a letter sent in 1908 to Colonel J. D. Fullerton, Secretary of the Aeronautical Society, Handley Page expressed a wish to meet Weiss after experimenting with wing types himself, hoping to publish a paper on the subject. After this, he was invited to the 'Wings Committee' of the Society where he had the opportunity to meet Weiss. Following a number of meetings, Handley Page became a shareholder in Weiss's company, the 'Weiss Aeroplane and Launcher Syndicate'. Handley Page's enthusiasm grew and he started to undertake experimental aviation work at his workplace without gaining prior permission; unsurprisingly, this resulted in him losing his job.

Shortly after this he set up his own business under his name, the premises consisting of a shed and small office at 36 William Street, Woolwich. He was commissioned by inventor G. P. Deverall Saul to build a quadruplane, which consisted of a pair of biplane wings (two sets of main planes) rather than all four mounted vertically together (as a conventional quadruplane—if such aircraft could be called in total seriousness—would have had). Deverall Saul's idea was that the design would be inherently stable. In order to complete the aircraft, Handley Page would need somewhere to fly it from; in December 1908, he went to view Noel Pemberton Billing's grounds at Fambridge, Essex. It was not up to Handley Page's standards as well as being too remote for him; he then leased an area of marshland, complete with corrugated iron shed at Creekmouth on the north bank of the Thames near the Woolwich ferry. The land also had flying rights for 2½ miles along the banks of the Thames eastwards, sandwiched between the river and the London, Tilbury and Southend Railway line. While at Fambridge, Handley Page met Weiss again and they started to work together, agreeing to have a joint stand at the 1909 Olympia Aero Show with Weiss's monoplane acting as a centrepiece. They also agreed that Handley Page would make Weiss a wing for his next glider and Handley Page would be able to use any of Weiss's patents for his designs. Work on the Deverall Saul quadruplane continued as well as producing components for aircraft. Handley Page had not flown himself, and so made a monoplane glider at his new premises with a foreplane instead of a tailplane, and Handley Page (or any other pilot) sat underneath the wing, above the undercarriage that consisted of three bicycle wheels. Handley Page's glider was not successful in leaving the ground, either by his hands or those of his two pupils (Handley Page was also already offering flying tuition). He did learn one important lesson at least—the need for a large landing skid underneath the fuselage. Although this would have been of use when landing after flight onto level ground, Handley Page actually discovered this as the glider went into ditches and broke the undercarriage before even getting airborne, and this would have caused serious damage to a propeller if one was fitted.

The planned joint stand at the Olympia Aero Show went ahead, and in March 1909 at Stand 30 Handley Page and Weiss displayed the Weiss monoplane. This plane was fitted with a 12-hp Anzani engine driving two propellers (the aeroplane had not yet flown, and never did), as well as a Weiss unmanned glider. The Deverall Saul quadruplane was still not ready at this stage so an artist's impression of it in flight, as well as a description of it on the stand, had to suffice. The quadruplane was completed in May and fitted with an 8-hp engine, but could not be persuaded to leave the ground, even when given help by a motor car towing it. In June, Handley Page launched Handley Page Limited—the first company in the United Kingdom registered specifically as an aeronautical engineering firm—with 500 shares of £20 each available, and four Directors (Frederick, his brother Arthur, and engineers Francis Dalton, and W. G. Magdalen). In early 1910 Handley Page was able to acquire three aircraft sheds that were built at Dagenham by the Aeronautical Society; they had planned to build a flying ground there, but this proved to be a failure. The sheds were moved to Creekmouth and re-erected. They were clearly visible from trains on the London, Tilbury and Southend Railway with 'HANDLEY PAGE LTD' painted in large white letters on the roof. Deverall Saul ordered another quadruplane, this time a two seater (and evidently not put off by the failure of the first one); orders were also placed for a 'pendulum stability' biplane and a monoplane wing with control surfaces for another aircraft. Handley Page also started construction of a powered aeroplane for himself, to be displayed at the next Olympia Aero Exhibition. This new design, which became the Handley Page Type A monoplane, was built with a Weiss wing design and a 20-hp Advance four-cylinder engine—the exposed cylinders were arranged in pairs in a 'V' shape and cooled by the air—and named the *Bluebird* as it was covered in blue rubberised fabric. The fuselage itself was boat shaped and tapered towards the tail, which was a cruciform shaped piece on a single joint that acted as both rudder and elevator.

Although not completed, it was shown at the 1910 Olympia Aero Show with a price of £375, but there were no takers. Trials afterwards showed that when power to the engine increased, the landing skid on the undercarriage simply dug in to the ground, the elevator not being large enough to make the tail lift. A fixed tailplane was fitted and the axle of the wheeled undercarriage moved slightly forward, which helped the issue, and after a number of 'hops' the *Bluebird* and Frederick Handley Page left the ground on 26 May 1910, but side-slipped and crashed after trying to turn across the wind. The crash showed the need for lateral control (which supposedly the Weiss design did not need). Handley Page reconstructed *Bluebird* with wing warping (common before ailerons started to be fitted) and made the rudder bigger. A new 25-hp Alvaston engine was fitted too, the changes being enough to warrant the *Bluebird* becoming the Handley Page Type C, but the aircraft would now not take off at all. An even larger engine, a 50-hp radial engine with five cylinders built by Isaacson, was fitted together with minor modifications to allow for the larger and heavier engine, but by this time work was progressing on other designs and so was put to one side. Of Handley Page's other designs, the monoplane wing that had been built for an Alexander Thiersch was incorporated into the rest of the aircraft and he successfully struggled to coax his completed design into the air, and it also crashed after managing an impressive 1,200-yard flight on the same day as the *Bluebird* took to the air. The biplane built for a W. P. Thompson and known as the Handley Page Type B achieved its 'pendulum stability' by having the engine and pilot (by far the heaviest parts of early aircraft) located underneath the wings. The 60-hp Green engine drove two propellers fitted level with the lower wing, the engine itself being located behind the pilot. Robert Fenwick who was Thompson's assistant was to fly the aeroplane, but the main wheels of the undercarriage buckled before it took off and, following gales that caused heavy damage to the Handley Page Limited buildings, it was damaged again while under repair; Handley Page did not deem it worth repairing and he considered it a failure, unsurprising given its nickname of *The Scrapheap*. Handley Page did allow Fenwick to rebuild it as long as Thompson paid, and in the summer of 1910 it was sent by train to Lancashire where after further modifications it flew, and Fenwick gained his Royal Aero Club certificate certifying him as a pilot. Fenwick returned back to Handley Page and became Handley Page Limited's first test pilot.

The Handley Page Type D monoplane was built, like the Type A, for the Olympia Aero Show, work starting in October 1910 with Fenwick assisting. The finely built boat-shaped fuselage was planked with mahogany and again used wing warping. Once more using a Weiss design, the leading edge of the wing curved backwards towards the tip producing a very handsome aeroplane, even though in order to have it ready for the 1911 Olympia Aero Show Handley Page had to borrow a 35-hp Green engine. The Type D was offered at £450, which included flying lessons; however, like the previous year, no one offered to buy one. With the engine returned and unable to fit the redundant 50-hp Isaacson engine from the *Bluebird*, a second Type D aeroplane was built using a fabric covered fuselage. Only the fuselage was used, the original wings and tail fitted onto it (the new wings and tail kept as spares) and it was fitted with the radial engine from the *Bluebird*. It was entered into the *Daily Mail*'s 'Circuit of Britain' race in July 1911, but it crashed a week before the race—on its first flight. Fenwick, the pilot, was uninjured; however, Handley Page was so angry that he fired him then and there, which led to Fenwick leaving in anger too, especially as the crash was not owing to pilot error and was almost to be expected in the early days of powered flight. The Type D was quickly repaired, but not until after the race (and even if it had been there was no one to fly it, Handley Page having realised he was better off on the ground rather than in the sky). The repaired aeroplane became known as *Yellow Peril* from the yellow varnish applied to the wings and tail. Handley Page gained a new test pilot, Edward Petre, who together with his brother Henry had come to Handley Page to ask about monoplanes after crashing theirs. Petre, who called the Type D *The Antiseptic*, made a number of flights in the aircraft. In the meantime Handley Page had been working on a new design, owing to new information on aerofoils that had come to light—this helped improve upon the Weiss design and brought up the possibility of a two-seat monoplane, and was aided by the availability of a wind tunnel at the Northampton Institute. A competition set up by the War Office for a two seat aeroplane for the Army was announced towards the end of 1911; initially Handley Page had already decided one of the rules was not achievable and the money offered not worth the effort.

In March 1912, Handley Page made a cheap offer (that was accepted) for the entire inventory of Aeronautical Syndicate Limited, which had entered liquidation (apart from four Valkyrie aeroplanes that had been presented to the Air Battalion, Royal Engineers of the British Army). This included four aeroplanes and a large number of aeroplane engines. It was quickly turned into a profit when, after cherry picking what he wanted (the Gnome aero engines), Handley Page sold the rest to George Holt Thomas of the Aircraft Manufacturing Company Limited (later 'Airco'). With this new found fortune and stock of suitable engines Handley Page now decided he would enter the competition and, together with Henry Petre, designed a new type of monoplane with the pilot and passenger seated side-by-side and matching the War Office specification as best as possible. The Type E was to still be built, though as a demonstration machine, and was fitted with the best 50-hp Gnome engine available. It first flew on 26 April 1912 and flights of increasing length took place thereafter, and although damage was caused from landing on rough ground the aircraft became stronger as it was rebuilt. After rebuilding, the wings and tail were finished in a yellow varnish and so the Type E also acquired the *Yellow Peril* nickname, and was a striking sight together with the blue finish to the fuselage. The Type E initially flew to Brooklands in late July where it stayed until 5 October when it was flown to Hendon.

The Type F, the two-seat monoplane built for the War Office competition, used a more powerful 70-hp Gnome engine and was the last aircraft built at the Handley Page site at Creekmouth. Handley Page's pilot Henry Petre didn't like Handley Page's preferred curved wings and so had a second set of wings built to his specification; these still swept back, but had a straight leading edge, and, as Handley Page and Henry's brother Edward were busy with moving the company to Cricklewood, Henry Petre got away with having the Type F built with them. When his brother found out he warned Henry of the likely dire consequences for him if Handley Page discovered the change of wings; Henry refused to fly the aircraft with Handley Page's wings so Edward Petre took his place as pilot for the trials. The second set of wings, as well as the move of location, delayed the construction of the Type F, which meant there was no time for a test flight or proper tuning of the engine. Therefore, the crated aircraft that arrived at Larkhill, Salisbury Plain, in August 1912 was untried and also late—almost missing the deadline for the arrival of entrants. The first flight of the Type F was on 21 August and fortunately it flew well, despite the hiccup of the landing skid getting caught while taxiing back to the hangar after landing, nearly pitching the aircraft up onto its nose that could have broken the propeller.

The next day resulted in disaster—there was to be an official three-hour endurance test. Edward Petre took the Type F up for a short flight, to make sure all was well on what was the aircraft's second ever flight. After take-off the engine started to misfire and the engine cut out, forcing Petre to land near the aircraft sheds used by the Bristol Aeroplane Company. The aircraft almost ran into chains surrounding the sheds and had to dodge people on the ground. A gust of wind lifted one wing, resulting in the landing gear and the other wing getting smashed as they hit the ground. The Type F could not be repaired at Larkhill and could not continue to take part in the competition. Completely new wings and landing gear were built for the aircraft at Cricklewood and it was back in the air in November, flown by Lieutenant Wilfred Parke who was very impressed by it; he considered it suitable for use by the Royal Navy as a scout aircraft. Parke's suggestions were taken seriously to the extent that two drawings were made, one by Petre (which was essentially the same as the Type F) and the other by Volkert (which was an improved Type E, using a 110-hp Anzani engine). It was to be called the Type H and presented to the Admiralty following Parke's recommendations. Parke took passengers up in it whenever possible and would fly to and from Brooklands. Parke planned to fly to Oxford on 15 December 1912 with A. A. Hardwick, the works manager for Handley Page, but after take-off the engine, which Parke had already mentioned to be sounding rough, seemed to be a lot more underpowered than it should be and was slow to gain height. It was said to only have been a few hundred feet in the air when over Wembley, and as the aircraft crossed a number of trees the engine cut out, the aircraft going into a spin after the aircraft stalled and then crashed, killing Parke and Hardwick. The loss hit Frederick Handley Page hard and reinforced his belief in the need to make flying as safe as possible, especially with regards to aircraft design itself—this would become a key part of Handley Page's designs and experimental work.

By this time, Handley Page had closed the works at Creekmouth and moved to larger premises in a 20,000 square feet converted riding stables at 110 Cricklewood Lane, North London (with access to a hangar at Hendon for flying); this move came from the idea to increase production, especially in hope of acquiring the contract to build Royal Aircraft Factory BE2 aircraft. On the last day of October the Type E, which by now had returned to Hendon, had been damaged when the propeller, a wing tip, and undercarriage wheel were broken. One of the pilots invited to try it out, Desmond Arthur, scraped the aircraft on the characteristic white railings that surrounded Hendon aerodrome. During the repairs a new tailplane was fitted at Cricklewood and it flew again on 1 February 1913, returning back to Cricklewood to be prepared for the 1913 Olympia Aero

Show, which was to start on the 14 February. For display at Olympia it was fitted with a Stolz Electrophone to enable the pilot and passenger to speak to each other, which interested King George V when he visited the stand after opening the show. After the show a new pair of wings were built and fitted to the Type E based on plans made by George Volkert, which used ailerons for lateral control instead of wing warping—the first flight with the ailerons taking place on 1 May.

George Volkert was formerly a student at the Northampton Institute, where he gained a degree in mechanical engineering and attended the aeronautical lectures that Frederick Handley Page gave. After completing his studies he joined Handley Page Limited full time as chief designer after having already worked during term breaks. The Type E was again used to showcase Handley Page's skills as a manufacturer and took part in air races and exhibition flights around the country, including one peculiar incident in Hull. Despite being banned from flying within the boundary of the City of Hull on a Sunday (after the mayor invoked the Lord's Day Observance Act of 1625), the pilot Ronald Whitehouse, a new staff pilot for Handley Page—the Petre brothers had both left in 1912—had little choice after he had completed repairs following an unfortunate taxiing incident involving a ditch. Around 7,000 people were reported to have cheered him on his way as he took off. A large number of them, supposedly half of those in attendance, had their names taken by police, but it was later found the take-off had actually happened outside of the city limits and any charges had to be dropped. After the successful tour, Whitehouse and the Type E returned to Hendon at the end of August 1913. With the new Type G nearly completed, Handley Page let the Type E go to George Beatty who had just formed a flying school at Hendon, the aircraft being converted by Beatty into a single-seat aircraft until the war broke out.

The hoped for contract to build the Royal Aircraft Factory BE2 biplane did materialise in 1913, but for just five aircraft. Even this small contract did not go well. Part of the specifications required that a specific type of high tensile steel was used; although it was available from the giant armament and shipbuilding firms, they charged a high price for small amounts, which the ever-frugal Frederick Handley Page was reluctant to pay. He told the War Office he would not accept other contracts unless they were for significantly larger numbers of aircraft. The completion of the first two aircraft was delayed, and meanwhile Volkert was instructed by Handley Page to design a biplane that would be at least as good as the BE2, but using the materials and skills that the company already had available. The third BE2 was delayed until 1914, and the War Office cancelled the last two.

Known as the Type G, the new type of biplane was shown to men of the Northern Aircraft Company who were looking for seaplanes to teach pilots in the Lake District. They offered to buy the Type G if it could be fitted with floats and so it was built with an undercarriage using twin skids so that the wheels could be removed and floats fitted. Handley Page was keen to finish it as a landplane, persuading the prospective buyers that with the design giving it a short take-off and landing, with the ability to climb quickly on take-off and make a steep approach to landing, it would be well suited for flying from open spaces such as parks where obstacles could easily get in the way. Although essentially a biplane version of the previous monoplanes with the fuselage mounted between the two wings, it was fitted with a 100-hp Anzani radial engine when finished. The pilot sat in the rear cockpit and the front cockpit was big enough to fit two passengers in. The first flight was made by Whitehouse on 6 November 1913. After a number of flights, he took the aircraft to the Royal Aircraft Factory at Farnborough on 12 December, flying back two days later. The Royal Aircraft Factory only had one suggestion to make to the design—to slightly increase the tailplane surface area. In early 1914 small improvements were made to the design, and on 29 April 1914 Rowland Ding of the Northern Aircraft Company took delivery of the aircraft. Ding continued to fly the aircraft, which included taking Princess Ludwig of Lowenstein-Wertheim from Hendon to Paris on 21 May (although bad weather meant the journey had to be cut short at Calais, where the Princess took the train onwards and Ding returned to Hendon the next day). Ding spent the summer giving exhibition flights in the north of England, and after damaging the undercarriage while landing at Northallerton Carnival it was returned to Hendon for repairs. On the outbreak of war, it was requisitioned by the Royal Naval Air Service and used for training and anti-Zeppelin patrols, armed solely with the pilot's revolver.

A new design of biplane was started by Volkert in late 1913, a single seat smaller version of the Type G to be known as the Type K. However, development was cancelled just as the summer of 1914 beckoned when Princess Ludwig of Lowenstein-Wertheim placed an order for a large single engine biplane to win the *Daily Mail*'s £10,000 prize for the first non-stop crossing of the Atlantic Ocean by air. Rowland Ding was to fly the machine, known as the Type L, with Princess Ludwig as co-pilot, sitting side-by-side with dual controls in an enclosed cockpit cabin that had a third seat for resting. The streamlined fuselage was to have a 200-hp Canton-Unne radial engine at the front and, as well as the engine and crew, would have capacity in tanks for 350 gallons of petrol, 35 gallons of oil, and 35 gallons of water. The design was taken from the Type K, but doubled in size, giving an impressive 60-foot wing span. The unassembled aircraft was more or less complete when the war broke out apart from the engine, although when the engine did arrive the Admiralty requisitioned it.

The war with Germany was announced on 4 August 1914. Handley Page possessed a wealth of experience and had achieved a reputation for innovative design, though only a small number of aeroplanes compared to their contemporaries had been built—fourteen in total, eight of them to their own design. The large factory at Cricklewood meant the company had fairly good prospects on paper at the start of the war; however, the delays and cancellations of the BE2 aeroplanes built under contract the previous year did not paint Handley Page Limited in good light. Frederick Handley Page offered his services and his factory to the War Office and Admiralty. Unsurprisingly, the War Office politely declined, but Captain Murray Sueter, the Director of the Air Department at the Admiralty called Handley Page immediately and asked Handley Page and Volkert to meet him. The enterprising Handley Page offered the Type L, still sat in bits at Cricklewood, to the Admiralty as a coastal patrol landplane or seaplane, and by reducing the fuel capacity it would be able to seat five. The lack of available 200-hp engines (owing to them all being requisitioned) resulted in a redesign initially using two 100-hp engines, one on each side, and later using two water-cooled engines mounted in the nose with the propellers fitted outboard of the fuselage, chain driven.

Sueter's consulting engineer was Harris Booth who preferred a larger seaplane design. This resulted in the White of Cowes built Admiralty Type 1000 seaplane, the prototype was even larger than the Handley Page 0/100 when it flew in 1916; not all of the planned prototypes were built, owing to poor performance and excessive weight. On 3 September, Sueter wrote to Handley Page telling him they did not plan to order any of his proposed types—this included the Handley Page Type N, a single-seat scout aircraft. The reality of modern industrial war was to change Frederick Handley Page's fortunes before 1914 was over.

2

Prototypes

Commander Charles Rumney Samson was one of the first of the Royal Navy Officers selected to learn to fly in 1911, and after a total seventy-one minutes of flying experience, gained his certificate on 25 April 1911. He later became the first Royal Navy pilot to take-off from a ship, when he flew a Short S27 biplane off a ramp fitted to the front of HMS *Africa* on 10 January 1912, and then became the first pilot ever to take-off from a moving ship on 9 May, with the same aircraft from HMS *Hibernia* during the Naval Review in Weymouth Bay. When the Royal Flying Corps was set up he was put in charge of the naval wing, originally part of the RFC, and when the Royal Navy decided to separate the naval wing from the RFC in July 1914 he became the commanding officer of Eastchurch Squadron, which duly went to France on the outbreak of war.

Eastchurch Squadron, which changed to become 3 Squadron RNAS in September, helped support the Allied armies on the ground along the French and Belgian border. Lack of replacement aircraft following the inevitable downing or accidental damage to machines resulted in Samson taking the initiative to arm some of the private motor cars some officers had brought with them, not just to harass the Germans, but also to rescue downed airmen behind or near enemy lines. The Belgians had been employing armoured cars successfully at this time and so two of Samson's fleet were partially armoured. Further armoured cars were built with armour plating rather than locally acquired boilerplate steel, and fitted with proper vision slots and hatches. Loopholes were fitted on larger armoured vehicles to allow accompanying Royal Marines to fire their rifles in comparative safety. By this point Samson's armoured cars, along with 3 Squadron, were operating in the areas between Dunkirk and Antwerp, his armoured cars, with the Royal Marines, accompanied the fleet of London buses to Antwerp in an attempt to relieve the siege there. Unfortunately, the armoured cars and reinforcements were not enough to save Antwerp from falling to the superior numbers of Germans and their siege artillery.

His involvement in trying to break the siege inspired Samson to request an aeroplane capable of bombarding the German forces, perhaps envisioning a form of aerial bombardment when conventional heavy artillery was not immediately available. The request, supposedly for a 'Bloody Paralyser' as Handley Page claimed, was supported by First Lord of the Admiralty Winston Churchill, and the official requirements were issued in December 1914 for interested aircraft manufacturers. Handley Page and Volkert went back to Sueter, and work started on what would be the Handley Page Type O.

The required specification ultimately drawn up was for an aircraft with a crew of two, carrying six 100-lb bombs, and a speed of at least 75 miles per hour. It had to fit into an aircraft shed with dimensions of 75 feet by 75 feet and 18 feet high, so if the aircraft was to be larger than that, it would require folding wings. The Admiralty ordered four prototypes in February 1915 with Handley Page receiving a £20,000 advance for the work. He then demanded and received the same amount in an overdraft from his bank.

As it was to be fitted with two engines, the drawing office at Handley Page explored various ideas as to how to mount them; ultimately, they decided on fitting one on each side of the fuselage, with the propellers rotating in opposite directions so as not to affect the performance (this effect was known as torque). Harris Booth also required armour plating to protect the crew against rifle fire. The weight of the armour plate alone would come to 1,200 lbs. The design was for an aircraft with a gross weight of 13,500 lbs—an achievement considering the average weight of an aircraft in 1914 was a quarter of that. Booth had limited the design team to a wing loading of 51 lbs per square foot, which required a lifting area for the wing of 1,500 square feet. This would give an upper wing span of 100 feet, resulting in the first Handley Page Type O becoming known as the Handley Page O/100. The lower wing had a span of 80 feet. Where possible, weight was saved in every area; it was discovered that even the grain direction on the wood made a difference, and so some parts were rebuilt. The Handley Page staff, which consisted of just twelve men when the initial prototypes were ordered, worked for nine-and-a-half hours each day, seven days a week, all through 1915. Sueter was so impressed with the work that he ordered an additional eight aircraft in the same month that the prototypes were ordered, later increased to forty aircraft with the order of twenty-eight more in April. The aircraft were so large that even Handley Page's Cricklewood factory could not cope and so, as well as hiring more staff, the Lamson factory at Kingsbury was used for assembly of the aircraft—it was twice the size of the Cricklewood factory. At the same time, work was going on using a wind tunnel at the

Northampton Institute where models were used to make sure the design would be both stable and react well to the controls.

The engines, two Rolls-Royce Eagle 250-hp engines, were the first of a new design. Those fitted in the first aircraft were just the second and third examples. These were put in nacelles with the fuel tanks behind the engines, and the whole nacelle armoured. The aircraft was built in sub-assemblies, and when completed looked drastically different to the characteristic shape of the Handley Page bombers of the First World War.

Whatever the real background to the nickname 'Bloody Paralyser', it was an apt description for the aircraft that emerged from a factory in Kingsbury, North London, on the night of 9 December 1915. This aircraft was the prototype Handley Page Type O, serial number 1455—it had an upper wing span of 100 feet, with the wings folded backwards offside of the 250-hp Rolls-Royce Eagle II engines, one fitted each side of the fuselage.

The cockpit was glazed, unusual for the period, and looked like a greenhouse with the pilot sat centrally inside on a then-conventional wicker seat. As November 1915 was drawing to a close the first prototype was nearing completion, by which time Handley Page's staff had increased from a dozen to 150. Alongside the Lamson Factory, a Rolls-Royce repair site in Cricklewood Lane and a skating rink at Broadway had been acquired and put into use. The fuselage of the first prototype was put together at Cricklewood then towed along Edgware Road to Kingsbury by Frederick Handley Page using his Arrol-Johnston motor car, where it was fully assembled with the wings, engines, etc. The aircraft was covered in doped Irish linen, as other aeroplanes at the time were, and would have been in a natural off-white/cream colour.

When the first aircraft was complete it needed to be moved to the nearby aerodrome at Hendon for its first flight. By now it was too heavy to be towed by Handley Page's car, so as a Royal Naval aircraft, it was moved by Royal Navy ratings with petty officers and officers in charge. On the night of 9 December the journey started, the folding wings of the aircraft coming in useful, but even with the span significantly reduced the size of the aircraft still caused plenty of issues on the journey, which used the main roads to Hendon. The Admiralty had already ensured obstacles would be removed where possible, but there were still unforeseen circumstances. There were several occurrences of the undercarriage tyres bursting, which were not easy to change given the configuration of the undercarriage. When the journey took the aircraft down Colindale Avenue, street lamps blocking the route were dismantled—the local gas company were understandably not pleased, but were simply told to take it up with the Admiralty. After these obstructions were cleared, trees in people's front gardens still impeded the progress and so the offending limbs were chopped off (including by Mr Handley Page himself who was more than willing to climb them and do the work to allow his machine to progress). After five hours, Handley Page 1455 arrived at Hendon and the next week was spent on final preparations for its first flight, which included fine tuning the engines and adjusting the rigging.

In the early afternoon of 17 December 1915, Lieutenant Commander J. T. Babington and Lieutenant Commander E. W. Stedman, pilot and passenger respectively, climbed into the aircraft and the engines were started. As the brand new Rolls-Royce Eagle engines did not have starting handles (and starter motors were as yet unconceived) and they were too high off the ground to be started by hand, a wooden double ramp had to be built. This enabled the ground crew to run up it, swing one of the four blades on the propeller closest to the ground, then run down the other side, followed by another and another until the engine was primed, allowing Babington to start the engine by turning the magneto in the cockpit. Babington taxied the aircraft to the downwind end of the aerodrome for take-off. Pushing the throttles forward, at 50 mph the aircraft became airborne for the first time, and Babington flew the aircraft straight in a long 'hop', putting the wheels down still within the perimeter of Hendon aerodrome.

Babington took the aircraft up again the next day, but was not able to accelerate much past 55 mph. The slow speed was ascribed to the drag caused by the large radiators fitted over the engine, so these were removed and different radiators were fitted along the sides of the engine nacelle. The third flight was on 31 December, which showed an improved performance with an increase of speed up to around 65 mph, but the design still needed work, the rudders were overbalanced and the ailerons and elevators were too heavy. Sueter was becoming impatient; on his orders the aircraft was flown to Eastchurch on the Isle of Sheppey, Kent, by Squadron Commander Longmore on 10 January 1916 so that further testing could take place there by the RNAS. The flight there showed some issues too—the windscreen part misted up and the port engine lost power owing to issues with the magneto.

After arriving at Eastchurch, Longmore flew the aircraft to its performance limits to see what its potential was. In trying to attain the maximum speed of the aircraft, the tail disconcertingly started to vibrate and then violently twisted at around 70 mph, forcing Longmore to land immediately. This warping caused damage to the rear fuselage, with the longerons bent and crushed in places, and the control cables had gone slack, meaning that the control surfaces would not be able to control the aircraft in flight. Frederick Handley Page and George Volkert arrived at

Eastchurch and set to work to fix the problems by reinforcing certain areas. However, that did not stop the issue and actually resulted in the aircraft being unable to take off.

The issue was eventually solved and the aircraft could fly, but not above 75 mph when the tail would start vibrating again. These design flaws were fed back to Handley Page who were still building the three other prototypes. Other modifications were implemented to address these issues and the unpopular enclosed cockpit would not appear again. The second prototype, HP 1456, was built with a longer nose, the pilot's cockpit being exposed to the elements with room for two sitting side-by-side with a small windscreen in front of them. Forward of the pilot's position there was a gunners position, which raised the possibility of defending the aircraft with a machine gun rather than a rifle.

To improve the handling of the machine the armour plate was removed too, which together with the removal of the heavy enclosed cockpit saved around half a ton in weight—the longer nose was important to ensure the centre of gravity stayed the same. As well as saving weight, it would soon be found that the superb performance of the Rolls-Royce Eagle engines meant the aircraft could easily operate at heights well above the range of small-arms fire. Additional weight savings were made with the removal of some, but not all, of the armour fitted to protect the engine and petrol tanks in the nacelles. The second prototype was moved to Hendon after completion and on 23 April 1916 took off, piloted by American freelance test pilot Clifford B. Prodger. Prodger flew the aircraft up to 75 mph and reported no major issues.

A week later, Prodger took the aircraft to 10,000 feet with ten willing passengers on board; this performance impressed Handley Page so much that he invited the RNAS to the acceptance trials two weeks later (7 May) when a total of seventeen people were flown at 3,000 feet, the height being gained in eight-and-a-half minutes. Not content with this, twenty Handley Page employees were taken for a flight by Prodger a few days later—a world record at this time. The RNAS accepted the aircraft, flying it to Manston, Kent, at the end of May (Manston replacing Eastchurch as the Handley Page base as it was larger). It was found that the issue with the tail started to emerge on HP 1456 too, this time at speeds of around 80 mph. Static tests were run with the third prototype, HP 1457, which had a newer and stiffer fuselage than the previous two, but tests on the ground could not induce the problem to occur. HP 1457 first flew on 25 June; it was the first type to have an additional crew position behind the wings. From this position it was possible for an observer to get a better view of the tail twisting, which again occurred during a flight on 26 June when the aircraft speed indicated 80 mph. Engineer Frederick Lanchester who had been involved in the issue made a number of recommendations that included the rear elevators, which had worked separately on each side, being yoked together to work as one among other changes.

Fortunately for the RNAS and Handley Page the changes were a success. The fourth and final prototype, HP 1458, was built with the new Rolls-Royce Eagle III engines, which, at 320 hp, gave an impressive 70 hp extra than the original Eagle II engines fitted to the other prototypes. It was also built to be fitted with armament, which would prove to be the standard fitting of all the Handley Page Type Os—a Scarff ring in the nose position (a superb machine-gun mounting devised by Warrant Officer F. W. Scarff, using an elevated bungee cord suspension to offset the weight of the Lewis machine guns very quickly, while at the same time able to rotate 360 degrees). The mid-upper position behind the wings had two pillar mountings for a Lewis gun each, and a ventral mounting in the floor to allow a Lewis gun to be fired below and behind the aircraft.

Handley Page 1458 arrived at Manston in August, and in September the Handley Page Training Flight was set up with HP's 1456 and 1457, while 1458 was used to test new lighter engine nacelles with less drag. The first prototype, HP 1455, was reconfigured to match the other three. As air crew were trained on the Handley Page prototypes and production aircraft started to arrive, so the grandiosely named Handley Page Squadron was set up. The Handley Page Squadron was under the command of Squadron Commander J. T. Babington and when ready was to be attached to the 3rd Wing, Royal Naval Air Service, based at Luxeuil, France.

All pilots had to undergo conversion training on any new aircraft types that they would serve on, but the Handley Page would have been very different from anything they would have flown before. Twin-engined aircraft such as the Caudron G4 were available to train on, but they were of nowhere near the same size or power. Flight Lieutenant Horace Austen Buss was to be one of the first pilots to fly the Handley Pages:

> They frightened me so much, the size of it. I thought, I hope they never ask me to fly one of these. The next thing of course, notice to transfer to the Handley Page wing formed at Manston.[1] [He later remarked that] it was a delightful aeroplane to fly and I was very fond of her.[2]

Flight Lieutenant Horace Austen Buss, Handley Page Squadron, RNAS

Buss was a man of considerable experience. Before the war he had worked as a mechanic at Hendon in exchange for flying lessons, and gained his pilot's certificate flying a Blackburn monoplane in February 1913. Joining the RNAS, Buss found himself as one of the first home defence pilots after the first aerial raid on Britain on 21 December 1914, armed with a sawn-off shotgun with three balls attached by chain, designed to wrap around and destroy an enemy aircraft's struts. Buss ended up at Manston following his transfer to the Handley Page Squadron, and flew a Handley Page for the first time on 8 December 1916, when he took HP 1457 up for fifteen minutes.

Lieutenant Paul Bewsher was one of those who trained at Manston before going to France with the first Handley Pages to cross the channel, albeit as an observer, having transferred from patrolling the coast in seaplanes. He described his feelings on arrival at Manston, with the aircraft already on site:

> When I arrived at the Handley-Page aerodrome I realised that, for the second time in the war, I was to have the good fortune to be attached to a pioneering branch of the Air Service, and that, instead of going to a cut-and-dried task, I was to assist in operations which had been untried and were entirely experimental. I had been, as a second-class air mechanic, a balloon hand on the very first kite balloon used by the British, and had accompanied it to the Dardanelles on a tramp steamer early in 1915. Now I was to be the first observer on the huge night-bombers, which were to prove of such tremendous value to the British.[3]

Lieutenant Paul Bewsher, Handley Page Squadron RNAS

The first production aircraft, HP 1459, had arrived at Manston on 11 September, seventeen days later it was joined by HP 1460. The next didn't arrive for almost a month, by which point it was decided that HP's 1459 and 1460 and their crews were ready to go to 3 Wing. The weather delayed them leaving until November and on 4 November 1916, the first Handley Page left Britain's shores for France.

3

The Bloody Paralyser

The completed Handley Page Type O was unlike any other aircraft used by the British aerial forces up until that point. The arrangement of the aircraft such as the crew positions seems to modern eyes more like that of a Second World War bomber than a First World War aircraft. The following description shows just how complex and impressive these aircraft were, and the role each crew member had. The information pertains to the O/400, the main type in use following on from the O/100. The main visible difference between the O/100 and O/400 were the length and design of the engine nacelles, however there were also other changes. The O/400's structure was strengthened, allowing an increased payload, and two main fuel tanks each holding 130 gallons of fuel were carried in the fuselage above the bomb crate. These were supplemented by two 15-gallon tanks in the upper-wing centre section, with the fuel lines running down into the engines by gravity when selected. This system replaced the fuel tanks behind each engine on the O/100, this itself supplemented during production by a single fuel tank above the bomb crate. Wind driven fuel pumps fed the engines. Both engines turned the propeller the same way on the O/400 as opposed to counter-rotating on the O/100, to help with a believed requirement. Counter-rotating propellers seemed to cause directional instability as well as increasing maintenance and supply issues, owing to two types of propellers being needed rather than one and extra gearing for one engine to reverse the shaft's rotation. To offset potential torque issues, the fin was offset slightly to compensate. The more powerful Rolls-Royce Eagle VIII 360 hp (later 375 hp) engines and other changes not only increased the speed, but also enabled the Handley Pages to operate up to an attitude of 13,000 feet.

The main structure of the aircraft was a braced wooden frame with fabric covering to enclose it and ply floor panels were required inside. This was the typical way that aircraft of the time were constructed—to make them as light as possible. The curved nose of the aircraft had a light shaped plywood fairing covered in fabric, over the formers. This was the standard aircraft construction of the time, giving a strong, light structure able to be lifted by the engine. The main fuselage of the aircraft was built with four longerons, long lengths of wood that stretched (although not one continuous piece of wood) the whole length of the aircraft. There were two on each side and four in total, with other wooden posts placed vertically, with wire and tie rods from each joint corner to brace it as a set of box structures. The fuselage was built in four sections: the nose and front of the aircraft forward of the wings in Section Cd; the fuel tanks, bomb crate, and rear gunner position comprised section Cc; the heaviest area of the fuselage was the rear and was four bays long, was designated Section Cb; and finally the tail unit itself, which contained the tail planes, was Section Ca. The fabric covering the aircraft was Irish linen, which was impregnated by panting with a chemical known as nitrocellulose dope that varnished, sealed, and tightened it. Doping the fabric surfaces of aircraft was and still is vital to ensure they remained as tight and streamlined as possible, and also to give some waterproofing. The chemicals that made up 'dope' were volatile, poisonous, and could very quickly make the person doping an aircraft light-headed, nauseous, and cause severe headaches— it could even result in death. Deaths occurred predominately among the female workers engaged in the task of doping.

The aircraft were painted in what was known as Protective Colouring Number 10 (PC10). PC10 was the dark green colour applied to many British aircraft of the First World War. The exact shade of PC10 has caused debates for many years and will no doubt continue to do so, but it is highly likely that the colour differed in different batches from different manufacturers, and also the amount of time and weathering an aircraft was exposed to. Preserved wings from First World War Handley Pages in the Royal Air Force Museum's stores certainly show a dark green shade to the fabric, as do other still-surviving remnants of fabric from Handley Pages kept in various different conditions. For identification purposes the upper wing was marked with the British roundel of red (in the centre) then white then blue, and then again often a thin white circle surrounding. Photographs show the size of the roundel, and the size of the circles within the roundel to differ. Typically the upper wing would have the roundel both on top and underneath the wing—the roundel painted underneath the wing was on the part that was outboard of the shorter lower wing and was therefore visible from below. There would also be a roundel on either side of the rear fuselage and, depending on unit and period, an identifying number or letter. Further to the rear, the white-marked 'LIFT HERE' with prominent directional arrows. These were in part required due to operations starting or finishing at night to assist the ground handling crews, ensuring they lifted and turned the aircraft at the wood supported areas, not the unsupported fabric. Some aircraft had these vertical ribs' positions marked as vertical white lines. There was also a rudder flash, another nationality identifying feature of vertical blue, white, and red bars either entirely covering the rudder or in a square inset on the rudder. Rearmost would usually be the aircraft's serial number, on the part of the tail that protruded further behind than the tail plane assembly. At some point in 1918, the white of the roundels on night bomber aircraft was abolished, and so the roundels became simply blue and red.

Other markings sometimes included nose art, examples such as a fearsome devil complete with red horns and sharp teeth on O/100 1466, elaborately decorated *Split Pin* (Flight Lieutenant Sieveking's nickname) HP 3127 and the simple, but elegantly painted *Ivy* on O/400 D8323. No. 7 Squadron RNAS, later 207 Squadron RAF, were known as the Black Cat Squadron and the black cat is sometimes seen on images of their Handley Pages. The origins of this do not seem to be recorded, however the black cat was a suitable good luck symbol for a night bomber. The blank canvas offered by the nose of the Handley Pages was used on non-operational Handley Pages too—American O/400s were often artistically decorated such as *The Galloping Goose from Kelly Field* featuring a goose in flight, and the post-war Handley Pages converted for passenger use had the elegant Handley Page logo of 'HP' intertwined and enclosed in an oval with wings adorning the top of the oval.

The gunners position at the front of the aircraft was fitted with a Scarff ring mounting for one or two Lewis guns—the arrangement of twin, rather than single, Lewis guns was also done on other aircraft fitted with a Scarff ring, such as the Bristol F2b Fighter or the Royal Aircraft Factory RE8; the combination was known as 'Huntley & Palmers' after the famous biscuit manufacturer of Reading, Berkshire. The Lewis gun itself was a splendid weapon invented by an American, Colonel Isaac Newton Lewis in 1911. He struggled to find a buyer for it, although the Belgian army decided to adopt it in 1913. With the German invasion in 1914, production moved to the Birmingham Small Arms Company in England and officially adopted for British Army service in October 1915. Using a forty-seven round drum magazine it was a fantastic light machine gun for the British infantry. Before being used by the British Army, it had already been in use with the Royal Flying Corps and Royal Naval Air Service; by mid-1915 the RFC had already ordered over 1,000, with about 250 delivered by this point. At a weight of 28 lbs (13 kg) it was not light, except in contrast to the water-cooled Vickers machine gun. In an effort to reduce weight, the bulky cooling jacket and aluminium cooling fins around the weapon were usually removed for aerial service, as the rush of air over an aeroplane flying through the air would negate the need for the original cooling system.

The drum magazine could be emptied in five seconds if fired all off in one go, and although it was usual just to fire off three to four round bursts, it would still not last long. Especially for aerial service, a ninety-seven round drum magazine was developed (based on using one forty-seven round drum stacked on top of another) and was in widespread service by the time the first Handley Pages entered service. In total, seventeen of these newly developed drums were carried on the Handley Page, divided between the front and rear compartments. As with other aircraft, where the engines were mounted behind the guns, (usually 'pusher' aircraft such as the Royal Aircraft Factory FE2b), bags were fitted underneath the guns to collect the empty casings, so that they wouldn't fly into the propellers and foul the propeller or engine. Some Handley Pages show the gun ring built up to give quite a pronounced 'snout' to the aircraft, over the fuselage longerons. The increase in height of the position came about following trials of the 6-pounder 'Davis' shell gun fitted in the nose of Handley Pages.

The Davis shell gun (which was also built in 2-pounder and 12-pounder versions) was an early recoilless rifle design. When the shell was fired, it simultaneously discharged a lump of lead and Vaseline of equivalent weight of the shell from the rear of the gun, compensating (balancing) the recoil. This configuration meant that the weapon was not loaded from the rear, but part-way down the length of the weapon, the barrel for the discharge swinging to the side. A large bracket was made to fit the weapon to the nose of HP 3127. The weapon was to be used against ground targets, for if the weapon was fired horizontally or at an elevated angle the discharge could easily damage the aircraft severely. Even while firing downward, between 30 to 60 degrees below horizontal, it could still cause damage, and in July 1917 HP 3127 had the gunner's position raised by 8 inches following damage to the upper wing. The increased height of the position was kept with a horizontal upper deck level rearwards until the front leather surround of the cockpit was reached, and this became a production standard on Handley Pages for the rest of the run of Handley Page O/100s and through to the production of Handley Page O/400s until the spring of 1918. Later production O/400s returned to the original lower position of the nose gun mounting. After HP 3127 was converted, three others (HPs 1459, 1461, and 1462) were also modified and fitted with the Davis gun and sent to France. Although the gun saw use against ground targets, such as supply convoys and railways, it was not deemed worth the effort and they were replaced with Lewis guns. A major issue was the storage and additional weight of the bulky ammunition—weighing just over 12 lbs for a 6-pounder shell, owing to the compensating discharge— and the fact the weapon was an unwieldy 10 feet long, and weighed 200 lbs including the mounting. The four Davis guns were officially withdrawn in February 1918 with 500 rounds of 6-pounder shells remaining; they do not appear to have been used any later than August 1917. The 1918 'Handley Page Bomber, Type O/400, Descriptive Handbook' issued by the Ministry of Munitions Technical Department mentioned the Davis gun even though it was no longer being carried when it was produced:

> Every endeavour has been made to overcome the disadvantages of mounting this gun, as it was considered to be the first really practical proposition in heavy gun mountings for Handley Pages. A gun was mounted and fired in the air at practice targets and enemy objectives with a reasonable amount of success; but when a comparison Is drawn between a machine carrying a gun and ammunition which can only be fired downwards, and one carrying bombs only, the decision is undoubtedly in favour of the latter.[1]

As originally designed, the bomb aiming position was behind and underneath the pilot. The improved sight coming into widespread use by 1917 meant this was often abandoned, and the observer would stay in the front nose position as the handbook for the type states:

> Experience showed that this gun pit was the best position for bomb dropping as it gave the observer a perfect forward view. A bombsight was therefore fitted to the nose of the machine and a bomb release handle provided in the gun pit.[2]

Handley Page Bomber, Type O/400, Descriptive Handbook

Occasionally located in the nose when it entered service in late 1918 was the High Altitude Drift Sight. This was developed by Lieutenant Commander H. E. Wimperis and used three scales, set with the aircraft's height, airspeed, and estimated wind speed to set up the bombing angle, and would be fitted to the extreme front of the aircraft, forward of the Scarff ring. By the end of the war another type of sight, which was more accurate, was being designed. Known as the Gray sight it used gyroscopes to remain horizontal, giving accurate data as to where the bombs would fall, rather like a ship's gimbal compass. Being stabilised at the same pitch and roll angle as the aircraft, this sight was a lot more accurate than those that were fixed. This meant that if the aircraft was not flying absolutely level the bombs would go off target simply because the observer's aiming point was some distance to the side of what was actually directly beneath the aircraft. However, the sight, if it had actually entered service, would have been fitted in the rear gunners position of the Handley Page with the observer further separated from the pilot; without an intercommunication system, it is likely they would have adopted a more refined version of the green, white, and red lights already used by observers to guide pilots while on the bombing run. The lack of intercommunication systems was also being addressed, with a telephone system starting to be fitted as the war ended so that the isolated rear gunner could speak to those in the nose. Some crews improvised:

> Well, in the Handley Page's, some of us would have a container on a piece of string, which would work backwards and forwards or we might fit up a tube. I fitted up a tube like they have on board ships. You know, speaking tube. I fitted one of those up on one of the machines, but otherwise, of course, we hadn't got any communication.[3]

> Sergeant Leslie Alexander Dell, 214 Squadron RAF

The method (container on a piece of string) mentioned by Sergeant Dell was used by crews to run hand-written messages on notes of paper between the two compartments. Although, as this necessitated the writer taking off his gloves to write the message, it was far from perfect.

The nose gun position was accessed by a small swing door underneath the Scarff ring and so the ring and the draught from the opening could be closed off. Directly behind the nose gun position was where the pilot and observer sat—two small windscreens were fitted side-by-side, as well as two seats—the observer's seat lifted up so the observer could go to the rear. The pilot sat on the right (unlike on modern fixed-wing aircraft where the pilot in command sits on the left), with the dashboard in front of him with instruments for the air speed indicator, altimeter, compass, watch, engine radiator thermometers, and switches for the lighting. The pilot controlled the aircraft with a wheel connected by control cables to the elevators, which pushed away and pulled towards the pilot to change the pitch of the aircraft downward and upward respectively; this was connected to the ailerons to influence the angle of bank and enable rolling manoeuvres when the wheel was rotated. His feet moved a rudder bar, connected to the rudders to move the aircraft in the yawing plane. There were leather straps to keep his feet on the bar. To the right of the pilot (mounted on the inside of the fuselage) were the engine throttles and mixture control for the engine carburettors—the mixture needing adjustment as the aircraft climbed through the air getting thinner with less oxygen component for combustion. On the left side of the fuselage were levers for adjusting the angle and thus aperture of the radiator shutters for temperature control (and not just if they got too hot; depending on the altitude or outside temperature it could be advisable to close them). These were usually operated by the observer. In the floor of the cockpit, partly offset towards the observer's side, was a negative lens giving a good view of the ground below, with a fore and aft line to give an indication of how much the aircraft was drifting to one side when flying in a crosswind.

Behind the cockpit was a bay that the observer used when dropping bombs from this original position (it was kept as an alternative when the position for bomb-dropping moved to the nose). In the original position the observer lay on the floor facing forward, with the bomb-release gear on his right and a steering indicator to guide the pilot left or right. Behind the observer were some ancillary engine controls, a manual, rotary petrol pump, petrol cocks, starting magneto, accumulators, flow gauges, ignition advance, and retard levers, which the observer would operate on the pilot's instruction. Behind this lay the main spars for the lower wing. The trapdoor to enter the cockpit was located in the floor in this area; it was a triangular shaped flap and access almost always seems to be with a ladder. The warning 'keep clear of propellers' was painted on the trapdoor for those approaching the aircraft to be wary of the propellers close by. If they were running, it would only take one or two steps to the side to result in a lethal accident. Between the spars were the bomb cells; the bombs were held vertically, suspended by the nose. A small square clear panel on either side of the fuselage allowed some light to come in to this otherwise enclosed area. Bewsher describes the area for the observer as he takes us on his journey from his seat alongside the pilot to the position to be assumed during the bombing run:

> ...I lifted up my seat and crawled to the little room behind, which vibrated fiercely with the mighty revolutions of the two engines. I stood on a floor of little strips of wood, in an enclosure whose walls and roofs were of tightly stretched canvas which chattered and flapped a little with the rush of wind from the two propellers whirling scarcely a foot outside. Behind was fitted a round grey petrol-tank, underneath which hung the twelve yellow bombs.
>
> I lay on my chest under the pilot's seat, and pushed to the right a little wooden door, which slid away from a rectangular hole in the floor through which came a swift up-draught of wind. Over this space was set a bomb-sight with its sliding range-bars painted with phosphorescent paint. On my right, fixed to the side of the machine, was a wooden handle operating on a metal drum from which ran a cluster of release-wires to the bombs farther back.[4]

Lieutenant Paul Bewsher, 3 Wing RNAS

The sight for the negative lens bomb was essentially a box that sat in the floor of the aircraft, a concave design giving a wider view of the ground below than if it was a normal straight-sided box. Three wires stretched across the lens for the height settings, which were set at certain criteria, also relating to the speed. The altitude could be taken from the pilot's altimeter, however speed was not so easy; the airspeed indicator would give an air-speed, but this would often be different to the actual speed the aircraft was flying over the ground, depending on how fast and in which direction the wind was blowing. If the wind speed making the aircraft faster or slower could be determined, there was allowance for this on the sights, but it was not perfect and a lot harder to do at night than at daytime when visual references below could be used.

The original design was for a rotating bomb bay that was revolutionary for its time, but this was dispensed with in favour of a far simpler option. The cells were designed to hold sixteen 112-lb bombs. Although the Royal Laboratory 112-lb bombs could only be carried singly by operational aircraft, they were already in use at the outbreak of war and through its duration. It was designed at the Royal Laboratory at Woolwich, as were the majority of bombs used by the RFC, RNAS, and later RAF. In planning operations for 1918, a programme was set up based on the assumption that 7,000 112-lb bombs a week would be required (as well as 20,000 20-lb Coopers, 8,000 50-lb and 2,000 230-lb or 250-lb bombs); however, the introduction and growing use of the Handley Pages meant production of 112-lb bombs was to be increased to 12,000 a week by the time it was approved in October 1917. By June 1918 it was actually found that these figures were far too high. March had been the busiest month for bomb dropping. On average, 100 tons a week and a maximum amount of 2,000 112-lb bombs a week dropped up until June (and this would not solely be Handley Pages, but also DH4s, DH9s, FE2bs, etc.). By August, a new rate of 5,000 112-lb bombs required a week was agreed upon, with a reserve of 50,000, this lasting until the end of the war. Shortages of metal meant that a number of 112-lb bombs (as well as 25-lb Cooper bombs) were made from cast iron instead of steel, especially when the tank building programme in 1918 increased, diverting steel supplies.

In the case of the 112-lb Heavy Case Mk III and V bombs, the actual weight of the bomb case itself was 79 lbs, with the explosive weighing 27 lbs, when filled with amatol 80/20 (or 38 lbs if filled with amatol 40/60). The description of amatol, and for the proportions quoted, are given as follows in *Details of Aerial Bombs*, issued by the Air Ministry in September 1918:

Amatol is a mixture of TNT and ammonium nitrate. It is used in filling bombs in two forms; these are known as 40/60 and 80/20 amatol. The figures 40/60 and 80/20 denote the proportions of TNT and ammonium nitrate contained in the amatol. The first figure represents the percentage of ammonium nitrate, the second the percentage of TNT; thus 40/60 amatol represents a mixture made up of 40% ammonium nitrate and 60% TNT.

The reason for employing amatol in place of simple TNT is due to the growing scarcity of the latter.

The density of amatol is somewhat less than that or TNT and on this account bombs filled with amatol will contain a relatively smaller bursting charge than TNT filled bombs.

In illustration, the case of the 112lb bomb is taken. This bomb, when filled with pure TNT, contains approximately 35 lbs of explosive, but when filled with 80/20 amatol it contains approximately 28 lbs of explosive. From this example it is seen that bombs filled with 80/20 amatol will contain 25% by weight less explosive than bombs filled with TNT.

These figures are not exact; they are obtained by striking an average, but are sufficient to afford an approximate illustration. It should be noted that bombs filed with TNT, or 40/60 amatol, are cast filled, i.e. the mixture is melted and poured in liquid, while bombs filled with 80/20 are stem filled, i.e. the dry powdered mixture is pressed in.[5]

Details of Aerial Bombs

As well as the explosive and the metal casing, a further two vital pieces of equipment were needed to make the bomb do its job—the detonator and the exploder. As it was, TNT and amatol were 'insensitive to any, but the most violent mechanical shock', so were relatively safe in transportation and storage. The detonator consisted of a few grains of highly explosive material, containing fulminate of mercury in a copper capsule. This could be detonated by the smallest shock—designed to be from a striker when the bomb hit the ground. It could be fitted in the fuse and struck directly on hitting the ground, or, alternatively, it could be fitted with a time-delay that was fired by a flash started by the fuse. Despite the explosive nature of the detonator it would definitely not be enough to detonate the main explosive filling; an exploder between the detonator and the explosive was used, using 'a pound or more of some more sensitive explosive, such as tetryl, surrounding the detonator and itself, and surrounded by the main charge. The exploder is detonated by the firing of the detonator when the bomb strikes, and in its turn detonates the main mass'.[6]

The same book gives further details of the effect a 112-lb bomb may have:

The penetration and size of fragments from 112lb RL bombs are shown by an experiment in which a bomb was fired 6 feet from a ½-inch steel plate about 8 feet by 4 feet. Of the fifty-six pieces which passed through, twenty-eight made holes of less than 1½ square inches area, and the ten largest made holes between 2 and 4 square inches. Two of the fragments penetrated a second ½-inch steel plate placed just behind the first.[7]

Details of Aerial Bombs

The damage done to railways by 112-lb and other sized bombs was also tested—a direct hit on a permanent railway line could be repaired by a party of men in one to one-and-a-half hours, the blast damage usually breaking just one rail and damaging 15 feet of permanent way (ballast, sleepers, ground underneath, etc.). The crater would need 10 to 12 tons of filling; however, it was also noted that no damage whatsoever to the railway, including the ground underneath, would be caused by a 112-lb bomb falling greater than 7 feet away from the centre of the tracks. These tests did, however, assume that men and materials to repair the damage were close by. If it were possible to drop a bomb that would derail a train, the damage could be exacerbated by the train causing further damage, and also necessitating clearing of the line of the rolling stock and locomotive or locomotives.

When stowed in the vertical position, as in Handley Pages, the 112-lb bombs could only be fitted with tail fuses, as the nose was fitted with a lug to hold the weapon on the release gear. The safety pin from the fuse was removed before flight. When dropped, the vane on the fuse rotated, which armed the bomb (a locking arm on the bomb gear stopped it from rotating while stowed in the aeroplane). The vane soon spun off once the bomb was released and started to fall through the air. On impact with the ground, or an object, the striker continued to move forward even though the main body of the bomb had stopped; this compressed a striker spring, which in turn fired the igniter. This burnt for either half a second, or two and a half seconds (depending on the type fitted), which then detonated the exploder and main explosive of the bomb. In August 1916, when bombs for the Royal Flying Corps now started to be supplied via the Trench Warfare Supply Department, there were around twenty types of bombs of various sizes in use. By the time the Handley Pages started to see action it had been halved, but there was still an administrative complication of the RFC and RNAS (despite mostly using either similar or the same bomb, such as the 25-lb Cooper, 112 lb, and 230 lb). They were having them supplied separately, the Admiralty retaining supply control for RNAS bombs.

The Admiralty was highly reluctant to have to rely on someone else for anything, but by September 1917 it was finally agreed after months of attempts (and by August 1917, the decision that it was essential to do so following recent developments in aircraft design and production, which led to the formation of the Bomb Committee of the Air Board) that all aerial bombs would be obtained via the Ministry of Munitions. This was with the exception of those bombs used by the RNAS that were stowed on naval vessels, such as on seaplane carriers, and also bombs used by the RNAS for attacking submarines.

Eight 250-lb bombs could be carried or eight converted 9.45-inch Trench Mortar bombs. These bombs, nicknamed 'Flying Pigs' were originally made for firing from mortars, which required a substantial timber base and traversing mounting; they were fitted with larger fins and a nose fuse with a vane, which could not be done with the 112-lb or 250-lb bombs that could only use a tail fuse when carried on Handley Pages. Converting a mortar bomb for aerial use so late in the war may seem surprising, but it became necessary owing to difficulties in production of larger bombs such as metal supplies. They were not particularly effective though, as it was found that due to the shape of the bomb half of the casing was embedded in the ground by the time the explosive went off, limiting possible damage from metal shards of the casing. Other large bombs dropped by Handley Pages included the 520-lb light-case and 550-lb heavy-case bombs, which would take up even more space.

The bomb-carrying gear, officially known as the 'Bomb Crate', consisted of four bomb beams running across the width of the fuselage. Four brackets were fitted to each beam, with adapters 9 inches long running vertically down from them. At the end were the bomb slips themselves, which the bombs were hung from. Four metal tubes (bomb guides) also hung off the brackets, wide enough to accommodate the size of the nose of the bomb, and below which was the aluminium (reinforced with wood) 'honeycomb' design that fitted the size of the bomb fins. The idea of the bomb guides was to direct the fall of the bomb once released, and to stop it from rotating while still inside the aeroplane. Originally the Handley Pages had bomb doors for each cell, spring-loaded and opened by the bomb itself as it fell. In the field it was found that they were not reliable and so they were removed, and the honeycomb was papered over. This helped to maintain what streamlining the Handley Pages had, but was also a useful guide for the ground crew when the aircraft landed, an easy indication to show if all bombs had been dropped or if any were still being carried.

Holding the bomb in place was done via the bomb slip, which had a metal suspension hook that would either be opened or closed. It was held open while loading and, when the top of the bomb's suspension lug touched the top of the hook, it pushed the arm of the hook against a trigger—a spring then closing the hook. It would be opened again by the trigger being pulled back by control cables from the bomb dropping gear.

To fit the eight 250-lb or converted 9.45-inch Trench Mortar bombs, two of the bomb beams were removed and associated equipment. The actual loading of the bombs was done from beneath; for the 112-lb bomb, the men were taught to place the number of bombs desired to be carried at a 'convenient' distance from the Handley Page, after they had been fused and with safety pins fitted. The release slips for the bombs should be tested and then the suspension hooks placed open. They were pushed up from hand by two or more men, and the bombs loaded in the order they should be dropped, from left to right. As the bombs were fitted and safely inside the bomb crate, the safety pins were removed as the arming vane on the tail fuse was safe from rotation by the locking arm—in the case of bombs with a nose fuse, the suspension lug being held in position stopped the vane from rotating. Once the lug on the nose of the bomb fitted onto the release slip suspension hook, the hook instantly closes and locks into place; an NCO or officer would be supervising the loading and would check the loading was correct.

The bombs could be dropped in either salvoes of four at a time, or individually. Each bomb slip had a control cable linked to the suspension hook and connected to a pulley nest block, and then to a control box. On top of this box, made of cast aluminium cylinder, there was a ratchet and a release handle. The ratchet had eight points and the release handle had two stops. The handle travelled a quarter of the circumference of the box in total. The eight points of the ratchet equated two bombs and so being moved two points meant the release of four bombs when the release handle was fully moved. To drop two bombs, the release handle would only be pulled halfway back (so an eighth of the entire circumference) then pushed forward again. As the technical leaflet for 'Bomb Gear in Handley Page Machines' stated, 'to release bombs singly is a matter of guess work, and cannot be relied upon'.[8] There were also additional racks for two bombs mounted on the outside of the aircraft underneath the fuselage, often used for carrying the Baby Incendiary canisters.

The Baby Incendiaries pretty much describe themselves. They were contained in a cylindrical canister weighing 140 lbs, with around 270 Baby Incendiaries inside. The action of the Baby Incendiary was described in the instructive leaflet:

On impact the cartridge sets down on the striker point in the base of the body, and the functioning of the cap simultaneously ejects the cartridge and causes ignition of the charge; the latter consists of a species of thermite, which burns with a very fierce flame, and after the flame has subsided the white-hot slag residue continues the incendiary action.[9]

Details of Aerial Bombs

If used together with heavier explosive bombs and landing on the right areas the result would be a large conflagration. The canister was protected with two walls of 18- and 20-gauge steel plate; however, it was advised that if the aircraft came under attack by machine-gun fire at close range it was better to get rid of all of them as soon as possible. For use on Handley Pages they would additionally be used to the main load and dropped at around the same time, although those dropping the bombs were instructed to allow one second's delay for each 1,000 feet the aircraft was flying at, before releasing them once the target was in the sights. When dropped, the spread of bombs from one canister would come down as a large shower, giving a good chance for a number of them to hit something that would combust. Even roofs (unless 'unusually strong') were likely to be penetrated by the bombs, and then the cartridge would start to burn underneath. As well as buildings in built-up areas, the Baby Incendiaries were also suitable for use against wooded areas—the list of targets suitable for this weapon was wide; 'towns, aerodromes, forage, stores, aircraft factories, explosive and chemical works, woods, forests, and crops'[10]—a lucky hit on a food store would not only mean it had to be replaced, but cause further morale issues for the German population who were already suffering the consequences of the Royal Navy's effective maritime blockade. Unsurprisingly, the nasty sounding little bombs had to be handled with care, and the instructive leaflet (other bombs did not have this) came with a sincere warning for those who would deal with them:

It is pointed out to all who may be concerned in the handling and use of these bombs, that although they are small, they contain all the essential features of a large offensive appliance. They must, therefore, be treated with that respect and care which is due to such articles, observing that undue familiarity, or lack of care, may cause as much damage to our own as to enemy material.[11]

Details of Aerial Bombs

Second Lieutenant Roy Shillinglaw of 100 Squadron was one of the observers who dropped Baby Incendiaries, following the unit swapping its Royal Aircraft Factory FE2b's for Handley Page in August 1918:

There are 272 bombs in each canister. Little bombs in a little case, but they were devastating things. They had a loose bottom with a rod, which held the bottom in to the top, which was tied with string. When you pulled the control a knife came across and cut the string, the rod fell away with the bottom and these bombs showered out. At 5,000 feet one of these canisters would cover 500 by 100 yards, it would smother the ground with 272 of these incendiary bombs. Vicious things. I've seen them burn through corrugated iron just like it was silver paper. We carried fourteen of these canisters sometimes. Well, one bullet in that lot and that would have been it, wouldn't it?! Never thought of it at the time...[12]

Lieutenant Roy Shillinglaw, 100 Squadron RAF

The Baby Incendiaries were not the first incendiary bombs used by the British during the war. In 1914 there were already two types of petrol bomb in use, but it wasn't until October 1916 when experimental types were manufactured. This included the Baby Incendiaries that were developed that year for naval use; they were produced in a specially built factory at Roslin, Scotland, under the supervision of Commander Francis Ranken (previously responsible for the Ranken dart, designed to be dropped on Zeppelins, with arms on springs keeping the dart in place with the explosive part of the weapon just inside the Zeppelin's skin so it could combust with the aim of setting light to the hydrogen and air as it escaped). Despite difficulties in the design and production of this weapon, the Baby Incendiaries were ready for wide-scale use in early 1918, and by July 1918 they were reportedly causing panic amongst the Germans. As well as being able to penetrate any type of roof covering, they could even burn underwater—if submerged to a depth of up to 2 feet the flame would still break the surface of the water. Although it would be possible for Handley Pages to carry large amounts of solely Baby Incendiaries, for best results they were dropped with high explosive bombs, especially when using the smallest bombs available with the largest:

It was found that the maximum, strategic, moral, and material effect was obtained by dropping a 1,700lb (referring to the SN 1,650lb) high explosive bomb closely followed by thousands of 'Baby' Incendiaries.[13]

The Official History of the Ministry of Munitions, Volume XII, The
Supply of Munitions

At the other end of the scale was the SN 1,650-lb bomb (it is also described as a 1,600-lb, 1,660-lb, 1,700-lb or 1,800-lb bomb, however as they were officially known as the 1,650-lb bomb this is how they will be referred to in the text), introduced in 1918 and the largest piece of aerial ordnance dropped by the British (the SN supposedly stands for 'Essen', one of the industrial targets had in mind for the bomb) and like the Handley Pages that dropped it, a large and surreal looking weapon compared to its smaller contemporaries. The bomb itself was a large cylinder shape, with a pointed cone at each end and with large rivets holding it together. The tail consisted of four large fins with brackets to hold them in place. The explosive content of the bomb was around half the entire weight of the bomb, and was known as the 'one tonner' even though it was shy of that weight by some way. They were first produced in around February 1918, and although originally termed 1,650-lb bombs as this is how heavy they were, the explosive filling was increased when proven that the aircraft would be able to carry it, being increased to 1,700 lbs and later 1,800 lbs. The bombs were filled with a 70/30 mix of amatol and ammonium nitrate. The bomb was 8 feet and 4 inches long even without the tail and so would not fit in the Handley Page's bomb bay—it had to be carried underneath instead. This arrangement also meant an unusual way of arming the weapon before it was dropped:

This bomb was underneath the fuselage and ten minutes before the target I had to crawl back into what we called the engine room, lift a hatch, and there was the nose of the bomb. I'd unscrew the vane, pull it out, and then I had a lot of cartridges, things about this length [indicates a length of about a foot with his hands] two or three lots of these. And I'd ram them in, they were to prime the bomb, and when they were all in, I'd put the nose cap on, screw it up and it was set to drop. Then I'd go back to the front of the machine when we were on the target, use the bombsight, pull the lever, and away went the bomb.

They used to go down tail first with their nose up, then they'd turn over and you could see them go straight down for the first 100 yards or so, then according to the height you were, sometimes it was, oh half a minute if you were at 10,000 feet—I was only at 10,000 feet once, but at 3,000 to 4,000 it would probably take about 20, 30, or 40 seconds, then just burst on the ground, on the target.[14]

Lieutenant Roy Shillinglaw, 100 Squadron RAF

An added possible reply to German 'frightfulness' were gas bombs. These were looked at, but it was considered that high explosive bombs were more effective for destruction purposes, and also morally on very shaky ground; another factor was the safety aspect if an aircraft loaded with them crashed, a factor always considered in aerial bomb production. Arrangements were made that in the case of the Germans using them, that the design and immediate production and use of them could be put into place very quickly by the British, although the need never arose.

Above the bomb crate were the fuel tanks—two of them, mounted transversely across the fuselage, cylindrical in shape. The fuel was pumped via pipes into two tanks mounted in the upper wing and then ran down to the engines by gravity. The wings themselves were not staggered, the upper wing being directly above the lower, and of unequal span. The upper wing was 100 feet wide as per the specification and the designation O/100 (the O/400 had the same wingspan), and the lower wing 70 feet wide. As was standard at the time, the wings were made up of a number of 'ribs', which took the profile of the wing as viewed side-on, set a certain distance apart with fabric covering. As well as the large wooden struts connecting the two wings, rigging using streamlined heavy-gauge wires made the biplane unit secure. The way an aircraft handled while in the air owed a lot to the rigging, the ground crew's expertise in ensuring it was not too tight or too slack had a great impact on the aircraft's performance. Immediately on both sides of the fuselage as the lower wing joined the spar, was the undercarriage, central between the engine nacelles and the fuselage. Each of the two undercarriage chassis had two wheels, and was joined where the main spars joined the fuselage and where the joints for the folding wing were. Unlike most aircraft of the time, the wheels were not on the outside of the undercarriage, but between the vertical pieces that joined them to the wings. The arrangement of two separate undercarriage chassis units allowed the underneath of the fuselage to be uninterrupted, which was to prove useful for carrying the SN 1,650-lb bomb in 1918. Palmer wheels and rubber pneumatic tyres were fitted as well as shock absorbers. The wheels, as standard at the time, were wire spoke, but covered in fabric to aid streamlining.

The engine nacelles were the main visible external giveaway to tell an O/100 from an O/400. On both types they were mounted mid-way between the two wings. The nacelles for the O/100s were a lot longer, and extended slightly to the rear of the wings (some early O/100s had nacelles so long the tip itself had to be able to fold 180 degrees so it did not foul the wings when folded back), as on the O/100 there were fuel tanks in the rear of the nacelles. On the O/400, where these were not present, the nacelles were much shorter and it also had a different, flat-fronted style of radiator. The vast majority of Handley Page O types were fitted with Rolls-Royce Eagle VIII engines. The Eagle was a superb engine, based on the engine fitted to one of their best known products, the Silver Ghost automobile, with twelve cylinders (as opposed to the six cylinders of the car's engine) and an increased stroke.

The first flight of the engine was in the prototype Handley Page O/100 1455, but it served in many other types. The Airco DH4 two-seat day bomber was designed to be fitted with the Eagle and served the RNAS, RFC, and then RAF extremely well. The only issue was supply throughout the war; Rolls-Royce simply could not build enough of them to meet demand; the design required a large amount of hand fitting and owing to the precision engineering employed by Rolls-Royce, it was not well-suited to mass production. By January 1918, the situation was getting so desperate that the Ministry of Munitions Supply Branch set up a separate section, under the authority of Sir Alfred Herbert, to deal with Rolls-Royce engine production. Production was, despite Rolls-Royce's reluctance to do so, sub-contracted, but was closely controlled. The Clement Talbot Motor Works in Ladbroke Grove, London, the National Shell Factory at Derby (who made the engine cylinders), part of the National Projectile Factory at Dudley, and part of the White and Poppe works at Coventry, among a few others, were to build parts of the Rolls-Royce Eagle and Falcon engines. The Supply Department of the Ministry of Munitions provided the machine tools and Rolls-Royce provided jigs and gauges. They also placed the contracts with the companies rather than have to go through the Supply Department, and provided members of staff to oversee the work being done elsewhere.

Another attempt was made by placing a contract with companies in the USA to 1,500 Eagle engines in part form and have them assembled in Derby, a factory being taken over and fitted out with assembly shops in anticipation for the arriving parts. The first American Eagle in kit form was expected in February 1918, but owing to various issues not a single one was completed before the Armistice. Despite the effort, the aimed production rates of 200 Eagle and twenty Falcon engines a week never came close to being met, which affected supply of Handley Pages during the summer of 1918. This was a disappointing result, especially as Rolls-Royce had been given the highest priority for machinery and materials, prioritising them over other aero engine manufacturers. By July 1918 Handley Page O/400s were coming out of factories well before engines were available, the excess aeroplanes being put into storage at the American Assembly Factory (again, a large building built in anticipation for large numbers of American-built aircraft being shipped to Britain for final assembly then flying to the front) while production of the aircraft had to be slowed down. Other engines were trialled not just for the Handley Page O/100 and O/400s, but other types too, including the Airco DH4 and also the Bristol F2b fighter, which used the downsized Falcon. Sunbeam Cossack engines were used on a number of Handley Pages and other types, including Sunbeam Maori, Fiat A12, and Hispano-Suiza; Galloway Atlantic engines were also trialled, however, they were not as good as the Rolls-Royce Eagles. The excellent American-built Liberty L12 engines were fitted to some aircraft (a type used to great effect in the Airco DH9A, following the failure of the Airco DH9 using the disappointing Siddeley Puma engine), including the Handley Page, and it was planned that these would be fitted in lieu of the Rolls-Royce Eagle.

The Liberty engine was designed following the entry of the USA into the war—a commission had toured Allied countries to ascertain the best type of engine suitable for mass production in the USA. The Rolls-Royce Eagle was chosen as well as the excellent, but untried Lorraine Dietrich engine. As the Eagle was not suitable for mass production, a completely new engine was designed in eight cylinder 200 hp and twelve cylinder 300 hp versions. The Department of Aircraft Production ordered 3,000 and production started in August 1917; however, by the end of March 1918, no deliveries had been made so the British asked for fifty to 100 complete sets of parts to be sent over for assembly in Britain. In June an additional 2,500 were ordered, but were told that just 980 of those could be spared out of the amount needed for the American programme up until the end of 1918. It was estimated that 16,000 of both types would be produced by the end of the year, but 14,000 were needed by the Americans, leaving 2,000 for the French and British who had both ordered similar amounts; the British wanted it for the DH9A, the Handley Pages, the Vickers Vimy, Airco DH10, and the Felixstowe flying boats. Despite difficulties with supply, the lack of suitable replacement available in quantities meant that the Rolls-Royce Eagle was fitted to the vast majority of the Handley Pages. The Eagle VIII was rated at 360 hp, and gave the O/400 a quoted cruising speed (although it would be impossible to accurately gauge, and would also depend on the age of the aircraft, rigging, and whether it had been left outside for long periods in which case rain could soak the fabric covering the aircraft making it heavier, etc.) of just below 100 mph at ground level or 80 mph at the maximum ceiling (an increase of 20–25 mph on the O/100). A ceiling of 10,000 feet was also attainable when loaded and eight hours duration with 2,100 lbs of fuel.

To get to 10,000 feet it took around forty-five minutes—two minutes and forty-five seconds for the first 1,000 and then eventually ten minutes for the last 1,000. While on operational service, this would mean the aircraft would have to circle continually gaining height before crossing the lines, often remarked as the dullest part of a flight by the crews.

Further out along the wing from the engine nacelles, where their supporting struts met the wings, was where the wings folded backwards. This was one of the original specifications of the design, essential so that they could fit in the hangars at the time that were designed for much smaller types. The main type in use was the Bessonneau hangar, which was designed by the French manufacturer Les Établissements Bessonneau in the 1900s. It had a wood frame with a canvas body and was an excellent temporary hangar; they were supplied as a kit and made of bays, so they could be extended if needed, and inspired temporary hangars seen today, but made with more durable materials. Not only could they be assembled and disassembled relatively easily, they could be moved as a whole, witnessed at least once by Lieutenant Bewsher.

Their design was perfect for the conditions experienced by flying units of the British and French air forces during the war. The wings folded towards the rear of the aeroplane. The joint was not at the trailing edge of the wings, but slightly inwards, where the struts were, meaning that this would be the strongest joint on which to hinge the weight of the wings. A triangular section on each side of the wing folded in to allow for this. A false strut was fitted to the portion of wings folded back, near where the engine nacelles would be, to keep them stable.

Out on the wingtips of the upper wing were navigation lights, which were red on the port (left) side and green on the starboard (right) side. On the lower wings, Holt's wing-tip landing flares were fitted, two each per wing. These were fitted to night-flying aircraft to aid landing in bad weather, or in case of forced landing when uncertain of the state of the ground beneath. There were two types, and ideally one of each type would be fitted on each wing—red, suitable for use when flying in mist, and white. Switches on the pilot's instrument panel controlled these. Michelin parachute flares designed for use in lighting up the ground at night in preparation for bombing could also be carried and dropped, although as their delay only allowed for a drop of 800–1,000 feet they were not particularly suitable for high-flying Handley Pages, and of better use on the FE2b night bombers that operated at lower altitudes.

Rearwards of the bomb crate was the rear gunner's mid-upper position. In this position, where the gunner stood on a platform mounted above the floor of the fuselage (when stood up, he would have a clearer view over the top of the aircraft than those in front) giving the gunner (or gunners) a fine, clear view of the rear. There were mountings for three Lewis guns; two were on pillars covering the upper rear of the aircraft, and the third (accessed by a platform lower down and further to the rear) was a lower, ventral gun that had a small trap door to be opened before the gun was pointed underneath and to the rear of the aircraft. Interestingly the *Handley Page Bomber Type O/400 Descriptive Handbook* mentions that this Lewis gun is a land pattern one, i.e. with the aluminium cooling fin and jacket fitted, presumably as the gun would mostly be out of the slipstream when fired from this position and therefore would not get the same cooling effect the other, more exposed, Lewis guns would have. As well as the racks mounted on the side walls for Lewis gun drum magazines, there was also a small hinged seat for the gunner. On some sorties, more than one gunner would be located in this position and operationally it was standard practice for new pilots and observers to undertake their first few raids from this position to get accustomed to the experience of a night raid. Despite the Lewis gun covering the rear and underneath, the position did not afford a great deal of visibility for the gunner to be able to aim the weapon if the aircraft was more to the rear than directly underneath the aircraft. However, if this did happen, there was another option, despite the Handley Page's relative lack of manoeuvrability:

> They could get under your tail. We had that several times but if you had a good pilot he could spiral out of that alright. Then you could both bring your guns on in any trouble.[15]

Sergeant Leslie Alexander Dell, 214 Squadron RAF

An additional sting in the tail for the Handley Page was the carriage of 25-lb Cooper bombs from this position; these would be thrown by the rear gunner himself at any targets of opportunity below, especially searchlights if one happened to be more-or-less directly underneath. Like the originally intended bomb dropping position, the rear gun layer position also had clear panels to allow light into the compartment. The rear gunner almost gained another item of munitions for his armoury—a grenade. The Royal Air Force in 1918 requested a design for firing grenades from Handley Pages, specifically to protect the rear of the aircraft from attack. The Munitions Inventions Department came up with a design based on the small No. 34 'Egg' bomb (during the First World War, British service grenades were termed 'bombs') already in use with the British Army as a hand bomb. The first design drawing was dated 19 August 1918, and the new type of bomb was known as the No. 48 bomb; the main body was 64 mm in diameter and was designed to be fired from a projector, which was a cup discharger attached to a much-shortened Short Magazine Lee Enfield rifle. A normal .303 bullet would be fired down the barrel, which would make contact with the base of the bomb, then fire it out of the cup discharger. This was a rather unusual design. Although rifle bombers in the army used cup dischargers—in order to fire bombs over longer distances than those achievable by hand—they always used blank cartridges, using the gas from the blank round to fire the bomb rather than the bullet itself (although the French used rifle bombs with standard rifle rounds to propel them). A No. 48 Mk II bomb was designed with a slightly lengthened body and a larger fuse, to give the bomb a longer range (in this case 350 yards). There is no evidence for these being fitted to Handley Pages during the war, although on 5 March 1919 a request was made for 300 No. 48 bombs filled with sand to match their weight as if filled with explosive, and 300 igniters, each of different lengths (100 each of 4.75 seconds, 6.8 seconds, and 9.4 seconds). Nothing further is known of their aerial experimentation, but the bomb and discharger were later tested in tanks during the inter-war period.

At the end of the fuselage, the tail was also a biplane, with both planes 20 feet wide including the elevators. In common with aircraft of the period, a single wooden (ash) tail skid was underneath the tail and a cable hand-grip at the extreme rear of the fuselage for ground crew to manoeuvre the aircraft with. Although the Handley Page could be moved by men, a large number were needed, and so the Handley Page became the first aeroplane to need a motorised vehicle to efficiently move it. Not only did this vehicle have to be able to do the job of a large number of men, it also had to have cross-country ability to move over the grass airfields these aircraft were operated from, and have adequate traction. Fortunately, in 1916 the well-known manufacturer of agricultural equipment and steam traction engines, Clayton & Shuttleworth of Lincoln, produced a 35-hp 'crawler' tractor, using caterpillar tracks. Caterpillar tracked vehicles were of ever-increasing popularity, especially during the First World War as they were put to good use as artillery tractors by the British (and as general supply trailer tractors in the middle east campaigns).

The Clayton 35-hp crawler was perfect for the role of aircraft tug, and they were purchased for use with Handley Page units. The introduction of the first aircraft tug did not bring the first tow bar with it (although, again in common with other aircraft of the time, a two-wheeled dolly with long handlebar was produced to accommodate the rear skid and again aid the ground crew in moving the aircraft) and so a rope was tied around each undercarriage chassis then to the rear of the tractor for haulage. Clayton & Shuttleworth were also one of the manufacturers of Handley Page O/400s during the war, as well as Sopwith Triplanes and Camels, and the tractors had an interesting role after the war when used as the first launching tractors by the Royal National Lifeboat Institution lifeboat stations around the British and Irish coast.

The production of the Handley Pages was split over various companies. Handley Page Limited simply did not have the capacity to build the amount wanted, and so other companies were contracted. To increase capacity, Handley Page opened a new 11-acre factory at Somerton Road in Cricklewood, with drawing offices nearby on Claremont Road and requisitioning land from Clitterhouse Farm for an aerodrome for the new factory. In total 840 Handley Page O type aircraft were ordered, but owing to cancellations at the end of the war, the total built came to 600. There were forty O/100s, six 'intermediate' aircraft, and 281 O/400s built by Handley Page Limited, with the remaining 273 built by other companies, these being the Royal Aircraft Factory at Farnborough, the Metropolitan Carriage & Wagon Company, the Birmingham Carriage Company, British Caudron (the British branch of the French aircraft manufacturing firm), and Clayton & Shuttleworth of Lincoln. The cost to the government of each Handley Page O/400 was £6,000, but that was without the cost of guns, aircraft instrumentation (altimeter, speed gauge, etc., which would be supplied by other manufacturers), and engines. The cost of a single Rolls-Royce Eagle VIII engine was £1,622 and 10s.

The Handley Page was also selected for American mass production. In August 1917 a set of drawings was shipped to the US Signals Corps Engineering Division where it would be adapted to use the Liberty engine for use by US forces (in addition to the plans for the Liberty engine to be fitted to British Handley Pages). An aircraft was sent over in January 1918 (actually an O/100, but featuring many O/400 parts—anything that would need changing to O/400 standard was signified by being painted red). In 1917 the possibility of building the aircraft in the USA and having them fly across the Atlantic owing to the U-boat threat to shipping was discussed, but later dropped, and so instead they were to be shipped to Liverpool in component form and assembled for flight in Britain. Originally 500 Handley Page O/400s fitted with the Liberty engine were ordered, with the addition of a second batch of 1,000 in August 1918 to equip thirty American bombing squadrons; however, by the end of the war, only 100 incomplete sets were ready to be shipped to Europe. The first American Handley Page was first flown on 1 July 1918 and later named *Langley*, and seven further O/400s were built, flown, and entered service, but never left the USA. Apart from numbers of individual US airmen who joined British Squadrons and flew on operational missions or were based close by and went on raids (including, on the last night of the war, an all-American crew of a Handley Page O/400), the Americans did not get to fly the Handley Page during the war. Owing to the delay in American-built aircraft being produced, a number of British-built aircraft were to be fitted with the Liberty engine and flown by American Squadrons, however, owing to the Armistice, this did not happen.

Whereas a 'normal' sized aircraft of the time could be relatively easily transported on specially designed trailers, towed by lorries or tenders with the wings alongside or on another trailer (in the rear of vehicle if space allowed), the Handley Page needed something rather different. Although the wings were very large, they were also light, and so a new design of trailer was specially constructed of a deep box girder construction covered with a canvas sheet to protect against the elements and an axle on springs with twin (pneumatic, unlike the solid ones used for lorries) on each wheel. To tow the trailer, 25-hp motor cars were used, with the body removed and the front of the trailer mounted upon it, creating a very early form of articulated lorry.

Into Action

The Handley Pages were to join 3 Wing at Luxeuil, which formed part of an Anglo-French bombing force. The origins of 3 Wing were linked to the introduction of the Sopwith Land Clerget Tractor, the prototype of which first flew in December 1915. The Sopwith Land Clerget Tractor soon became known as the 'one-and-a-half Strutter' owing to the configuration of one pair of struts between the upper and lower wing, and one pair of half struts (from the upper wing to the fuselage) on each side. It was designed as both a fighter (Admiralty Type 9400) and a bomber (Admiralty Type 9700). Both types became the first British aircraft to be successfully fitted with synchronisation gear for a forward-firing machine gun, firing through the propeller arc with a single Vickers gun; the fighter version had a Lewis gun mounted on a Scarff ring behind the pilot and the bomber, solely crewed by the pilot, had an internal bomb bay with a capacity for four 65-lb bombs. One RNAS plan for the Sopwith 1½ Strutter bombers was to attack the German industrial towns of Essen and Düsseldorf, targeted due to the steel works producing materials used in the U-boats (hence the naval interest). The planes were based from RNAS Detling, near Maidstone in Kent. The four-hour range of the Sopwith 1½ Strutters made this a possibility, but there was the small matter of neutral Holland being on the flightpath to the intended targets. A detour would be possible to avoid overflying neutral territory and the political ramifications that may follow (as well as the possibility of being shot down by Dutch forces, a very real threat to aircraft of both sides during the war), however it was argued that this may not always be possible, especially given the stress pilots would be under while on operations.

Following the abandonment of this plan, the French were asked if a joint bomber force would be desirable; they agreed, and so in mid-June 1916 Captain W. L. Elder and a naval party started to construct a camp at Luxeuil—originally planned for a force of sixty aircraft, and later increased to 100. No. 3 Wing and its Strutters moved to RNAS Manston (also in Kent, but closer to the coast) in preparation for the move to France. Owing to the preparations and commencement of the Battle of the Somme, and the increased demand for aerial operations in the area to support the ground offensive, there was a call from Hugh Trenchard for more fighters, especially the Sopwith 1½ Strutter, which was also in service with the Royal Flying Corps. Production of the bomber Strutters was put on hold and 3 Wing was not ready to commence operations until October; this caused severe delays to both the British and French side of the Anglo-French bomber force—they were using a French-built version of the Strutter, known as the SOP 1B1 when crafted as a bomber. Although these were built in French factories, they were lacking engines. The French-built Clerget engines, used for both British and French-built examples, were in high demand by the RFC, so most of the supplies were being diverted to the Somme area. The French had also been promised a third of the Strutters delivered to Luxeuil from Britain. To fill the gaps, both the British and French were using Breguet Bre 5s. The Breguet, designed as an escort fighter, allowed the gunner an uninterrupted field of fire above and forward when in 'pusher' configuration; however, they proved unpopular and unsuccessful as a bomber, and were limited in supply. It was considered that they needed at least one escort fighter for each bomber, if used on day bomber work. The French were also making do with obsolescent Henri Farman 'pusher' biplanes with a very limited bombing capacity, and 3 Wing also had two Short Bombers. The Short Bomber was a landplane derivative of the extremely successful Short 184 seaplane. The Short Bomber had a longer range than the Strutter at six hours, but was underpowered.

On 30 July 1916, despite not being at full strength, 3 Wing's first raid was on German barracks and petrol store at Mulheim, near Freiburg, with three Strutters joining six French bombers—one of the Strutters was one of the two-seat fighters also used by 3 Wing. After this, Captain Elder was ordered not to fly on operations until more aircraft arrived, pushing the next raid to 12 October; the Breguets arrived in the two months prior to this date. Sixty-two aircraft in total took part in the raid, including Breguet Bre 5s, of the French and British units, and Sopwith 1½ Strutter bombers and fighter escorts from 3 Wing. The French were also escorted by the Nieuport Scouts of the American volunteer Lafayette Escadrille, but could not fly all the way to Obendorf so had to return for fuel then rejoin the bombers on their return leg. Not all aircraft bombed their target and there was no damage done to the Mauser works, although ten German civilians were killed or wounded. The disappointing results of the raid certainly did not justify the twenty-one pilots and observers lost to anti-aircraft guns and German scouts engaged on home defence, who hounded the aircraft as they returned—the arrival of the Lafayette Escadrille almost certainly saving the day from becoming an even bigger disaster. On 23 October, following up from the French raid the previous night (they had decided to stick to night bombing following the Obendorf raid), the steel works at Hagindengen were attacked by thirteen Strutter bombers escorted by seven fighters. Fortunately there were no losses this time, helped by little anti-aircraft fire and no German aircraft attacking them.

There were three further raids in November and one in December, but bad weather hampered operations for much of winter; snow and fog from a particularly cold winter proved problematic at the airfield, and also obscured the low-lying valleys in which the enemy industrial areas were located. Nine of 3 Wings best pilots were moved to Dunkirk at the end of January, following a request to support Royal Flying Corps operations in that area. The first raid of the year occurred on 23 January when twenty-four aircraft set off for the Burbach blast furnaces near Saarbrücken. On their return, a bomb that had got stuck in the bomb bay dropped and exploded while the aircraft was taxiing after landing, killing two groundcrew immediately and a third dying of injuries. Even when the weather started to clear in February, low temperatures caused oil to freeze in the Strutter's Clerget engines. The blast furnaces were attacked again, once in February and twice in March. On 7 March an order came through for more men, and also machines, to go to Dunkirk—six Strutter fighters, as well as nineteen pilots and 100 ratings. The arrival of the Handley Pages would have improved morale immensely.

The first Handley Page to make it across to France, 1459, had observer Lieutenant Paul Bewsher among the crew of the aircraft who had previous experience of reconnaissance missions around the coast. He described the build-up to the ferry flight:

> The great machine was prepared. Heavy tool-boxes, engine spares, tail trolleys, and a mass of material were packed into its capacious maw. The tanks were filled with petrol, oil and water. The engines were tested again and again. The day came. A pile of luggage stood on the ground beneath the machine; farewells were said—gloves, goggles, boots and flying caps were collected—and it rained.
>
> Back into its hangar went the machine. Back into the tents went the luggage. Back into the mess went the disappointed airmen. For three or four days this happened, but at last a gentle breeze, a clear horizon, and a blue sky greeted the morning. Once again the suit-cases and trunks were packed inside the machine. I put my little tabby kitten into her basket and tied a handkerchief over the top, and lashed the whole on to the platform in the back of the aeroplane. The six airmen dressed themselves

in their sky-clothes and took to their places—the C.O. at the wheel. A whistle was blown; farewells were shouted; the engines roared, and we mounted triumphantly into the air over the countryside of Thanet.[1]

Lieutenant Paul Bewsher, 3 Wing RNAS

Bewsher went on to describe his feelings during the flight on 4 November 1916:

I was leaving England behind! I had to look back over the rail to see the white line of the cliffs and the sweep of the Isle of Thanet coast from Birchington to Ramsgate. I began to feel a lump in my throat. I was not eager to look forward to see the first glimpse of France through the sea mist. My thoughts were full of the sadness of bereavement. I knew not what lay ahead—what France and war might bring me. I knew not how long I would be from my own well-known country, or even if I would ever return.[2]

It was not long before Bewsher thoughts were distracted by an escaped passenger:

To my horror I suddenly became conscious of the kitten sitting beside me carefully cleaning her paws, and probably supremely unconscious that she was 6000 feet in the air, half-way across the Dover Straits. Apprehensive for her safety I gave her no time to learn her position, but quickly pushed her into the basket, and, undoing my flowing coat and my muffler, I took off my tie, which I tied across the top of the basket to prevent the spirited young lady from emerging once more.[3]

Lieutenant Paul Bewsher, 3 Wing RNAS

Despite the cold, Bewsher became more and more absorbed into reading his copy of H. G. Wells' *The History of Mr Polly* before the aircraft flew over the outskirts of Paris and landed at Villacoublay. The second aircraft, HP 1460, followed not long after HP 1459, and more Handley Pages followed as they were prepared and tested at Manston. One more, HP 1461, made the crossing that year on 15 November, but weather again delayed crossings so that it was not until 1 January 1917 that the next two Handley pages left Manston.

Before the operational career of the Handley Page bombers had even started, the Germans were to know all they needed to know about the design itself. When HPs 1462 and 1463 attempted to fly from Manston to Villacoublay on the first day of 1917, despite HP 1462 making the journey with no problems, HP 1463 landed 12 miles behind German lines, delivering a fully intact brand-new Handley Page O/100 complete with two officers and three air mechanics to a German airfield at Chalandry. The flight was described by Air Mechanic Higby:

> Both aeroplanes eventually got away at about 1100 hours in clear weather with fresh winds, but crossing mid-channel at 6500 ft we were skimming heavy billowing clouds. Then we saw Lieutenant Sands' machine dive. We circled for a time, then Lieutenant Vereker put the nose of our machine down. We carried on until our altimeter showed 200 ft and we were still in heavy cloud. The pilot immediately put the nose up again and after about thirty minutes of heavy going with first one engine boiling and then the other, we came out at about 6000 ft. We tried in all directions to find a break in the clouds in order to get our bearings, and this manoeuvring went on for about two hours until we came out of cloud at 500 ft. We landed in what turned out to be a ploughed field overgrown with grass. We had no opportunity to destroy the machine as German troops separated us from the aeroplane before we realised we had landed in German territory. We were 12 miles behind the German lines. Afterwards we found out that our compass was sticking and that we were lucky to have landed without mishap.
>
> Air Mechanic Higby, 3 Wing RNAS

One version of events is that the pilot, Flight Sub-Lieutenant Vereker, ran back to the aircraft in an attempt to take off, but as his head and shoulders were just inside the fuselage he was pulled down again by a German. The men were interrogated and then spent the rest of the war as prisoners. As well as the aircraft itself, there were technical reports and other paperwork that proved interesting to the Germans, and, after being dismantled and transported to Germany, 1463 was reassembled and flown by the Imperial Air Service, complete with insignia. It was written off in a crash on 22 August that year, apparently due to the cabling for the ailerons being reassembled wrongly. *The Flying Book* 1917 edition includes the Handley Page O/100 in its list of modern aeroplanes—owing to the need for secrecy there is nothing particularly modern about the list, the more modern British types being the Airco DH1, the Sopwith Tabloid, and the Avro 504 all retired from front-line duties by 1917. The inclusion of the new, state-of-the-art Handley Page is explained in the description of the type, described as a '500-hp Twin Tractor Biplane':

The most important war-time product is the giant twin-engined tractor biplane, the most powerful weight-carrying land machine in the world. As, unfortunately, it is definitely known that one of these machines is in the hands of the enemy, it is possible to give few general details without divulging information of military importance.[4]

The Flying Book, 1917

Handley Page 1463 was believed to have returned to England—only briefly, and without landing—on the morning of 16 March 1917. At 05.20, in the early morning light, an aircraft appeared near Westgate, Kent, and dropped twenty 5-kgs bombs. The German crew, from Seeflieger Abteilung 1 based at Zeebrugge, had intended to attack coastal shipping, but when they emerged from low cloud decided to attack what they thought were the railway station and sheds at Margate. Most of the bombs landed in open fields and just £45 of damage was caused, mostly broken windows in nearby buildings, with no injuries to the population. A number of eye-witnesses identified the aircraft as a Handley Page, perhaps some of them aware of HP 1463 being captured, and one special constable reported seeing the British red, white, and blue markings on the tail. Although this convinced the British intelligence services that the raid had been carried out using the captured Handley Page, it actually appears to have been a single engine floatplane.

There were claims later that the Handley Page design was used as a basis for the Gotha G.IV and G.V bombers, a myth that still exists today. Apart from a very basic likeness in design, i.e. both being large, twin-engine biplane bombers, there were no real similarities in the two designs. Apart from the setback of losing one aircraft before the first attempt at putting the aircraft into action, the plans continued. More and more Handley Page O/100s were being ferried to France through the early months of 1917, and the first operational use of the 'Bloody Paralyser' was to come on the night of 16–17 March 1917, the honour falling to HP 1460, based with HP 1459 at Ochey—the operational home of 3 Wing since November 1916.

The Handley Pages were operated by the Handley Page Squadron, and in charge of the Handley Page Squadron was Squadron Commander John Babington, who made an impression on Bewsher:

On one occasion he wished to move an enormous hangar, complete with its canvas curtains and covers, a hundred feet long and forty feet across, about four times as big as an average cottage. The whole was extremely heavy, and weighed many tons. The C.O. called a bugler, and the call Clear Lower Deck was sounded. When every hand, from cook to clerk, had fallen in, he distributed the men round the hangar and gave the order, 'One, two, three, Lift,' and marched the unwieldy structure across the ground to its new position in a few minutes. In this way he rearranged the whole aerodrome.[5]

Lieutenant Paul Bewsher, 3 Wing RNAS

The first Handley Page raid was on the railway station at Moulin-les-Metz on the night of 16 March, the momentous occasion being described in full by Sub-Lieutenant Bewsher who was at Ochey, but not taking part in the raid:

The little triangular door on the floor of the machine was shut. The blocks of wood were taken away from beneath the wheels. The engines roared out, and the machine moved slowly across the grass. It turned slightly, its noise leapt up suddenly again, and with a beating throb the huge craft began to move across the aerodrome with its blue flames and showers of red sparks shooting out behind it. Faster and faster it went— every eye watching it, every mouth firm and voiceless. At last it roared up into the air.[6]

Lieutenant Paul Bewsher, 3 Wing RNAS

To those on the ground, the noise of the engines appeared to cease after it took off and a red glow appeared beyond a slope that the aircraft would have had to fly over. Fearing a crash, pandemonium then ensued with shouts encouraging others to leap into action. A motor car, fully loaded with would-be rescuers armed with Pyrene fire extinguishers, sped off as quickly as it could, however it was not long until the tremendous noise of the Handley Page returned as the aircraft flew over the airfield. It circled the airfield for around ten minutes before heading towards enemy territory. A change of wind and red landing flares had, no doubt combined with stress, fatigue, and excitability of the men on the ground, caused the false alarm. Eleven bombs were dropped over the target with the twelfth jamming and having to be released by the crew. Afterwards, Handley Page Squadron Commander J. T. Babington who had flown the Handley Page sent a report to Captain W. L. Elder (commanding 3 Wing) stating that the Handley Page had no difficulty in lifting the load of twelve 100-lb bombs and enough fuel for five-and-a-half hours flight, and that he thought the aircraft would be 'entirely satisfactory and reliable' in its intended role as a night bomber. Elder then reported to the Admiralty on 18 March, requesting as many Handley Pages as possible be sent to Ochey (he stated they had accommodation to easily house sixteen to twenty of them), mentioning that Ochey was a very suitable aerodrome for night bombing and how 'the vast majority of industrial Germany should be within comparatively easy range'. He also mentioned how the initial raid had taken place despite poor weather conditions and lack of spares, which was hampering the operations of the Handley Page Squadron.

The next raid was on the night of 5–6 April, with both Handley Pages due to bomb the railway junction at Arnaville. The first to leave had to circle Arnaville four times owing to thick mist—all the while facing anti-aircraft fire and searchlights—but reported dropping all twelve 100-lb bombs on target before returning. The other Handley Page had to turn back after flying into thick fog before reaching the lines; Sub Lieutenant Bewsher was on board, and described how the French observer gave his verdict:

> The almost inevitable word brouillard. He thought it was too misty. He stood up and leaned back to the pilot, and shouted his words of explanation—'Trop de brouillard! No good! It will be very bad by Metz!'[7]

Lieutenant Paul Bewsher, 3 Wing RNAS

At some point, possibly at Ochey, HP 1459 was photographed wearing a very curious looking paint scheme. The normal all-over PC10 dark green had been replaced on the undersides of the wing and fuselage, and also the struts joining the two wings, in a mottled camouflage. Although designed to conceal the aircraft better while flying at night, it was deemed unsuccessful or not worth the effort as it was not seen on other Handley Pages.

The third raid was on 13–14 April, using both aircraft again, this time the target being an iron works at Hagendingen. Take off was delayed as they waited for the moon to rise to give them better visibility, the first one not taking off until 02.17. Just under an hour later they arrived at the target, dropped all twelve bombs and returned. The second aircraft, crewed by Flight Sub-Lieutenant E. B. Waller, French airman Lieutenant le Couteau, and Lieutenant Paul Bewsher didn't leave until later owing to a problem with one of the engines. Nearing the target, Bewsher left his seat, went to the compartment behind the pilot and lay on the floor, looking through the negative lens sight, with the bomb release gear on his right.

> The edge of the door framed now a rectangular section of dark country, on which here and there glowed the intermittent flame of a blast-furnace. I could not quite identify my objective, so I climbed forwards to the cockpit and asked the French observer for further directions. He explained to me, and then suddenly I saw, some way below the machine,

a quick flash, and another, and another—each sending a momentary glare of light on the machine. I crawled hurriedly back, and lay down again to get ready to drop my bombs. Below me now I could see incessant shell-bursts, vicious and brilliant red spurts of flame. I put my head out of the hole for a moment into the biting wind, and looked down, and saw that the whole night was be-flowered with these sudden sparks of fire, which appeared silently like bubbles breaking to the surface of a pond. The Germans were firing a fierce barrage from a great number of guns. They thought, fortunately for us, that we were French Breguets, which flew much lower than we did, so their shells burst several thousand feet beneath us.

I was very excited as I lay face downwards in my heavy flying-clothes on the floor, with my right hand on the bomb-handle in that little quivering room whose canvas walls were every now and then lit up by the flash of a nearer shell. Through the quick sparks of fire I tried to watch the blast-furnace below. Just in front of me the pilot's thick flying-boots were planted on the rudder, and occasionally I would pull one or the other to guide him. The engines thundered. The floor vibrated. Below the faint glow of the bomb-sights the sweep of country seemed even darker in contrast with the swift flickering of the barrage, and here and there I could see the long beam of a searchlight moving to and fro.

Then I pressed over my lever, and heard a clatter behind. I pressed it over again and looked back. Many of the bombs had disappeared—a few remained scattered in different parts of the bomb-rack. I looked down again, and pressed over my lever twice more,—my heart thumping with tremendous excitement as I felt the terrific throbbing of power of the machine and saw the frantic furious bursting of the shells, and realised in what a thrilling midnight drama of action and force I was acting. I looked back and saw by the light of my torch that one bomb was still in the machine. I walked back to the bomb-rack, and saw the arms of the back gunlayer stretching forwards, trying to reach it. I put my foot on the top of it and stood up. It slipped suddenly through the bottom and disappeared.

In a moment I was beside the pilot. 'All gone, Jimmy! Let's be getting back, shall we?'[8]

Lieutenant Paul Bewsher, 3 Wing RNAS

As they returned, Bewsher noticed that Metz—which had been brilliantly lit up with no attempts of a blackout—was now not to be seen at all, hidden in darkness. The raid was to be relived again and again on their return, discussed over coffee and biscuits with excited colleagues. The German anti-aircraft gunners in the area of Metz had the unusual distinction of being the first to fire at the Handley Pages, and as the operational use of Handley Pages increased, so did the numbers of anti-aircraft guns and gunners to meet them.

When it came to ground-based anti-aircraft defences, the Germans had already started the war on a good footing. They had actually been the first users of anti-aircraft artillery, years before powered heavier-than-air flight had even taken place, with the 3.7-cm Ballonkanone of 1870, five of which were made and mounted on four-wheeled, horse-drawn carts. These were used against the balloons that the French operated as a forms of communication to and from Paris, which was under siege during the Franco-Prussian war. As early as 1906, an armoured vehicle with an anti-aircraft gun on the rear had been designed and built, and so by the outbreak of war the German Army already had a number of anti-aircraft guns on horse-drawn wagons and also armoured, motorised chassis. The standard gun in use was the 7.7-cm BAK (BallonAbwehrKanone) and although there were only six up-to-date motorised anti-aircraft guns, two horse-drawn ones, and a number of older anti-aircraft guns on various mountings it was still more than the Allies had. With the coming of the war, more were soon ordered and older and captured weapons were brought into service, as well as field guns being put on mountings—often made in the field—to make them able to fire at the high angles to put them into service as anti-aircraft guns.

The most often mentioned anti-aircraft weapon by the night fliers of the FE2bs and Handley Pages were the 'flaming onions' (also termed 'green balls' or similar terms), which seemed to rise slowly towards the aircraft as if they had been fired very closely together or at the same time. They were also seen by pilots operating at day time when attacking enemy observation balloons. Opinions differed as to their nature:

Archies burst around and strings of balls of fire known as flaming onions shoot up at one. If these were to wrap themselves around one's tail. Well. Amen.[9]

Lieutenant Leslie George Semple, 207 Squadron RAF

Seemingly linked together, and made of flaming phosphorous, these grim fireworks formed a terrifying defence against the approach of aircraft. This was the 'flaming onion' battery at Roulers, and I very soon learned what a nightmare they could be when spurting up within a few feet of a machine, threatening to envelop it in flames.[10]

Second Lieutenant Denis Hugh Montgomery, 101 Squadron RFC

Others found them less intimidating:

> You would see their guns start up and down there and they looked just like little peas and they would come up like this in rows you see. Perhaps two, four, six at a time and I think that by the number of these things that came up. They were directing the barrage all round you see because they seemed to fire more at those onions than they did at you in a lot of cases and I think they were just a direction guide for the guns. Well, when they passed you they were bigger than a football each. They were only just like little peas you see and they would gradually get bigger and bigger and you would watch them coming up like that and around they would go. I have never been hit with one but I have had scorches. Where something has fallen on the wings and scorched the fabrics see. It might have been from shrapnel or from high explosives but some people were hit I believe with it but nobody had a direct hit that we could find anything out about. They didn't do any harm.[11]

Sergeant Leslie Alexander Dell, 214 Squadron RAF

> Of greater and invaluable assistance to us was a device used by the Germans to guide their men who were working over our territory. They were called 'flaming onions', balls of fire shot up several thousand feet and were in code. As they never changed position we dismissed them as a defensive measure and recognised them as signals.[12]

Lieutenant Hugh Baird Monaghan, 215 Squadron RAF

The 'flaming onions' were not designed as signals, but were actually artillery rounds, fired by the 1872 3.7-cm Hotchkiss (built under licence in Germany) five-barrelled revolving anti-torpedo gun, taken out of storage and used as anti-aircraft guns. As the name implies, they were introduced to combat torpedo boats in the late nineteenth century, and similar in appearance to the smaller calibre Gatling gun and were also hand-operated, using a crank to revolve the barrels and fire each barrel in turn. It had a fairly slow muzzle velocity, each round leaving the barrel at 1,620 feet per second (compared with over 2,000 for the larger anti-aircraft guns) and fired a rate of around forty rounds per minute—depending how fast the gunner was cranking the handle. Although the rounds were not linked together at all, and indeed designed to do harm to the aeroplane, there was at least one claim that 'an FE2b returned one night with a long strand of copper wire trailing from its wing. Attached to the wire were two tufts of charred metal'.[13] Although this was attributed to the 'flaming onions', some anti-aircraft shells (including those fired by the 8.8-cm guns) were filled with more unusual fillings—such as incendiary pellets, wire with barbed hooks, or even pieces of chain—owing to small explosive contents of the normal shells, which may explain what was seen on the FE2b. Bewsher, who wrote articles for the *Daily Mail* in his poetic style on the topic of Handley Pages, often mentioned the green balls and in an article published on 30 December 1918, admitted he finally found out what they were. Over lunch, he mentioned them in passing to someone who promptly replied that he had some in his possession.

> Calmly he brought me a small pointed pom-pom shell about an inch across and three inches high, weighed a pound or so. As I handled it reverently he continued: 'We found lots at Tournai. We did not know what they were. We put them on a fire, and they flared up and gave off a brilliant greenish light which lit up the whole of Tournai. They burnt for about ten seconds!'
>
> It seemed a reasonable solution of the apparently insoluble. The strings of 'Green Balls' were hundreds of pom-pom shells filled with phosphorous, and we had laughed at them as they went rushing by our wings! If we had known that each contained a weighty piece of metal going up at a terrific speed, we would have taken them far more seriously. I thought that it seemed wonderful to know at last. Then I began to feel sorry I had found out.
>
> I wish I did not know. I wish the mystery had never been solved, but had always been inexplicable and fascinating. I wish that for ever I could think about those beauteous bubbles of airy light floating up like unreal phantoms of loveliness into the dim gloom of the pool of the October lights.[14]

Captain Paul Bewsher, 207 Squadron RAF

As well as the five-barrel revolving guns there was 100 of the Maxim 3.7-cm automatic cannon, the same as the pom-pom guns used by both the Boers and British during the Second Boer War of 1899–1902. By late 1917 there was the 3.7-cm automatic Sockelflak (Flak-FliegerAbwehrKanone) gun, a short-barrelled weapon with a large curved magazine containing ten rounds, originally fitted as a defence weapon to Zeppelins, but removed following the successful efforts by the British in shooting Zeppelins down in the autumn of 1916, resulting in a reduction of their use. Captured field guns were put into use as anti-aircraft guns with 400 of the French '*Soixante-Quinze*', the quick-firing 75-mm gun of 1897 being relined to 77 mm and used to fire German ammunition against enemy aircraft. The Russian 76.2-mm field gun was used too, but the gun barrels were too brittle to be changed and so were kept as built, firing captured ammunition; however, when this ran out, the Germans simply made new 76.2-mm ammunition for them. The 7.7-cm BAK continued to be made and fitted to vehicles as armoured anti-aircraft lorries, and were located close to the front line where they had an interesting role as tank destroyers during the Battle of Cambrai in late 1917.

In 1917 Krupp and Rheinmetall both started production of an 8.8-cm anti-aircraft gun known as the 8.8-cm K Flak. It was built on a large four-wheel trailer with a sturdy pedestal, and towed behind a motor tractor. It was the predecessor of what became the dreaded '88' of the Second World War. The shell left the barrel at 2,355 feet per second and, fired at a 70 degree angle, could reach a height of over 20,000 feet, putting the Handley Page and the high-flying day bombers and reconnaissance types well within reach. Leutnant Fritz Nagel was one of the officers chosen to train on the new gun and to use them, having transferred from a motorised 7.7-cm anti-aircraft unit:

Our training course took three weeks and was quite pleasant. The new 88-mm gun carried a considerably more powerful punch than the 77-mm gun. Now we could engage enemy fliers much earlier while they were still far away from their targets. We had two guns, each drawn by a tractor that was equipped with a steel rope to pull the gun out of any ditch or deep mud.[15]

Leutnant Fritz Nagel, Heavy Kraftwagen-Flugzeugabwehrkanone
Battery 179, German Army

Built in fewer numbers, a slightly smaller 8 cm was also built by Krupp and had a performance that was very close to the 8.8 cm's. Larger still was the 10.5-cm anti-aircraft guns, built again by Krupp and Rheinmetall. These were found to be too heavy for mobile use on the roads and were either put in fixed positions or mounted on railway wagons, in which use they were called Eisenbahnflak.

The lack of raw materials towards the end of the war caused issues for the anti-aircraft artillery just as it did for all areas of the German armed forces. Gunpowder for the artillery became a problem to supply, and so the charge was reduced where possible to save what they had. This did not have such a negative effect, as the larger anti-aircraft guns would not be fired unnecessarily at individual aircraft (especially at night time), but usually as part of a barrage, firing into a set space and wait for the aircraft to hopefully fly into that area of sky. As long as the first shell was fired early enough for the aircraft to be expected near the area, and the momentum of fire kept up, it would have the same effect as a full charge. Scarcity of brass meant that other options were used for the cartridge cases for the artillery, but the use of other materials was always found to be inferior. Owing to the nature of anti-aircraft artillery (i.e. it would only be in use for a short period, firing as rapidly as possible at the passing aeroplane) it was decided that anti-aircraft shells would continue to be supplied with brass cartridge cases.

Despite the arrival of the Handley Pages and their success on operations, the days of 3 Wing were numbered. Already on 25 March 1917 a telegram had been received stopping daytime raids and informing them that the Wing was to be shut down. The disbandment was postponed on 1 April, with orders for a reprisal raid on a German city as revenge for U-boat attacks on two British hospital ships. No Handley Pages took part in the daytime raid, which involved two attacks with the aircraft returning, refuelling, rearming, then heading off again, but involved twenty-five British and fifteen French aircraft, who were happy to join their British counterparts despite previously deciding to stick to night bombing. Freiburg was the target, with civilians as the main intended target, dropping leaflets as well as bombs to inform those on the ground that the raids were as a response to the German U-boat *UC-66* torpedoing the British hospital ship HMHS *Asturias* on 20 March, killing thirty-five, and also *UB-32* torpedoing HMHS *Gloucester Castle* on 31 March, with three dying during the transfer to safety. These were among nine British and Commonwealth hospital ships torpedoed by German U-boats during the war, causing immense outrage not just amongst Britain and her allies, but in neutral countries too.

The effects of 'Bloody April' on the RFC and RNAS Squadrons operating in the Arras area were being felt, and the aircrew, ground crew, and aircraft of the component units were needed elsewhere. The disbandment of 3 Wing didn't just help the British aerial forces to move aircraft, crews, and supplies to elsewhere where they were to be put to better immediate use, it also helped the Germans too, and not just by the ceasing of bombing industrial areas—although still in their infancy, their home defence units were able to move to the Arras area and join the fight there. Their aircraft may have been out of date, but the valuable pilots would soon be put to good use. The Handley Pages and their crews were to move north to join 7 Squadron who had been in service with their aircraft since early April.

Another Start

The two Handley Page bombers from Ochey went to RNAS Coudekerque, joining other Handley Pages that had started to arrive from March onwards. At Coudekerque, the Handley Pages were under 5 Wing, which consisted of 5 Squadron that operated Sopwith 1½ Strutters and 7 Squadron who had been created as a Handley Page Squadron in November 1916, to operate four Handley Pages, although the first didn't arrive until 4 March 1917. Bad weather hampered the arrival of the aircraft; on 4 April, Flight Lieutenant Buss tried to fly HP 1466 to Coudekerque, but had to return to Manston, although the next day he was able to complete the journey, bringing three other men with him. Bewsher arrived at Coudekerque from Luxeuil on 23 April, learning upon landing that the Handley Pages there were out on a coastal reconnaissance.

Since early April the Handley Pages of 7 Squadron had undertaken daylight reconnaissance of the coast, going as far north as Zeebrugge. Despite the use of 3 Wing's Handley Page Squadron showing how suitable they were for night bombing (especially given their size, slowness, and lack of manoeuvrability compared to the performance of the single or two-seat aircraft employed during daytime), it was no doubt surprising to the men from Luxeuil that 7 Squadron were using them in this way, even with a single-seat Scout escort. However, on 23 April, one aircraft observed direct hits on a German destroyer with 65-lb bombs, with unknown damage caused. Buss described carrying fourteen 65-lb bombs on the 'hostile shipping patrol', dropping all the bombs, but coming under attack from a small green aeroplane off Ostend, however, this 'was easily driven off'.

Several days later on the 26 April, it was soon proved that the Handley Pages were unsuitable in this role. Four Handley Pages bombed four German destroyers off of Ostend, dropping thirty-two 112-lb bombs. No hits on the vessels were seen, but shortly after one of the Handley Pages was attacked by a German Rumpler 6B single-seat floatplane scout. The Handley Page, flown by Flight Sub-Lieutenant T. S. Hood, had its petrol tanks hit, so Hood attempted to head towards land. He ran out of fuel and ditched around 2 miles offshore, near Nieuport, and came under fire from German shore batteries. Despite the attention from German gunners on land, two French FBA flying boats attempted to rescue the crew. One of them rescued Gunlayer Kirby, but the other was shot down as it tried to take off, presumably with all three other Handley Page crew. The other three were later presumed killed. This put an end to the daytime operations of the Handley Pages and henceforth they only flew at night. Four Short Bombers undertook a raid on the seaplane base at Ostend on the night of 3 May, with two of the aircraft returning after dropping their bombs, rearming, and heading off again. The first night-time Handley Page raid for 7 Squadron came on 9 May with a moonlit trip to Zeebrugge. Buss was airborne that night taking HP 1466, along with Lieutenant John and Petty Officer Powell, to the docks at Bruges and dropped ten 112-lb bombs from 6,000 feet, the round trip taking two hours and two minutes. The need for moonlight was important as the crews had little experience of night flying, however, as the experience grew darker conditions became acceptable to fly in. Buss described the situation as he saw it:

I think the naval people were so impressed they thought well, fine, they will send us up the coast in daylight to bomb any shipping we could see which they did. We were all horrified because they knew obviously they, the Handley Page was most vulnerable to a fighter picked up on the tail and being slow and our CO who was Squadron Commander Babington tried to get out of it but no, they insisted that we should go up in daylight. So the next afternoon we went up in daylight up the coast as far as Zeebrugge. Nothing happened that time. So they sent us the next day. Next day of course, one of us got shot down and the next day I think another one. Well, that depressed us so much. We thought well, we shall all be finished before we have a done a night raid at all. Well, after that they did stop the daylight work. We got on to our proper job of night bombing which was mostly up the coast bombing the submarine bases. Any shipping we could see and the bombing mostly at the huge dock where the submarines were based at the Zeebrugge Mole.[1]

Flight Commander Horace Austen Buss, 7 Squadron RNAS

Initially, German coastal bases for seaplanes, U-boats, destroyers, and torpedo boats were targeted, aiding the Royal Navy's work undertaken in the vital English Channel supply route; it also hampered the destructive work being done in the coastal waters around Britain, the Mediterranean, and Atlantic Ocean by the U-boats, whose unrestricted submarine warfare was taking a heavy toll on Allied shipping. Around half-a-million tons of shipping had been sunk in February and again in March (which came to around a quarter of all shipping heading to Britain), with 860,000 tons of shipping sunk in April for the loss of only nine submarines in the first three months. Although the campaign brought the United States of America into the war on 6 April on the Allied side, this would not save the desperate supply situation in Britain. It was calculated by the Admiralty that if the German submarine campaign continued at such a pace, Britain would run out of supplies and be forced out of the war in six months. Merchant shipping was being lost quicker than ships could be built to replace them. Any damage or disruption to the U-boats in their home ports by the Handley Pages or other RNAS bombers was vital, and perhaps just as importantly made it seem that something was being done with the most powerful aircraft available. The U-boats were protected in hardened concrete shelters at Bruges and gained access via the canals to the North Sea at Zeebrugge and Ostend. From here they had a much reduced transit time to areas where they would encounter Allied shipping, so after using their limited supply of torpedoes (as well as shells or mines) not much time would be lost in returning to base, refuelling, rearming, and going back on patrol. Although difficult, if not impossible, to destroy them in their shelters, if the actual access to the sea could be stopped (i.e. damaging the sea lock gates and making them inoperable), it would provide a much needed respite. Despite the frequent raids, it did not seem to affect the exhausted submariners much:

British bomber aircraft came over almost every night and the German 15-cm AA guns, which ringed the town rent the dark skies with splinters of steel, their heavy salvoes shaking the very foundations of the barracks in which we slept. But this was insufficient to disturb the slumber of a U-boat man.[2]

Oberleutnant Zur See Werner Fürbringer, Submarine *UC-70*

Following the raid on 9 May, attacks on Bruges, Ostend, and Zeebrugge were almost nightly as both the weather and the experience of the men improved.

Of course, it was an experience but we got so used to flying and we always had one thing of flying at night we felt more comfortable than we would have done flying in day. Not being able to be seen so easily and the anti-aircraft didn't worry us so much but it got a bit hot when we were over the target. There was that relief when you had finished and turned for home and you opened the engines up and climbed up and came home. Well, I always had a feeling anyhow we were in a much more comfortable position up there than sitting down, the poor fellows down in the trenches down below who we could see getting strafed.[3]

Flight Commander Horace Austen Buss, 7 Squadron RNAS

As the men got used to flying, they flew raids when levels of moonlight gave the greatest possible visibility. However, the amount of raids steadily increased until June, when they were mounted on most nights. An event in May was to add another type of target for the Handley Pages attention—the Gothas. The Gotha G.IV bomber was vaguely similar in appearance to the Handley Page. Its crew of three were located in the fuselage—a forward observer in the nose, pilot behind (although sat on the left rather than on the right), and a gunner rear of the wings. The Gotha was also a twin-engine aircraft, but with the engines in the 'pusher' configuration, facing the rear. With a wingspan of 78 feet and a length of 40 feet they were smaller than the Handley Pages, but had a higher ceiling of 15,000 feet when fully loaded. The rear gunner had an ingenious method of defending the underneath of the aircraft. Where the Handley Page had a lower trapdoor, the Gotha had a 'V' shaped tunnel from the top of the fuselage to the bottom, allowing the rear gunner to fire through the fuselage with an adequate arc of fire to deter aircraft attacking from below. The bomb load of the Gotha was smaller than a Handley Page, but still powerful. They were specifically designed for long-range daylight bombing work. A squadron was set up, known as Kagohl 3—although also known as the England Geschwader or England Squadron—and based at St Denis-Westrem and Melle-Gontrode, close to Ghent in Belgium. Although British Intelligence was aware of the aircraft and the unit's formation and location, it was thought they would be used for attacks on the Western Front rather than Britain.

Following the defeat of the Zeppelins in the autumn of 1916, London and the south-east of England had been relatively untouched from the air, the Zeppelins instead attacking less well defended areas in the Midlands and the north of Britain. This was to change on the afternoon of 25 May 1917, when twenty-three Gothas took off for London. Reaching land over Essex, hazy weather necessitated a change of target, so the Gothas swept over Essex, right over the Home Defence aerodromes at RFC Stow Maries and RFC Rochford, who had been notified far too late to be seriously effective, over the Thames Estuary, and over Kent. Some bombs were aimed at the South Eastern and Chatham Railway's network at various locations, but no real damage was done, and six bombs were dropped on

Ashford, where the railway's vital works were (which as well as building and repairing locomotives, were also making items for the war effort such as gun carriages). Other locations had a number of bombs dropped on them, but with no major damage, until coastal town of Folkestone and the nearby Shorncliffe Camp was reached. No warning was given to the population here, and as it was such a busy area with military movements it was assumed the formation of aircraft at 15,000 feet were British. Over Shorncliffe Camp where a large number of Canadians were stationed, six 50-kg bombs and twenty-one 12.5-kg bombs were dropped, killing seventeen and wounding almost 100 more. Shortly after, Folkestone itself was hit, most of the bombs falling on part of the old town, packed with women and children shopping. At least two 50-kg bombs fell in Tontine Street, a particular busy street. One of them fell amongst a busy queue of shoppers outside a greengrocers, which then brought the roof crashing down onto those inside. Many shops were seriously damaged, and around sixty people were killed or seriously wounded. Bombs landed elsewhere in Folkestone, too, including at Folkestone Central railway station.

The Gothas headed to nearby Dover, but by now there was heavy anti-aircraft fire from Royal Garrison Artillery anti-aircraft units and also the Royal Navy vessels were opening up. Although it had little effect on the bombers, as it was set to explode several thousand feet below the aircraft, it did have the effect of dissuading them and they returned to Belgium. Understandably there was massive uproar, both within the Government, Navy, and Military, but also among civilians. The pressure was on to attack the Gothas at their bases, as the RNAS had done in 1914 against Zeppelin bases when they were in range from Allied-held territory. The Gothas at St Denis Westrem had in fact already been bombed by the RNAS on the day before the raid, when Airco DH4s from Dunkirk had raided the aerodrome, although caused little damage despite the DH4 crews reporting bombs exploding close to the large aircraft on the ground.

The frequent raids continued through June, with St Denis Westrem and Gontrode added as prime targets, with important railway stations and junctions as secondary targets. On 3 June, ten Handley Pages and four Short Bombers took off with St Denis Westrem the main target. Nine aircraft bombed the Gotha base, with two attacking the secondary target of Zeebrugge, three turning back with engine trouble. The steady flow of Handley Pages and crew meant that more and more aircraft were flying each night, both the flight crews and ground crews were becoming more experienced and so potentially unnecessary time spent on the ground was constantly being reduced, helped by the influx of men with experience from 3 Wing. Accident rates owing to inexperienced pilots were also reducing, and the number of Handley Pages now available nightly meant

that it was possible to set up a second unit, known as 7(A) Squadron—
to avoid confusion, 7 Squadron became known as 7(N) Squadron. The
official formation of 7(A) Squadron was on 23 July, again at Coudekerque,
with eight Handley Pages. Most of the men were new to France and, in
Squadron Commander Richard Pink's view, would not be allowed to take
part in raids until they had had enough training and experience, especially
in flying a Handley Page at night as some had not done this before. They
would need to be thoroughly familiar with this before being released on
operations—better for them to have a landing accident without a full
load of fuel, bombs, and Lewis gun ammunition than with, and so 7(A)
Squadron men would fly in 7(N) Squadron machines on raids.

Meanwhile, 7(N) Squadron continued raiding German naval and aerial
bases, although towards the end of July targets further inland tended to
replace coastal ones in support of the Army's campaign in Passchendaele,
the Third Battle of Ypres. The actual objective of this battle was to break
through and capture the Belgian ports, particularly the U-boat bases;
however, despite an initial start in good weather, unseasonal rainfall soon
slowed down the advance, which turned into a battle of attrition rather
than one of opportunity to significantly disrupt the unrestricted U-boat
warfare. The accompanying plan codenamed Operation Hush, for an
amphibious invasion on the Belgian coast to aid in the capture of the
U-boat bases, was postponed several times and then ultimately cancelled.
From now on, strategic targets to help the land forces, especially railways,
became more important targets, although the pressure on the Gotha
aerodromes was kept up.

Two typical raids are described in Buss's pilot's log—on the night of
13 July:

Raid on Aestryche Aerodrome. Unable to find aerodrome owing to bad
visibility. Six bombs dropped on row of lights showing at Bruges on
canal bend. Eight bombs dropped on Thourout railway junction.[4]

Flight Commander Horace Austen Buss, 7(N) Squadron RNAS

A week later on 21 July:

Raid on Middlekerke ammunition Dump. Glided down to 6000ft (from
8000ft) and dropped fourteen 112lb bombs. Bombs were seen exploding
in a line across dump and railway sidings.[5]

Flight Commander Horace Austen Buss, 7(N) Squadron RNAS

The 7(N) Squadron had received their first Handley Page fitted with the 6-pounder Davis shell gun in July, and first used in anger on the night of 11–12 July when eight rounds were fired on a raid on railway sidings at Zarren. The gun was used again on the night of 15–16 July against motor transport convoys, and the railway junction at Thourout was shelled on the night of 9–10 August, but after that they do not seem to have been used again. Enemy aircraft operating at night were starting to be encountered in the area. A report following a raid on the German Gotha bomber airfields at Gontrode and St Denis Westrem and the airfield at Ghistelles on 6–7 July, apparently encountering a formation of enemy aircraft after the Handley Pages had dropped their bombs.

Fortunately, without the heavy bombs, the Handley Pages were slightly faster and more manoeuvrable, and escaped without loss, although damage to the aircraft testified the determination of the enemy aircraft. The German aircraft that attacked them were likely to have been those in the area used to cover the return of the Gotha bombers based at these aerodromes. The next day, despite any effects of the raid, twenty-two Gothas bombed London on what was the second daylight Gotha raid on London, which resulted in fifty-seven deaths and nearly 200 injured. Nos 3 Squadron and 4 Squadron RNAS, based at Dunkirk, were sent up to hunt the Gothas on their return, but instead ended up in a dogfight with German fighters covering their return, the British aircraft claiming four enemy aircraft.

In early August 1917, Corporal William Edward David Wardrop arrived at 7(N) Squadron. He had joined the RNAS in 1915, and the 'gawky' (in his own words) just-under 6-foot-tall gun layer did not find life on an active flying unit to his expectations, despite the fact that the unit was heavily engaged on enemy raids. For starters, he had originally been due to be sent to the Mediterranean to serve in one of the units deployed there, but after being kitted up for this theatre of operations and being inoculated, he was instead sent to France. Wardrop described the situation when he arrived, with another new gun layer:

After the usual questions, medical examinations and formalities we were duly enrolled to the complement of No. 7 Squadron, No. 5 Wing, Royal Naval Air Service. During the week following we were given all kinds of work to do. We did everything except what we were sent for, namely, flying. After five days we found it was very humiliating, so we decided to put in a request to see the officer in charge of armaments, Lieutenant Wayne. This was granted and next day we had to interview. We told him we would like to go to a squadron where they needed gun-layers. He at once replied, 'We want you here, and in due course you will have a

machine'. After a little more conversation we left with the consolation
that one day we might be needed. Next day to our joy Jack Keen and
myself were allocated a machine each. This was on August the 11th,
seven days after our arrival.[6]

Corporal William Edward David Wardrop, 7(N) Squadron RNAS

Two days later, Squadron Commander Herbert Brackley took Wardrop
up for a familiarisation flight, so he could get used to the landmarks
they would pass on the ways (to and from forays) into enemy territory.
Wardrop soon found that, even at night, having a map in his mind of how
local roads, etc. looked would prove very useful. Depending how much
light the moon provided, roads, waterways, and railway lines would show
up clearly, and forests and woods would also be defined well enough to
navigate using a map. Wardrop thought much of his pilot:

> He wasn't flamboyant in any way, very quiet, very unassuming, an
> extremely fit man, a wonderful swimmer I remember, and so keen on
> all kinds of fitness tests and so forth. At the same time he was a very fine
> leader and commander. He expected all of us to give what he showed
> could be done. He led the way in all things. If we were moving from one
> aerodrome to another, which we did on one or two occasions, he would
> always lead the squadron and show the way.[7]

Corporal William Edward David Wardrop, 7(N) Squadron RNAS

Of the Handley Pages, Wardrop described how they made him feel:

> Absolutely secure, like a dreadnought, that's how I would describe it.
> One felt absolutely confident that the Germans or anybody else could
> never bring it down, whatever you did. The only way to bring it down
> was to hit it direct with another machine we could feel. But of course we
> were brought down.[8]

Corporal William Edward David Wardrop, 7(N) Squadron RNAS

Wardrop certainly joined 7(N) Squadron at the right time if he wanted to
see action. It was a busy month, with continuing attacks on airfields, but
also on strategic railway locations to aid the Army in the Third Battle of
Ypres. Fourteen Handley Pages took part in a raid on a Thourout area
on the night of 16 August, targeting the railways and an ammunition
dump nearby. The dump exploded several times, with fires being reported

in the vicinity of the railway too, a good sign that vital stores had been hit. Two nights later Thourout was hit again, with docks at Ghent and Bruges also being targeted. The gates of the docks were a prime target— one well-placed bomb could, theoretically, put a dry dock out of action for a significant time period, hampering repairs or just simple maintenance to enemy vessels, especially U-boats. Although there were occasions when the dock gates were hit, the lack of apparent results was puzzling the crews:

> We had bombed lock gates on many occasions, and we could never understand why although we went down very, very low on occasions, and had special commissions we were asked to do, like going down as low as possible to drop 50lbs bombs on the gates, and we knew full well we hit the gates. But the photographs were shown next day and there was no damage. This went on time after time and we were puzzled. A long, long time after we found, of course, that there was two gates. If one was damaged they put the other one out and repaired the other one. That was why we were puzzled about why we never managed to do what we thought we were going to do, smash them up altogether. It was very clever of them, but no good to us.[9]

Corporal William Edward David Wardrop, 7(N) Squadron RNAS

As mentioned, unrestricted submarine warfare conducted by the German U-boats was taking a heavy toll on Britain, sinking unprecedented numbers of merchant shipping. Not only were ships being sunk faster than they could be replaced, but their vital goods on board were desperately needed to supply the population, and also the factories. Aircraft were part of the Royal Navy's fight against the U-boats. After initially only possessing a few, airship development started in earnest from 1915 and by 1917 there were several types of various sizes in use, undertaking long patrols and armed with bombs and machine guns. Stationed around the country, their slow speed was not an issue for their anti-submarine role where they certainly would not be outpaced by their prey, and their endurance meant that patrols could last as long as daylight allowed them to. Although they were not quick to attack a U-boat once spotted, their presence alone was usually enough to keep the enemy submerged.

Aeroplanes were used too, both land-based and flying boats. Flying boats were preferred as they were able to land in case of difficulties and could patrol larger areas—it was believed that crews of land-based aeroplanes were less effective too, as the further they went away from land the less observant they were as they were nervous about the possibility of having to ditch in the sea in case of engine trouble. Aeroplanes and airships were aided by new ordnance, which had come into use in larger numbers. Aerial depth charges had been designed and were in use, with an explosive capacity of 35 lbs or 65 lbs depending on the type, but these were felt far too light to be of any use, and in 1917 the 100-lb (a new type, not to be confused with the pre-war Hales 100-lb bomb in use with the RFC) and 230-lb bombs were introduced; the 100-lb bomb being designed specifically for anti-submarine use and the 230-lb bomb being the next stage up in size of aerial bomb now that more powerful aircraft were being introduced with the capability to carry them. Most aerial bombs in use at the time had nose fuses, which detonated the instant they hit the ground (or indeed water), whereas the 100-lb and 230-lb bombs had tail fuses (although the 100-lb could be fitted with a nose fuse). These fuses allowed a delay of two-and-a-half seconds from impact with the water until it exploded, allowing them to sink to a depth of around 80 feet. The manual for the 230-lb bomb described how it worked:

> When the bomb is loaded on carrier, the vane of fuse is held from rotating by a stop on the carrier.
>
> When the bomb is dropped, the vane is free to rotate, and spins off.
>
> On impact the bomb is checked, but the striker being free to move forward compresses the striker spring and fires the cap of the 'detonator, aerial bomb'. This burns for 15 secs., 2.5 secs., or .05 sec., according to type and then fires its detonator, which in turn fires the 'detonator, H.E. bomb,' in exploder, and so sets off the bomb.[10]

Details of Aerial Bombs

The 230-lb bomb was specially fitted with a nose-cap for use against submarines, presumably to ensure the streamlining of the bomb was not damaged upon the impact with the water, and continued to drop straight.

Despite the improvements in aerial weaponry to deal with the submarines, most of the land-based aeroplanes employed on anti-submarine patrols were not quite of the same capability as those now being used on the western front. Understandably, the RFC and RNAS were reluctant to send valuable aircraft and their crews, such as the superb Airco DH4 day bomber, for use on often fruitless anti-submarine patrols when they were being used to much greater effect where they were. Owing to increased coastal activity of U-boats, the RNAS decided to send four Handley Pages from Couderkerque to the Royal Naval Air Station at Redcar (primarily a training station), near Middlesbrough in North East England on a temporary detachment. They were to be based at Redcar, principally to cover shipping leaving the docks at Hartlepool and West

Hartlepool (together known as the Hartlepools)—a large and important shipping area that had already been targeted on 16 December 1914 when it was heavily shelled by German warships—as well as other shipping in the Tees area. The chance of seeing a U-boat close to land was high; the day before the Handley Pages arrived, on the sunny evening of 4 September, a U-boat surfaced off of Scarborough, north Yorkshire, and after initially attacking mine-sweepers in the vicinity, briefly bombarded the town itself, killing three civilians and injuring six more. The four Handley Pages (HPs 3123, 3125, 3131, and 3136) and their crews arrived on 5 September, headed by Flight Commander F. T. Digby. An additional two Handley Pages were also sent to Redcar, both of them (HPs 3126 and 3127) fitted with the 6-pounder Davis gun in the nose cockpit, which could potentially be a lethal weapon against the vulnerable hull of a U-boat on the surface.

Flight Lieutenant Lancelot de Giberne (although known as simply 'Lance') Sieveking DSC made his first sighting and attack in 'his' HP 3123 *Split Pin* on 10 September when a U-boat was attacked 5 miles north-east of Long Nab (near Scarborough), and the next day a U-boat was spotted just 3 miles north of Redcar itself and six bombs were dropped from *Split Pin*. On 21 September *Split Pin* took part in its third U-boat attack, dropping three 100-lb bombs on a U-boat spotted on the seabed 3 miles east of the North Cheek (near Runswick Bay). Flight Sub-Lieutenant John William Beebee flying HP 3136 also took part in an attack on 24 September, when four bombs were dropped on a U-boat near Runswick Bay. In all, forty-two patrols were undertaken by the Handley Pages out of Redcar, with eleven sightings of U-boats, and seven attacks being made using bombs. None of the attacks made on U-boats resulted in the destruction of an enemy submarine, but the desired effects of the patrols was not just the destruction of enemy submarines, as beneficial as that would have been—just keeping the U-boats submerged and primarily occupied with escaping detection and destruction put further strain on their crews, and limited the time available to sink yet another merchant vessel. The Handley Pages had been considered a success in this role and it was hoped the detachment, or another one, would return to Redcar, but it did not happen and an interesting episode in the Handley Page's operational career came to an end in early October as planned.

The Handley Pages flew to Manston on 6 October and became the nucleus of newly formed A Squadron RNAS, which once built up to strength was to operate alongside RFC bomber squadrons in France. The use of Handley Pages on anti-submarine patrols was a stopgap measure, but throughout the war the RNAS had been developing seaplanes and flying boats to combat the threat; large twin-engine Curtiss and Felixstowe flying boats were being used at the same that the Handley Pages were being used at Redcar, and they were employed in large numbers for long-range patrols. As more of these entered service, the need for land-based aeroplanes, with their limitations compared to flying boats, diminished. The departure of the Handley Pages did not signal the end for large twin-engine landplanes operating anti-submarine patrols. In May 1918, the Blackburn Kangaroo (which at first glance looks like an awkward version of the Handley Page owing to the longer fuselage, although was in fact smaller) was introduced into service with 246 Squadron RAF at Seaton Carew, not much farther north than RNAS Redcar. This single squadron of Kangaroos, with a three man crew and 920-lb bomb load, took part in twelve attacks against U-boats from May to October 1918; on 28 August, a Kangaroo attacked UC II-class Minelaying U-boat *UC-70* that was spotted submerged. After initially having bombs dropped on it from the Kangaroo, it was then finished off with depth charges from the destroyer HMS *Ouse*.

While the Handley Page Flight at Redcar tried to stop U-boats, which were already out hunting, 7(N) and 7(A) Squadron continued to support the ground offensive by attacking railway locations, as well as coastal targets and enemy airfields. On 29 September, while eight other Handley Pages were detailed to bomb either Zeebrugge or St Denis Westrem, Squadron Leader Brackley, with Bewsher as the observer, and Wardrop as gun layer, were to bomb the vital railway bridge over the Meuse River at Namur. Disruption here would have a significant knock-on effect to the supply of men, guns, and ammunition at the front.

The time of preparation is one series of kaleidoscopic pictures—of crawling inside a machine unfamiliar to either of us; of being taught the operation of a new petrol pressure system; of watching the loading of the four huge 250-lb bombs, fat and yellow, which I have never before had the opportunity of dropping; of drawing a line from Dunkerque to Ghent, from Ghent to Namur, across the long green-and-brown map; of pondering the patches of the forests, the blue veins of the river, and thinking how in a few hours they will appear for me in reality, lying below in the moonlight, etched in dim shades of black and dull silver; of a strange dinner in the mess when semi-seriously, semi-facetiously I write out my will, leaving to one friend my books, to another friend my pictures; of having the document properly witnessed, and rushing out amidst cries of good luck; of the lonely dressing in leather and fur in my little hut; of the roar of the engines as we rise up at latest twilight towards the glittering companies of the stars.[11]

Lieutenant Paul Bewsher, 7(N) Squadron RNAS

HP 3130 took off at 19.59, with four 250-lb bombs and eight 65-lb bombs. The flight there passed without incident, but the pressure on the crew was certainly felt, knowing the importance of their mission. The relatively narrow width of their target meant accuracy was everything, and it would be easy to drop all the bombs and for them all to fall harmlessly into the water. Bewsher told Brackley that he wanted him to turn and face north-west, into the wind, and to throttle the engines back. The lack of noise would mean they would hopefully approach unheard, the wind keeping them aloft for as long as possible while gliding down, and then after releasing the bombs while flying directly over the bridge, to put the throttles on and escape homeward bound. As the aircraft went lower, and the target became closer, Bewsher was pleased to notice through his bomb sight the intermittent red glow of a steam locomotive's firebox. Bewsher directed Brackley using red and green lights in the cockpit when the aircraft got nearer to the bridge. Frustratingly, the direction bar would line up with the bridge, but then drift to the left. Bewsher brought the aircraft around, but again the same happened:

> Again I press the right button; again a green light glows; again the machine swings towards the bridge. The range-bars cross the base of it. I press over the bomb handle quickly…And again. Clatter-click-clatter-click-click-clatter sound the opening and closing bomb doors behind me as bomb after bomb slides out into the moonlight depths below. For a moment I see the fat yellow shapes, clear-lit in the pale light beneath me, go tumbling down and down towards the dim face of the country.[12]

> Lieutenant Paul Bewsher, 7(N) Squadron RNAS

The first bomb run had been completed. The importance of the mission continued to play on Bewsher's mind, knowing that every train stopped would make a difference, and if successful, the hard-pressed men struggling in the mud of the Ypres salient would suffer further:

> If I fail, that much-desired relief will not take place, and therefore many more British soldiers may be killed. That is not all, however—for failure means that this expensive raid is wasted; the reputation of the squadron is tarnished; the official approval of Handley-Pages as long distance night bombers is reversely affected…

> Lieutenant Paul Bewsher, 7(N) Squadron RNAS

Brackley brought the Handley Page in for another run.

> The machine ceases its leftward drift and swings to the right, and the two luminous range-bars are in line with the bridge. I grasp the bomb-handle

and once, twice, press it over. I look behind—the bombs are all gone.

I climb clumsily to my feet and look through the door beside the pilot.

All gone, sir, I… Oh! Look, look!

Upon the thin black line of the bridge leap out two great flashes, leaving a cloud of moonlit smoke which entirely obscures one end of it.

'Oh- damn good—damn good!' yells out the pilot excitedly. 'Hit it! Hit it! You've hit it! Oh—priceless-priceless.'[13]

Lieutenant Paul Bewsher, 7(N) Squadron RNAS

Wardrop, who in the back of the aircraft was isolated from the pilot and observer, was able in one way to communicate to those in the front:

In the back of the machine I see a sight which left the clearest image of this raid in my mind. There stands the moonlit figure of the tall good humoured gunlayer, and with a characteristic gesture I see him put out his arms with the thumbs pointing upwards—the most sincere expression of congratulation he can deliver.[14]

Lieutenant Paul Bewsher, 7(N) Squadron RNAS

In total, the men and their machine were airborne for four-and-a-quarter hours, and it was later reported that the target was badly damaged, with direct hits on the northern end of the bridge. Wardrop was later to describe the raid:

The proudest time or moment was, I suppose, when it was reported that it was the longest raid ever taken place, it was two-hundred miles behind the German lines. We managed to get there and back. I think we had one or two people shoot at us as usual, but that was one of those things that was just bound to happen. But it didn't do any damage as far as we were concerned. We got back all right, and it was reported by our agents that we were successful. It was successful, we stopped them from building up their ammunition and armaments.[15]

Corporal William Edward David Wardrop, 7(N) Squadron RNAS

On the same night a unique event was to occur in the history of the Handley Page bombers during the First World War—the use of a Handley Page O/100 as a gunship to seek and destroy the enemy. As early as June, following the aircraft raids on Britain and looking for new ideas to shoot them down, a suggestion was made by the Vice-Admiral of Dover

Command; this was for wireless transmission-equipped Handley Pages to patrol the coast where the Gothas were likely to cross whenever the weather seemed suitable for an enemy raid, and to report back to give early warning to anti-aircraft defences. The reply from Captain C. L. Lambe, the Senior Naval Officer at RNAS Headquarters Dunkirk, was that the aircraft were not suitable for the role, the newly introduced Sopwith Camels being a more potent defence than what would have been the forefather of Airborne Early Warning aircraft. A local initiative, which surprisingly proved successful was the use of a Handley Page to specifically search out Gothas in the air and attack them. On the night of 29–30 September, a Handley Page fitted with five Lewis guns (presuming the standard fitting of two on pillars in the rear cockpit, and a further one on the floor opening giving protection from below, the forward nose cockpit must have had two Lewis guns fitted on the Scarff ring) and crewed by pilot Flight Sub-Lieutenant Gibbs and four gun layers, took off for a four-hour patrol, flying at 10,000 feet 10 miles north of Ostende. That night, seven Gothas and three of the Zeppelin Staaken 'Giant' R Type aeroplanes left to bomb London. A raid had been attempted the previous night, but ended in disaster for the Germans—poor weather resulted in just £129 worth of damage, and none of it in London—for the cost of three Gothas lost and six further crashed while attempting to land.

Three of the Gothas that night were reported as returning without dropping any bombs over Britain, and of the seven aircraft remaining, some dropped bombs over Kent instead of the main target of London. Forty on the ground were killed and eighty-seven injured, with £23,154 worth of damage caused. The Home Defence Squadrons mounted thirty-three sorties to combat the aircraft, but just three of those resulted in a pilot briefly seeing and identifying an enemy aircraft. One of the issues with combatting the Zeppelin Staaken 'Giants'—with a wingspan almost double that of the Gotha G.IVs 77 feet—was that Home Defence pilots that had one in their sights could easily think they were actually attacking a Gotha and open fire despite being twice the distance away than they thought they were (and owing to the sting in the tail of the Gothas, an attacking pilot would understandably want to hang back). As the Gothas returned, three of them were seen by the Handley Page, which went in to attack. Two of them were actually engaged, the first one seemingly disappearing after the first attack. Better luck was had with the second machine, attacked from a range of just 50 to 100 yards. Five drums were fired from the Lewis guns of the Handley Page into the unsuspecting Gotha, and the Gotha was seen to descend in a steep spiral. The Gotha appears to have been Gotha G.IV 602/16, which force-landed just over the border into Holland, one crew member wounded and all of them interned. This remarkable little episode of the air war was finished off by the Handley Page then dropping a number of 65-lb bombs on Thourout airfield before returning home. The use of a Handley Page as a form of 'gunship' appears never to have been repeated again.

October continued with the same targets, Handley Page 3122 of 7(A) Squadron being shot down on a raid on the night of 27–28 October while raiding St Denis Westrem airfield, one of nine aircraft airborne that night. The next night, the same number of Handley Pages were airborne—six heading for the Cockerill Railway Works at Antwerp while one bombed the railways at Ghent and another Bruges Docks. The last to take-off was carrying twelve 112-lb bombs meant for Cologne, but bad weather meant it had to turn back and drop the yellow eggs on an inviting looking factory well lit up below. Worsening weather further hampered the return, and the aircraft came down safely at a Royal Flying Corps aerodrome at Droglandt after being airborne for over seven hours, flying back after a well-deserved rest. Nine Handley Pages were again aloft on the night of 30–31 October, some coming under attack from enemy aircraft, but fortunately without loss.

C. E. V. Wilkins arrived at Coudekerque on 15 November following training on the Handley Page course at Manston. By the time he arrived at Coudekerque he had had nine hours and thirty-eight minutes solo at the controls of Handley Pages, but was not to fly at Coudekerque until 5 December when he undertook a twenty-five minutes local flight in the afternoon. That evening he was in the rear of HP 3133 for a raid on St Denis Westrem, but had to return owing to the starboard engine boiling badly; the other five Handley Pages from 7(N) and 7(A) Squadrons were able to reach their targets. Two days later he took part as front gun layer on a raid on Bruges Docks, reporting 'excessive green-ball defence', as well as fifteen searchlights, but little anti-aircraft fire apart from the green balls.

No. 7(A) Squadron became officially known as 14 Squadron on 9 December, but otherwise the raids continued to the same locations as often as the weather allowed, mainly keeping up the pressure on the German bomber bases and hitting the tempting target of Bruges Docks when possible. The weather resulted in the loss of one aircraft and almost the crew on the night of 11–12 December—HP 3121 was returning from a raid on Bruges in heavy rain when it hit the ground at high speed, flipping upside-down with the pilot and observer trapped in the wreckage. Petrol spread over the men and the wreckage from a broken fuel tank while the weight of a Rolls-Royce Eagle engine pinned pilot Flight Lieutenant Darley's head into the ground. Fortunately the engine did not move and crush Darley, or the petrol catch fire, even though it took an hour for enough men to arrive to be able to get the two men out of their unpleasant situation.

The rest of the year saw just two more nights when aircraft were in action; the 18–19 when a factory was targeted by four aircraft (three actually dropped their bombs) and the 22–23 when aircraft from both 7 Squadron and 14 Squadron raided German aerodromes and Bruges. The first year of action for the Handley Pages had seen the aircraft trialled in a variety of uses and night bombing was by far the most suitable role for them. Despite having been in production for a fairly considerable amount of time, only three Squadrons in France were using them, although those equipped with them had by now settled into a good routine. No. 7 Squadron had worked out the logistical nightmare of dealing with the enormous aircraft on night raids, similar methods being adopted by other Handley Page squadrons. At the start of the night when raids would be taking place, the aircraft due to take part would be lined up with enough room to easily move around each other. The only lights visible would be red lights to indicate the boundaries of the airfield that the aircraft could manoeuvre in; the lights were dull enough so that they would not be noticeable above any appreciable height that an enemy aircraft would be flying at. Each aircraft would flash it's allocated letter by Aldis lamp to the control tower (a much more rudimentary structure—if indeed it was even a structure—than the building the term is now applied to) when ready, each crew already knowing which place they were allotted for take-off. A red light would be shown by control for ten seconds signifying the crews to 'stand by', next would be a green light shown for ten seconds, in which time the first aircraft would get underway and take off. Three minutes was allowed until the green light was shown again and the second aircraft would leave, and so on until all aircraft were airborne. If an aircraft missed its slot it would automatically go to the back of the queue. When airborne and clear of the airfield, the aircraft would turn on its lights—a tail light and starboard (green) and port (red) lights. There would also be the navigational lights and recognition lights, bright white with one on the upper wing on the centre section to signify it was a friendly aircraft to allied aircraft above, and one under the fuselage to those below. If these did not work and a Handley Page came under attack from friendly anti-aircraft guns, the Aldis lamp would be used to flash the letter of the night, or the crews would fire the colour of the night by Very light. Of course once the aircraft got close to the enemy lines all lights would be switched off until back again.

Lighthouses were in use to aid night flyers, and these were used by the enemy, too. They had been used since 1914, but the first proper ones were used from early 1917 when FE2b night bombers started their work in earnest. They were mobile so could be relocated if the location of night-bombing aircraft changed (particularly useful when operations started in the south of France), and were originally lit by acetylene (although were being replaced with electric arc lights by the end of the war). Thirteen were in use by June 1917, increasing to twenty-seven by the end of the war, ten alone supported the Independent Force operations.

> Along our front were six signal towers stretching over thirty miles which flashed in Morse the letters A, B, C, F, G, and H. We picked out the one nearest the aerodrome and oriented ourselves from there.
>
> If we got off course and wandered over toward Switzerland, a large, illuminated cross on the ground told us we were approaching the border and if we got too close the Swiss batteries would open up. I never saw one of our signal towers up close but they could not have been high off the ground because their flashes were barely visible from ten miles.[16]

> Lieutenant Hugh Baird Monaghan, 215 Squadron RAF

They were vital navigation aids for the night flyers, and the German ones could be just as useful as the Handley Page crews made their way to and from their targets. Lieutenant Aubrey Evelyn Horn describes a typical return from a mission:

> Having crossed the lines again you switched on all lights, had some chocolate, thanked your stars you were at least over the lines again and going home. You must then be careful not to pass over prohibited areas, which were clearly marked on maps in the mapping office for you'd be shelled, lights, signals or not for you are coming from Hunland and they took no chances. I got it one night over St Pol and Ladd and I never forgave them! The next light seen was 'Q' then you saw the dummy aerodrome lit up like nothing on earth.[17]

> Lieutenant Aubrey Evelyn Horn, 7(N) Squadron RNAS

To try and lessen the risk of German night fighters attacking them on their return, by the time it was a part of the Royal Air Force, 207 Squadron had taken elaborate steps to bring their aircraft home as safely as possible by constructing a dummy aerodrome, with the bright white landing 'T' lit up at all times. The returning aircraft would line up as if to land on the dummy aerodrome (having by now turned the recognition lights off, but with the port and starboard lights showing) and signal their letter by Aldis lamp to the dummy airfield (or with the recognition lights if the Aldis lamp was not working). At the dummy aerodrome, people on the ground would be in touch with the real aerodrome by telephone, keeping them updated as to whether they would accept an aircraft for landing. If they would accept the aircraft, the aircraft's letter would be flashed back at the aircraft and it would land on the real airfield, ideally without the airfield needing to turn any lights on—if the crew did want the landing 'T' turned on, they would turn their own port and starboard lights off. As soon as the aircraft landed, the 'T' would be turned off (if it was needed) and the aircraft either led to its hangar by torchlight from a petty officer on a ground (if it was believed enemy aircraft were in the air) or by shining the airfield's searchlight onto the hangar. The airfield then telephoned the dummy airfield to inform them they were clear for landing again.

If an aircraft lined up with the dummy airfield, flashed it's letter, but was not accepted for landing, it would receive no reply and have to circle around and start again, repeating the procedure until accepted. Red rockets would be fired by the airfield if it was under attack by enemy aircraft, and if an aircraft tried to land without following the correct procedure it would have the searchlight pointed directly at the cockpit to make it very clear he was not to land. In an emergency, such as the aircraft being damaged, running out of fuel, or with an injured crew member on board, an aircraft would flash its letter with a piece of red glass over the Aldis lamp, and it would be given priority over all other aircraft in the circuit, even if another had been given clearance to land (in which case it would receive the searchlight reception). If an aircraft crashed on the airfield blocking the runway or otherwise making it too dangerous to land, the airfield's searchlight would be pointed at the wreckage, which would also aid those going to its assistance. If an aircraft was overdue, the searchlight would be pointed directly upwards into the air and white rockets fired at intervals in the sometimes forlorn hope that it was lost and would head for the aerodrome once seen.

With 41st Wing

There was a Squadron Naval 'A',
Dumped down in Ochey one wet day,
The place was full of mud and muck,
Which was 'A' Naval's usual luck.
And the rain came in the cabins
And the rain came in the cabins
And the rain came in the cabins
Until they stopped the leaks.[1]

Verse of A Squadron, RNAS song written by Flight Command
McClelland, October 1917

Following the Gotha raids on London and the south-east, the backlash from
the British public prompted Prime Minister David Lloyd George to look for a
way of being seen to do something about it; he was particularly mindful of the
revolution in Russia, and perhaps mindful of the attacks on civilians at home,
as well as the mounting casualty lists of men serving on foreign fields. In an
ideal world, Home Defence Squadrons would be supplied with more pilots and
better aircraft, however, this just wasn't feasible when (as always) the newest
types were needed for, and were of better use on, the front line. The immediate
calling back of front-line Scout Squadrons could only ever be a temporary
solution; it was not a guarantee of them downing the enemy and would have
an adverse effect on air superiority over the Western Front. Commander of
the Royal Flying Corps Major General Hugh Trenchard was given the task
of considering the feasibility of whether the British bombing of German cities
would be suitable. Trenchard was mindful that this may backfire, especially if
the British response would be half-hearted and not thorough, and stated:

Unless we are determined and prepared to go one better than the
Germans, whatever they may do and whether their reply is in the air

or against our prisoners or otherwise, it will be infinitely better not to attempt reprisals at all.[2]

Major General Hugh Trenchard, Royal Flying Corps

Lloyd George set up a committee for 'Air Organisation and Home Defence Against Air Raids', in the charge of General Jan Christian Smuts, a member of the War Cabinet (Smuts had formerly fought against the British when he led the Boer Commando during the Second Boer War of 1899–1902). While the committee discussed evidence and compiled a report, Trenchard and French Air Commander Paul Fernand du Peuty looked at possible locations for aerodromes close to the German border in the Departements de Meurthe-et-Moselle and Vosges areas in the summer of 1917. These were far from the British held parts of the Western Front, the only other British unit in the area being the 6th Aircraft Park, but were no strangers to Handley Pages or other bombers as 3 Wing RNAS had been based in the area just a few months prior.

The committee was to propose a new air force, separate from control of the Royal Navy and the Army, which ultimately led to the creation of the Royal Air Force on 1 April 1918. Meanwhile, on 1 October 1917 (while the Third Battle of Ypres was still raging) Field Marshal Sir Douglas Haig was informed that the War Cabinet wished for immediate action to be taken by bombing aircraft operating from the area around Nancy, and that Trenchard was to be returned to London to talk with Lloyd George. Lloyd George was told the next day by Trenchard that he could expect that RNAS aircraft operating from Ochey (again) could expect to be in action just six days after arriving. Trenchard told Lloyd George that the men and their machines would not fail, however they would likely be hampered by poor weather, lack of experience, and size of the force. Unsurprisingly, given that air superiority had been won back only at such a high price after the debacle of Bloody April over Arras, Haig was adamant that none of the aircraft and crews under his command would be removed for operations elsewhere. He also declared that he would not be party to the killing of defenceless women and children. Unfortunately for Haig, Lloyd George was fond of new schemes whereby the Germans could be defeated by means other than directly fighting them on the Western Front and the plan went ahead.

The new force, 41st Wing Royal Flying Corps, was formed on 11 October with the headquarters at Bainville-sur-Madon, commanded by Lieutenant-Colonel Cyril Newall, and the aircraft operating from Ochey. Ochey was at this point home to two French bombing squadrons, and had previously been home to 3 Wing and their Handley Pages. Newall's target area had Cologne, Frankfurt, and Stuttgart as its eastern limits, with anything westward of that considered a target for the DH4s and Handley

Pages. The FE2bs could only be used on relatively short-range missions owing to their smaller fuel capacity—unlike the other two types at Ochey they had not been designed for long-range bombing work. The first five aircraft from 41st Wing to arrive were DH4 bombers of 55 Squadron. By this stage, 55 Squadron was a superb unit, very possibly the best day-bombing unit in the RFC or RNAS at this time, having been serving in France since March of that year and conducting long-range bombing through some of the RFC's most testing times against stiff opposition. The Airco DH4 was an excellent day bomber and superseded the Sopwith 1½ Strutter. The DH4 was designed by Geoffrey de Havilland, and, like the Handley Page, were mostly fitted with the Rolls-Royce Eagle engine, the crew of two separated by the fuel tank located in-between the two. Although this made communication awkward, the use of speaking tubes did help alleviate this. The observer was fitted with a Scarff ring and one or two Lewis guns, the pilot having a forward-firing Vickers gun (two in the case of some RNAS examples). The DH4 could carry two 230-lb bombs, although like the Handley Page and others could, and did, carry a variety of other types such as 25-lb Cooper and 112-lb bombs.

The second of three squadrons that comprised 41st Wing was 100 Squadron, a night-bombing squadron (indeed, the first dedicated night-bombing squadron to serve on the Western Front) who operated Royal Aircraft Factory FE2bs (by now obsolescent for day fighting, but found themselves highly suitable for night bombing until the end of the war). Commanding 100 Squadron was Major Wulstan Tempest who had risen to fame on the night of 1–2 October 1916, when he shot down Zeppelin L31 over Potters Bar in Hertfordshire, killing the whole crew including Heinrich Mathy, a renowned Zeppelin commander. The FE2b (nicknamed the 'Fee') was originally designed as a machine-gun-carrying day fighter, a 'pusher' design with the Beardmore engine powering a rear-facing propeller at the back of the nacelle. In front of it sat the pilot, and in front and below him was the observer, right in the nose of the machine—although unlike the Handley Page this was much more exposed, an observer standing up being almost entirely in the open air, the nacelle barely coming up to his knees. The FE2b and the FE2d (fitted with a 250-hp Rolls-Royce Eagle to improve performance at altitude, as well as increased carrying capacity compared to the 160-hp Beardmore engine of the FE2b) were not retired from daylight operations until the late Spring of 1917; although not in time to save the 'Red Baron' himself, Baron Von Richtofen, from being shot in the head and severely wounded by a Royal Flying Corps FE2d in June 1917. As well as being used as a Home Defence aircraft back in Britain, the FE2b was put to work as a night bomber following its retirement from daylight operations. It was successful in this role, and the black painted

FE2bs, fitted with accoutrements such as wingtip flares, navigational lights, and a flare chute underneath the observer's position, would undertake raids behind the German front line, dropping a mixture of 230-lb, 112-lb and under-wing 25-lb Cooper bombs on enemy supply dumps, railways, and even moving trains. The observer's Lewis gun would also come in useful for these, and two used by 100 Squadron were even fitted with Vickers Mk III 37-mm 1-pounder 'pom-pom' automatic guns, which were found particularly useful in attacking trains. Like 55 Squadron, 100 Squadron was highly experienced, having been on operations since April. Lieutenant Alfie Reginald Kingsford, an FE2b pilot with 100 Squadron, briefly summed up 100 Squadron's targets, and the others:

Our targets were mostly in Alsace Lorraine, Metz, Diedenhofen, Trier, Saarbrücken on the Saar Valley, Kreuzwald, Courcelles, and Conflans, enemy troops being in all of these towns, as well as anything of military importance, and later we gave many of his aerodromes a good smack up. The day squadron, flying DH4s, did as far as Cologne, and a darned good show too. The Naval squadron went a bit farther than we did. They had Handleys, but didn't seem to do a lot of flying.[3]

Lieutenant Alfie Reginald Kingsford, 100 Squadron RFC

Completing the initial set up was the newly formed A Squadron, RNAS, who brought Handley Pages back to Ochey after a six-month gap. Four of their Handley Pages were those that had been sent from Dunkirk to Redcar little more than a month previously and these aircraft and their crews formed the basis for the new unit. Along with six other Handley Pages, A Squadron was formed at Manston before departing to France. The first batch of ground crew left on 5 October, and the second crossing to France on 10 October. Following a miserable journey, mostly by railway (travelling in the ubiquitous 'Hommes 30 Chevaux 8' goods wagons that the vast majority of men serving on the Western Front experienced at one stage or another), the men preceded the Handley Pages—nine of the ten arrived safely on 21 October, the remaining Handley Page hitting a tree on the approach to the aerodrome and damaging the port wings. Before their arrival, and as promised, six days after the first aircraft arrived, 55 Squadron conducted the Wing's first raid on the iron foundry at Burbach, in the Saarbrücken area. Two flights of DH4s took off and unleashed just under 1,800 lbs of bombs on the area.

On 25 October, the Handley Pages made their first raid as part of the new force. Nine Handley Pages took part, but only six returned. Twelve FE2bs of 100 Squadron were also airborne that night, each of them dropping their 230-lb bombs as well as an additional twenty-three 25-lb Cooper bombs on railway lines and associated buildings. One of the Handley Pages that took off that night was piloted by Flight Sub-Lieutenant Linnell—with the lights of Saarbrücken visible in the distance, one of his engines failed and turned around in a vain attempt to reach Allied lines. Linnell could make out the shadow of a hill while he struggled to fly straight, despite the wind and torque from the one running engine, and at a critical moment was blinded by a German searchlight. This resulted in him pulling back on the control wheel too far, causing the speed of the Handley Page to drop off rapidly and putting it into a spin, the upper wing hitting the ground first and ending the career of HP 3141, but fortunately not the lives of the crew, who were made prisoners of war. One of the other Handley Pages, flown by Flight Sub-Lieutenant MacDonald, was shot down by German anti-aircraft fire, again with all crew surviving and entering captivity, and the third Handley Page was hit by friendly fire—a French anti-aircraft gun downing the Handley Page on its return and crash landed, although it was later brought back to Ochey and repaired. Two FE2bs were also lost that night, and were 100 Squadron's first operational losses since formation.

The weather hampered operations, as it did for 3 Wing the year previously. The conditions at Ochey further added to the misery of the crews. As they were far from British held areas, there was no Army Service Corps units nearby to supply their rations and they had to draw from French rations instead, which were, at least in the RFC and RNAS men's eyes (or bellies), not as good as British rations—especially the quality of the tea. The men soon became frequent customers of a French-run canteen on the airfield, using their pay to try and satisfy their stomachs. The winter weather at Ochey was harsher than that further north. As the Squadron song showed, mud featured heavily in the men's memories long after leaving Ochey:

It had rained steadily during the whole time of the arrival of the personnel. It was cold. There were no stoves and no means of making a fire. All the stoves that we were ultimately able to acquire were obtained from the French Sergeant Casernier after a good deal of skilful flattery and cajolery. The squadron was lodged in Adrian huts. These were unique in having one universal quality—they all leaked. With praiseworthy persistence the rain dripped steadily through the roof and down on one's face throughout the night. There were but few tools and no materials with which to stop the leaks. Gradually the ground round the huts became a sea of mud. There was mud everywhere—it got on the clothes, into the hammocks, into the food, and no matter what one touched or attempted to touch, the mud was there first.[4]

Unknown Officer, A Squadron RNAS

Another raid was mounted on 30 October, which resulted in another aircraft being shot down, the three crew being taken prisoner including a very experienced Handley Page pilot. This was HP 3123 *Split-Pin* flown by Lieutenant Lance Sieveking DSC, formerly of 7 Squadron, accompanied by Air Mechanic Brooks and Air Mechanic Dodd. Captain Lambe visited Ochey at the end of October following this unfortunate start to the 41st Wing—particularly A Squadrons activities—and found plenty to remark upon. One clear cause of problems was the lack of skilled ground crew, and for what they did have, there was 'no spares of any sort... and practically no stores'. [5] Upon the four Handley Pages (originally detached from Dunkirk to Redcar with accompanying air and ground crews) returning to France, at least twenty-three skilled ground crew were kept in England. Just half of the ten Handley Pages originally sent to Ochey were still in operation (it appears that by the time he made this report, the Handley Page lost on the night of 30–31 October was still in action). The two damaged aircraft could certainly be made airworthy with little effort, but there were simply no spares available to repair them with. Only one of the operating aircraft had radiator shutters, which were vital in cold weather to prevent the engines freezing while in flight.

Although weather and the issues above stopped the Handley Pages from doing much of any use, conditions for the men improved, with roads being built and the catering situation getting better, with Captain J. Loxley taking charge. Vehicles were allowed to be used by both officers and the rest of the men for trips into local French towns to enjoy themselves, which of course greatly improved morale. As things became settled for A Squadron and the rest of 41st Wing, Ochey was bombed for the first time on the night of 15 November 1917:

> Previous to this date it had been quite the common thing to stand outside the huts and listen to the bombardment, without any other remark than to commiserate with the actual sufferers. Suddenly the crash of the first bomb was heard. This was followed by a moment of general stupefaction. Life had hitherto been so normal, in effect so uneventful; here was a rude awakening to the facts of war—a brusque plunge into abnormality. [6]

Unknown Officer of A Squadron RNAS

Ochey was, at this point, defended by two French 75-mm anti-aircraft guns nearby, and a single machine gun of 100 Squadron placed between two hangers. The attack occurred in three stages, from 20.30 until around 00.00; unshaded lights lit up areas around the huts very well, presenting a prime opportunity for the first of the raiders, however, the first attack cut the mains supply. Air Mechanic Dolley of A Squadron was found dead during the raid, he had been standing up when a bomb burst around 10 yards from him. He was buried two days later at Choloy Military Cemetery, near Toul. Two other men of A Squadron were wounded. The raids could disrupt flying operations, returning aircraft being especially vulnerable if enemy aircraft were around. An attacking aircraft would find a Handley Page, likely low on fuel and with a tired crew, an easy target if spotted. The possibility of damage to the aircraft due to a damaged runway (when landing they could potentially hit these areas) or coming under fire from friendly anti-aircraft guns, mistaking them for German machines.

> Our 'drome was frequently bombed and we had to move all accommodation and planes into woods skirting the 'drome after cutting down many trees. Occasionally on returning from a raid we would find our 'drome being bombed and we would have to make ourself scarce until safe to land.[7]

> W. G. Hall, A Squadron RNAS

More raids followed, and trenches were dug to shelter men in case of attack. Additional anti-aircraft guns were brought in by the French. Aircraft were spread out across the aerodrome to try and protect them better—better one machine be damaged by one bomb, than two or more by the same bomb if the aircraft were in close proximity. Unfortunately this very scenario did occur to one of the French night-bombing Squadrons also based at Ochey, as on one occasion a hanger and three aircraft were destroyed by two direct hits.

> Things began to get rather uncomfortable, and soon through enemy raids the Squadron had a number of machines put out of action, while transport suffered likewise.[8]

> Lieutenant Cyril Gordon Burge, 100 Squadron RFC

Eventually, it got to the point where motor transport was moved 1 mile away from the aerodrome on nights where it looked suitable for the enemy to raid. Valuable equipment was removed from all hangers every evening and dispersed across the aerodrome too. Trenches were dug, as well as additional machine-gun emplacements. For all their attempts, the German raids did little damage to the aerodrome, many of their bombs failing to explode. Major Lambert of A Squadron and chosen armourers and gun layers would disarm the bombs, seen sat on them, using a hammer and chisel to break through the casing in the mornings following raids—often a disconcerting sight for the others.

As Christmas came, the weather deteriorated further and there were still shortages, men resorting to using empty sand bags as replacement footwear when boots wore out. There were just four Handley Pages serviceable, although the weather was still precluding any operations for A Squadron. Not so for 55 Squadron's DH4s who were having some success. On 24 December twelve aircraft raided the chemical works at Mannheim. Despite heavy anti-aircraft fire downing one aircraft to add to the two that had already turned back owing to engine trouble, sixteen bombs were dropped on the city from 13,000 feet, and the DH4s turned back for home, and successfully evaded five German fighters that did not dare to press home their attack. No. 55 Squadron's claim to fame for the raid came to light several days later when it transpired that the Kaiser and his staff had travelled through Mannheim on his Imperial train barely an hour before the station was bombed—the last to travel through Mannheim for some time.

Christmas day for A Squadron was memorable; there was no Christmas pudding (which arrived two weeks later), but the tail skid trolley for a Handley Page was put to good use by mounting a barrel of beer on it, taking it to each hut in turn and allowing the men a certain number of minutes to use the tap. Continuing the movement of the motor transport to outside the airfield at night in case of enemy attack, the transport men were to have dinner in the village of Crepey. *En route*, one lorry slid on the greasy roads into a ditch—a tender (likely one of the widely used Crossley tenders used in large number by the RFC, RNAS, and then RAF throughout the war) sent onward to Crepey to pick up dinner and bring it back for those trying to extract the stuck lorry. The tender skidded off the road, over a ditch and into a field just 4 miles further towards Crepey, and those on board headed back to the lorry. By now the lorry was back on the road and headed towards the stranded tender, several hours later extricating that too. Unfortunately the dinner for the men involved was ruined. On 28 December, 41st Wing became VIII Brigade Royal Flying Corps.

At home, the O/400 design, which took into account lessons learnt from the development, production, and first use of the O/100s, was now in full swing. Development had started on the O/400 as early as the summer of 1917, but was mainly held up—as production of many British Great War aircraft types were—owing to lack of suitable engines. This was finally solved in December 1917 when it was decided that the O/400 would not use right and left-handed Rolls-Royce Eagle VIII engines, but have them all rotating the same way, and production continued, to replace the existing O/100s in operational squadrons and equip new squadrons. Although initially showing no interest in the Handley Pages, it would not be long until the Royal Flying Corps started to request them too following the reported results of RNAS squadrons using them.

7

To the Dardanelles

At the outbreak of war, First Sea Lord of the Admiralty Winston Churchill had requisitioned two British-built battleships that were on the verge of completion for the Ottoman Government, the *Resadiye* and the *Sultan Osman-I Evvel*. The Germans took advantage of this by sending the battlecruiser SMS *Goeben* (which was transferred to the Ottoman Navy and renamed the *Yavuz Sultan Selim*) and the light cruiser SMS *Breslau* (renamed the *Midilli* after she too was transferred to the Ottomans) to Constantinople, which (among other factors) resulted in the Ottomans coming into the war on the side of the Germans. The Gallipoli Campaign of 1915 failed to break through the Dardanelles, which was supposedly to result in the British fleet bombarding Constantinople and forcing them to surrender, and so by 1916 with many thousands of British, French, Indian, Australian, New Zealand, and other Empire and Commonwealth dead on the peninsula for no gain, the German ships remained a constant threat to naval activities in the Mediterranean. At any time, they could come out of the Dardanelles and harass transport ships sending men, machines, animals, and stores to Salonika and the Middle East. A daring raid was suggested to send a Handley Page O/100 to bomb Constantinople from an RNAS base in the Mediterranean, targeting the formerly German ships. Commodore Murray Sueter originally asked for a version of the O/100 fitted with floats as most of the route the aircraft would fly was over water, but Handley Page declared this was not practicable after allocating the Type S designation to it.

Instead, Handley Page O/100 3124 was selected while still at the Cricklewood factory instead of going to undertake trials with the Davis Gun. HP 3124 was flown from Cricklewood to Hendon then Manston on 22 May 1917. Flight Commander Kenneth Savory of 2 Wing RNAS was chosen as the pilot, and recalled to England to familiarise himself with the Handley Page. Savory had already been awarded the Distinguished Service Order for raiding Constantinople on the night of 14–15 April 1916 in a single-engine Royal Aircraft Factory BE2c along with Flight Sub-Lieutenant Richard Sebastian Willoughby Dickinson as observer. They were one of three aircraft that raided Constantinople, a round trip of over 300 miles, with severe rain, wind, and even snow experienced on the return flight.

Savory flew the Handley Page on a local flight on the same day it arrived at Manston, declared himself happy with it, and then loaded up the equipment needed. As well as Savory, he was joined by Lieutenant McClelland who would be a second pilot, Lieutenant Rawlings as observer, Chief Petty Officer Adams as engineer, and Leading Mechanic Cromack. As well as the men's personal luggage, there were hammocks and bedding, tents, spare parts, tool boxes, almost an entire Rolls-Royce Eagle engine in component form, and two complete spare four-blade propellers that had to be tied down to the top of the fuselage. HP 3124 took off for Villacoublay, Paris on 23 May, then down to Lyons, Marseilles, then across to Pisa in Italy. Rome was the next stop where they were met by heads of Italian aeronautical staff who were no doubt eager to draw comparisons with their large Caproni bombers. While the hospitality was no doubt welcomed, it did mean that any hope of secrecy surrounding the raid was rapidly becoming rather forlorn. From Rome it was onto Otranto then across the enemy territory to Salonika. While at Otranto, the men were informed that there were spares there that were urgently needed at Mudros, but, once these were loaded, the weight was found to be too heavy and after two attempts it was found that the Savory could not climb high enough to cross the mountains. They returned to Otranto, offloaded enough spares to get the aircraft back down to a sensible weight, and the spare propellers were fitted onto the engines. On the third attempt the aircraft was able to cross the Alps, however the radiators freezing was not the only danger faced by the men:

> While flying across the Albanian Alps the airmen could see the hostile Bulgarian horsemen chasing them, in the hope that their machine might be forced to descend and give the crew as prisoners into their hands. Cross winds, clouds, and all kinds of atmospheric disturbances rendered the latter portion of the voyage most difficult and perilous. The mountain peaks range from 8,000 ft to 10,000 ft in height. Happily, the engines never failed for one moment, and even with the heavy load on board there was never the slightest fear on the part of the pilots that any trouble would arise.
>
> Flight Magazine, 20 December 1917

Although the sound of enemy cavalry giving chase to an aeroplane, taking pot-shots at it, may sound like the Bulgarians were wasting their time, given how low the aircraft was flying—just clearing the mountains—there was a real danger the aircraft could have been brought down by their fire. The Handley Page landed at the RNAS airfield at Amberkui near to Lake Tuzlu Geul. The aircraft left on 8 June for RNAS Marsh at Mudros where it was prepared for the raid on Constantinople. The original plan to attack the German ships with torpedoes was rejected, so HP 3124 was loaded with a full complement of sixteen 112-lb bombs and took off for Constantinople on 3 July. Part way through the flight, the engines overheated and started to lose power, so Savory dropped some of the bomb load to allow the aircraft to fly higher for their safety with less power and headed to an alternative target, dropping the rest of the 112-lb bombs on the Ottoman army camp at Bulair on the Gallipoli peninsula (scene of an Ottoman defeat in 1913 in the First Balkan War) and returned back to Mudros. Another attempt two days later ended in failure when a tyre burst as the fully loaded aircraft started its take-off roll; fortunately, this happened before the aircraft picked up much speed or the results could have been disastrous. The next night, and with a replaced tyre, bad weather forced Savory back, determined to try again the next day.

On the night of 7 July, Savory took off with a reduced load of twelve 112-lb bombs at 20.47, and just over three hours later arrived over Constantinople at 2,000 feet. Savory aimed for Stenia Bay where the *Yavuz Sultan Selim*, the *Midilli*, and other ships and submarines were in waiting. Three runs were taken over the vessels before Savory came in at 800 feet over the *Yavuz Sultan Selim*, Flight Lieutenant McClelland dropping four 112-lb bombs, missing the warship, though falling among the other ships nearby. The next four reportedly hit the warship. A further two bombs were dropped on the SS *General*, which was reported to be a German headquarters, and the last two on the Turkish War Office (one hitting a stables, the other just missing the main gates). As was reported in the newspapers after the raid:

By this time, considerable alarm seems to have been caused in Constantinople, and the guns, which had not been previously fired, were now loosed at the machine. In fact, the flight back down the Sea of Marmora was accompanied by an orchestra of guns.

Nottingham Evening Post, 14 December 1917

Savory headed back to Mudros via the Sea of Marmora, the same way that they had arrived from. At least twenty-six bullets had struck the aircraft, one bullet damaging the oiling system of one of the Rolls-Royce Eagle engines meaning the return flight was done on a single engine. The

Handley Page arrived back at base at 03.40. There were conflicting reports on what damage was actually done by the Handley Page, but the main target of the *Yavuz Sultan Selim* appeared to have actually been mostly untouched; it continued to serve through the rest of the war and with the Turkish Navy, up until it was scrapped in the 1970s.

Savory was awarded a bar to his DSO and recalled to England for further service on Handley Pages with A (later 216) Squadron. A celebratory lunch was held to celebrate the Constantinople raid, which was attended by various distinguished officers and engineers, headed by Lord Herbert Scott. Savory and McLelland could not attend, replying to the invitation that they were in France and 'we are too busy killing Germans', and so Frederick Handley Page told the story for them.

Handley Page 3124 remained with 2 Wing at Mudros, with Flight Lieutenant John Alcock (who would later fly the Vickers Vimy on the first non-stop transatlantic flight in 1919) taking it on a raid to Panderma on the southern shore of the Sea of Marmora on 7 August, then on 1 September attacking the railway station and related buildings at Adrianople, a major city close to the border with Greece and Bulgaria. The Handley Page was also used for patrols, and another raid on Constantinople was planned for 30 September, with railway stations there being the target for the deadly cargo, which included incendiaries.

After flying through anti-aircraft fire over the Gallipoli peninsula, the propeller on the port-side engine broke off and petrol from the auxiliary tank on that side started leaking. Alcock tried to gain—or at least maintain—as much height as possible on one engine, but the aircraft went from 6,000 feet to 1,000 feet in around 60 miles. Alcock decided to ditch the aircraft off Suvla Bay, hoping to be picked up by Royal Navy warships operating in the area. After the aircraft came to a quick halt in the sea, the three crew members clung onto the rear fuselage, but came under fire from Ottoman soldiers on shore. The fuselage floated for two hours; ultimately, the men had no choice but to swim to the shore, and hid there until the next day. At around noon on the 31 September, the men were discovered and taken prisoner, eventually getting to Constantinople, however, not in the way they'd hoped. Despite the aircraft's limited operational career, resulting in just one successful raid on Constantinople and one that did fairly minor damage, the propaganda value alone of the raid was extremely valuable, and ever the publicist, Frederick Handley Page, made frequent mention of the raid in advertising material from then onwards.

8

Flight to Damascus

The story of Colonel T. E. Lawrence, better known as 'Lawrence of Arabia', is well-known. Needless to say, by 1918 Colonel T. E. Lawrence's work in the Middle East was having a great effect. As well as the Arab forces to fight the Turks with, he also had an attachment of Rolls-Royce armoured cars accompanied by Talbot light tenders, some of them having 10-pounder mountain guns mounted on the back as mobile artillery support. In the air, Lawrence had the support of two Bristol F2b Fighters of 1 Squadron Australian Flying Corps.

The Rolls-Royce Falcon-powered Bristol Fighter was one of the best British aircraft of the war, and were a great asset to Lawrence with their ability to undertake reconnaissance, bombing, and strafing in support of the ground forces, as well as being sufficiently manoeuvrable, fast, and well-armed to take on whatever the enemy would send up against them. The Bristols were mainly involved in fast communication work between Sherif Feisal of Hedjaz and General Allenby as the Bedouins operated behind the Ottoman lines. Knowledge of the work the Handley Pages were doing was by now widespread and so Lawrence requested at least one heavy bomber to aid his forces in coming offensives. Lawrence felt increased air power was absolutely necessary to compliment the forces he already had at his disposal:

I explained our prospects, and how everything was being wrecked by air-impotence. He pressed a bell and in a few minutes Salmond and Borton were conferring with us. Their machines had taken an indispensable part in Allenby's scheme (the perfection of this man who could use infantry and cavalry, artillery and Air Force, Navy and armoured cars, deceptions and irregulars, each in its best fashion!): and had fulfilled it. There were no more Turks in the sky—except on our side, as I hurriedly interpolated. So much the better, said Salmond; they would send two Bristol fighters over to Umtaiye to sit with us while we needed them. Had we spares? Petrol? Not a drop? How was it to be got there? Only by air?

An air-contained fighting unit? Unheard of!

However, Salmond and Borton were men avid of novelty. They worked out loads for the Handley-Page, while Allenby sat by, listening and smiling, sure it would be done. The co-operation of the air with his unfolding scheme had been so ready and elastic, the liaison so complete and informed and quick. It was the R.A.F., which had converted the Turkish retreat into rout, which had abolished their telephone and telegraph connections, had blocked their lorry columns, scattered their infantry units.

The Air chiefs turned on me and asked if our landing-grounds were good enough for a Handley-Page with full load. I had seen the big machine once in its shed, but unhesitatingly said 'Yes' though they had better send an expert over with me in the Bristols tomorrow and make sure. He might be back by noon, and the Handley come at three o'clock. Salmond got up: 'That's all right, Sir. We'll do the necessary'. I went out and breakfasted.[1]

Colonel Thomas Edward Lawrence

Handley Page O/400 C9681 was selected in May 1918 to fly to Egypt and then onwards to Palestine. Brigadier General Amyas Eden Borton DSO (Commander of the Palestine Brigade of the RAF, which comprised the Fifth Wing and Fortieth Wing) was on leave in England at the time and asked the Air Ministry for permission to fly back to Palestine. After an introduction to flying the Handley Page at Cranwell in Lincolnshire, he left on 25 July as a passenger on the aircraft along with Sergeant Goldfinch and Air Mechanic First Class Francis. The pilot was Major MacLaren MC who brought his pet dog Tiny with him. The men went via Manston to Paris then roughly followed the route taken by Savory *en route* to Mudros in Handley Page O/100 3124 the previous year, and arrived Kantara, Egypt on 8 August, Borton taking the opportunity when possible to fly the aircraft.

The Handley Page arrived at Ramleh on the Suez Canal on 29 August to serve with 1 Squadron AFC after being serviced at Kantara, and flown by Captain Ross Smith it was used at first as a transport aircraft, bringing in petrol, ammunition, aircraft, and vehicle spares to Azrak. The arrival of the giant Handley Page amazed the Arab forces, who had never seen anything like it before—and certainly gave them a morale boost after coming under aerial attack from Ottoman forces. Lawrence described the scene when, with Feisal, he went to see the new arrival:

Twenty miles short of Um el Surab we perceived a single Bedawi, running southward all in a flutter, his grey hair and grey beard flying in the wind, and his shirt (tucked up in his belly-cord) puffing out behind him. He altered course to pass near us, and, raising his bony arms, yelled, 'The biggest aeroplane in the world', before he flapped on into the south, to spread his great news among the tents.

At Um el Surab the Handley stood majestic on the grass, with Bristols and 9.A--like fledglings beneath its spread of wings. Round it admired the Arabs, saying, 'Indeed and at last they have sent us the aeroplane, of which these things were foals.' Before night rumour of Feisal's resource went over Jebel Druse and the hollow of Hauran, telling people that the balance was weighted on our side.

Borton himself had come over in the machine, to concert help. We talked with him while our men drew from her bomb-racks and fuselage a ton of petrol; oil and spare parts for Bristol Fighters; tea and sugar and rations for our men; letters, Reuter telegrams and medicines for us. Then the great machine rose into the early dusk, for Ramleh, with an agreed programme of night-bombing against Deraa and Mafrak, to complete that ruin of the railway traffic which our gun-cotton had begun.[2]

Colonel Thomas Edward Lawrence

The arrival of the Handley Page was cited as one important factor that brought together other tribes to Lawrence's army. The first bombing raid took place in the early hours of 19 September 1918 when sixteen 112-lb bombs were dropped onto the Ottoman headquarters and telephone exchange at El Afule, severely disrupting communications and a good start to the Battle of Nablus, delaying reinforcements and news of the British attack on the Ottoman Seventh Army. Later that evening the railway and aerodrome at Jenin was bombed, with a second sortie in the early morning of 20 September. The success of the British forces resulted in the retreating Ottoman Seventh and Eighth armies becoming bunched up in the narrow Wadi el Far'a, allowing three squadrons of British fighter aircraft a great opportunity to strafe them and kill many. Meanwhile the Handley Page was used as a transport aircraft to move fuel and other supplies from Ramleh, as well as getting the chance to raid the airfield at Deraa on 23 September. HP C9681 certainly helped speed up the British and Arab forces on their road to Damascus, and on 31 October the Ottomans surrendered.

1. Prototype O/100 Handley Page 1455 in a hangar with the wings folded back, showing the unusual cockpit design. (*Fleet Air Arm Museum JMBGSL03801*)

Above: 2. Handley Page O/100 3123 *Split Pin* at RNAS Redcar, 1917, on anti-U-boat patrol duties. (*Fleet Air Arm Museum JMBGSL03841*)

Below: 3. Handley Page O/100 of 7 Squadron RNAS; the black cat nose marking can be seen on the front of the fuselage. (*Fleet Air Arm Museum JMBGSL03849*)

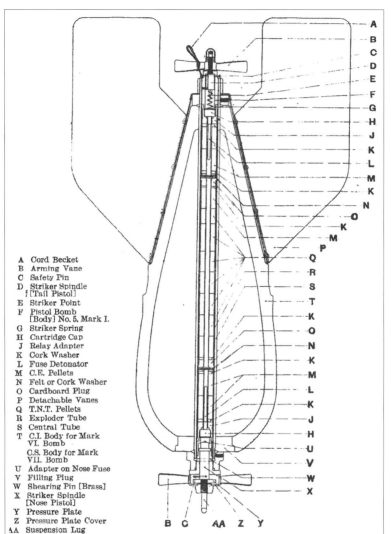

Left: 4. Drawing of a 112-lb bomb, dropped in great numbers from Handley Pages.

A Cord Becket
B Arming Vane
C Safety Pin
D Striker Spindle [Tail Pistol]
E Striker Point
F Pistol Bomb [Body] No. 5, Mark I.
G Striker Spring
H Cartridge Cap
J Relay Adapter
K Cork Washer
L Fuse Detonator
M C.E. Pellets
N Felt or Cork Washer
O Cardboard Plug
P Detachable Vanes
Q T.N.T. Pellets
R Exploder Tube
S Central Tube
T C.I. Body for Mark VI. Bomb
C.S. Body for Mark VII. Bomb
U Adapter on Nose Fuse
V Filling Plug
W Shearing Pin [Brass]
X Striker Spindle [Nose Pistol]
Y Pressure Plate
Z Pressure Plate Cover
AA Suspension Lug

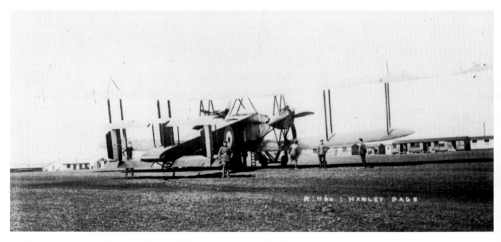

5. Rear view of a Handley Page O/100. (*Author's Collection*)

Above left: 6. A 1917 Handley Page advertisement following the raid on Constantinople.

Above right: 7. 'Bombing the stranded "*Goeben*" in the Dardanelles'—artist's impression of the daring raid on Constantinople in 1917. (*Flight Magazine, 7 February 1918*)

Below left: 8. 'What might have been, and even yet may be'—artist's impression of a Handley Page attacking a German town with a wrathful ghost emerging from the fires. (*Flight Magazine, 22 November 1917*

Below right: 9. 'Britain's biggest battleplane—the great Handley Page bomber at work'—an artist's impression of a Handley Page flying at night. (*The Sphere Magazine, 27 October 1917*)

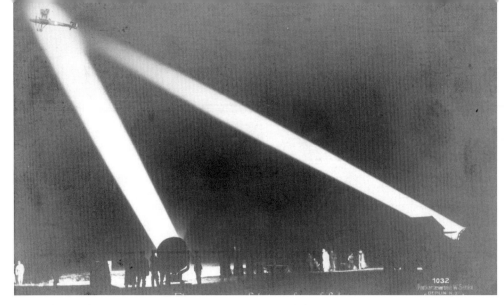

10. '*Scheinwerfer*'—a German postcard showing searchlights at night with an image of a Handley Page superimposed in the searchlight's glare. (*Author's Collection*)

Above: 11. Handley Page O/400 with the wings folded back. The forward gun position has two Lewis guns mounted on the Scarff ring. (*Author's Collection*)

Below: 12. Handley Page O/100 on a snow-covered aerodrome.

13. Front view of a Handley Page O/400 with the wings folded. (*Author's Collection*)

Above: 14. A crashed Handley Page O/400. (*North East Land, Sea and Air Museums*)

Left: 15. Artist's impression of a trio of Handley Pages flying at night. In reality, flying in formation at night was highly unlikely owing to the risk of collision. (*Flight magazine, 27 March 1919*)

16. Handley Page O/400 and crew. Judging by the uniforms, this is an ex-RFC squadron. (*North East Land, Sea and Air Museums*)

17. Side view of a Handley Page O/400 with the raised forward gun position. (*Author's Collection*)

18. Handley Page O/400 airborne giving a good view of the difference in size and shape between the upper and lower wings. (*Author's Collection*)

19. Front view of a Handley Page O/100 with wings folded back, giving a good comparison of the engine radiators on the O/100 engine nacelle versus the O/400 seen elsewhere.

20. Handley Page O/400 of 100 Squadron RAF. There appear to be a number of French civilians present. (*Fleet Air Arm Museum JMBGSL03898*)

Left: 21. Fuel tank and bomb 'crate' of a Handley Page O/400. (*Fleet Air Arm Museum JMBGSL03931*)

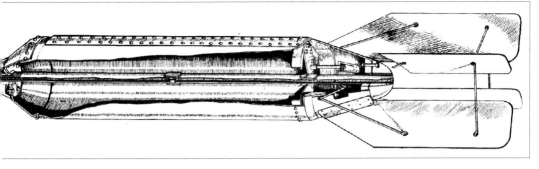

22. Cutaway view of an SN 1,650-lb bomb.

Below left: 23. Drawing of the Baby Incendiaries and their loading frame, container, and release gear.

Below right: 24. SN 1,650-lb bomb (described as a 1,700-lb bomb), a Baby Incendiary bomb, and a sergeant of the RAF for comparison. (*Author's Collection*)

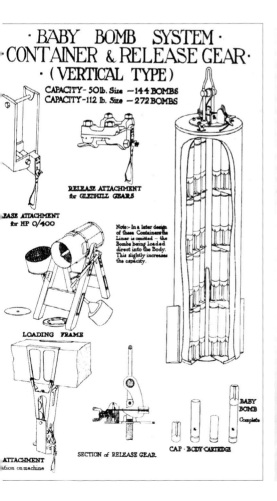

The Daily Mirror

CERTIFIED CIRCULATION LARGER THAN THAT OF ANY OTHER DAILY PICTURE PAPER

No. 4,490.   Registered at the G.P.O. as a Newspaper.   SATURDAY, MARCH 16, 1918.   One Penny.

GREAT BRITAIN'S REPLY TO GERMAN "FRIGHTFULNESS"

One of the famous Handley-Page bombing machines which are being used by British airmen to give to the Germans a taste of the medicine they have so freely scattered over London and the South-East of Britain.

A Handley-Page machine setting out for a flight to some part of Germany.

Mr. Handley-Page chatting with the pilot of a bombing machine.

Above: 25. Front page of *The Daily Mirror*, Saturday 16 March 1918. (*Author's Collection*)

Below: 26. Amusing Christmas card from 115 Squadron showing a Handley Page O/400. (*North East Land, Sea and Air Museums*)

27. Handley Page O/400 and men of 214 Squadron RAF. Note the SN 1,650-lb bomb positioned alongside. (*Fleet Air Arm Museum JMBGSL07540*)

Below left: 28. A 1918 Handley Page advert.

Below right: 29. 'Was England Will!'—German propaganda poster showing what Britain planned to do to German industry with flocks of Handley Pages to do it.

30. A 3.7-cm Gruson-Hotchkiss Revolverkanone, responsible for the 'flaming onions' reported by Handley Page and other British aircraft crews. (*Brett Butterworth*)

31. Rear view of 3.7-cm Gruson-Hotchkiss Revolverkanone manned by Luftschiffer-Bataillon No. 1, showing the anti-aircraft sight. (*Brett Butterworth*)

32. German Maxim 3.7-cm automatic cannon. (*Author's Collection*)

33. German 7.7-com Flak gun mounted on a motor lorry. (*Brett Butterworth*)

34. German 8.8-cm K-Flak anti-aircraft gun on trailer mounting. (*Brett Butterworth*)

35. Concrete U-boat pens at Bruges, a frequent target for the Handley Pages. (*North Eastern Railway Magazine, 1920*)

36. Handley Page V/1500. (*Author's Collection*)

37. Side view of a Handley Page V/1500. (*Author's Collection*)

38. 'Super Handley' in the air. (*Author's Collection*)

39. A 1919 advert for Handley Page Transport.

9

1918

New Year brought the promise of more aircraft and more squadrons. Now the Handley Page had proved itself and had been further refined with the O/400 version, powered by the Rolls-Royce Eagle VIII now in production (although would not enter service until around April 1918), the Handley Page Type Os were among the fleet of modern aircraft that would see in the coming formation of the Royal Air Force. In the south of France, A Squadron at Ochey was renumbered to 16 Squadron and their first raid of 1918 took place on the early morning of 6 January when two Handley Pages took off— one dropped twelve bombs on the railway junction at Courcelles, but the other returned with oil trouble. Two aircraft attempted to raid Thionville on the night of 21 January, but one returned owing to cloud cover, and the other dropped bombs over a large railway depot south of Metz. Three days later on 24–25 January, Captain Digby's Handley Page bombed Mannheim, the first time a Handley Page had bombed this major city. Reports received from Germany mentioned damage to a large factory, believed to have been the Schutte-Lanz factory, where the enormous R Type 'Giant' aeroplanes were built (these aircraft, powered with four or five engines, were twice as big as the Gothas and were also used to bomb England), as well as considerable damage to the Lindenhof area of Mannheim. Aerial photographs showed a burst on a munitions factory near the railway station. A heavy enemy raid took place on the aerodrome in mid-February, with some hangars damaged including one of the 16 Squadron hangars having a corner blown off. The camp was subsequently moved further south-west, with trees in the nearby wood used as concealment for living quarters, as well as new hangars put up on the edge of the wood. Until this happened, men were sent to other locations for safety, including some sent to the American camp at Colombey. The site at Ochey continued to receive attention from the Germans, the disused hangars becoming more and more damaged.

The Americans who also had ground forces in the area were very interested in the aerial goings-on at Ochey and came in large numbers to ask questions and try and get a flight. Another arrival, not long after the influx of Americans, came in the form of the Italians, bringing with them the huge three-engine Caproni CA5 bombers. The Caproni CA5 had one engine on each wing and at the rear of the engine a boom that joined at the tail; the fuselage itself ended with a rearward facing 'pusher' engine, between the tail booms.

> These machines were considered the very latest in bombers, having three engines and carrying a crew of four, and being capable of doing long shows with heavy loads. Whether they were hard to handle or whether the pilots were only mediocre, I don't know, but they had plenty of crashes, and one bird wrote his machine off the first day they arrived. We helped to pick up the pieces.[1]

Lieutenant Alfie Reginald Kingsford, 100 Squadron RFC

The relatively quiet start to the year continued for 16 Squadron with only two raids undertaken in February—two bombers attacking Trèves on the night of 19 February, with the raid repeated by one Handley Page on 26 February. Raids started even later in March, the first one on the night of 23 March when a Handley Page dropped ten 112-lb bombs on the railway centre of Konz, near Trèves. The next night, three aircraft took to the air; two were aimed for Cologne, Flight Lieutenant Digby dropped his bombs on the city, setting a large wood store on fire as well as damaging various other buildings; Digby landed after eight hours. A reliable source later informed the Allies that much more damage had been done to Cologne than the Germans admitted at the time, and it had significantly affected the local population. The second Handley Page, flown by Flight Lieutenant McClelland, turned around to return to base after the radiator temperatures rose to dangerously high levels after crossing the lines. After landing and believing the problem was solved, he headed off again, but near Metz one engine failed, so he dropped his bombs over Courcelles and flew back to Ochey on just one engine. The third Handley Page of the night dropped twelve 112-lb bombs on the railway triangle at Luxembourg. The prototype Handley Page O/100 HP 1455 was lost when a 100 Squadron FE2b was thrown by a bomb blast onto (and partially into) HP 1455 and wrote them both off. For an aircraft that had first flown in December 1915 and was a prototype aircraft, HP 1455 had certainly had a long and useful career after being rebuilt to production standard.

Raids on enemy airfields and the coastal targets that were more desirable to the Admiralty (who ultimately they were responsible to) were still the regular work for 7 Squadron and 14 Squadron RNAS in the north of France. As the men became more experienced, they devised ways to evade unwanted attention from enemy searchlights. During a raid on the Bruges docks on 17 February, C.E.V. Wilkins got caught in searchlights after dropping his bombs at 5,000 feet. He immediately headed to Holland, 'split-assing' (tight turning) while descending, levelling out at 3,800 feet after having successfully avoided the searchlights.

On the night of 18 February, seven aircraft from 14 Squadron attacked St Denis Westrem, dropping four 250-lb and ninety 112-lb bombs in total, the aircraft returned and raided a second time. Two aircraft from 7 Squadron were airborne and attacked Bruges. Lieutenant Horn was the rear gun layer on HP 3119, taking off at 1857 and loaded with four 250-lb bombs and six 112-lb bombs. After take-off they gained height to the west of Dunkirk, friendly searchlights bothering them, but most turning off after the colour of the day was fired by Very light. They crossed the lines at about 7,000 to 8,000 feet and skirted the south side of Ghistelles. Looking over the side of the aircraft, Horn saw a 'round dark blot' on the ground:

While wondering what town it was, a red rocket soared up and burst into a million scintillating stars. This was the signal for undisguised hate on the part of the Hun occupants of the town. They sent up a barrage which luckily was well on the port quarter of the machine, and could be plainly seen bursting into sharp spluttering flames leaving woolly puffs of white smoke. The smoke showed up clearly above the sharply defined horizon of the mist, for above the mist the sky is perfectly clear and the stars and moon are brilliant. Shrapnel was not the only thing which was fired up against us. Luminous balls of fire made their way upwards as well as the inevitable flaming onions.[2]

Lieutenant Aubrey Evelyn Horn, 7(N) Squadron RNAS

The bombs were duly dropped over Bruges—the 250-lb bombs having a very noticeable effect, Horn believing he could even just about hear the explosion. The job done, the pilot turned for home and followed a canal as a navigational aid. At this point the aircraft encountered a German scout, believed by Horn to have been an Albatros. The first he knew of the encounter was when the aircraft was put into a nose dive, followed by the sound of the forward machine gun opening up. Horn grabbed one of the Lewis guns at his position, but clearly the chance to aid the forward gun had been missed, but then realised the lower gun position may be a more suitable place for him:

I then scrambled down onto the lower deck and got behind the gun there, fully convinced that the Hun was on our tail, and we'd probably get it in the neck. This was no comfortable reflection to feast one's mind upon while waiting for bullets to come ripping up from the tail, raking us fore and aft. The tail is a blind spot and a machine firing into our tail from behind is practically immune from any of our gunfire.[3]

Lieutenant Aubrey Evelyn Horn, 7(N) Squadron RNAS

The expected attack never came, but isolated in the back Horn was not aware of what had been experienced by the pilot and observer at the front, finding out on their return:

It seems that Hudson startled a machine flying below us (at) about 200 feet and it deliberately turned, flew ahead of us, turned again and flew straight up at us. By this time Hudson dived from his seat, through the door and into the for'ard cockpit, fitted a pan and put a burst of about ten rounds straight into the fuselage of the Hun, who was about 50 feet below us then. At any rate he was close enough for Barker to see that the propeller boss was streamlined. The result of this burst was that the Hun's nose turned vertically upwards, stalled and did a vertical nose dive. A second burst immediately after the first also went into the Hun, who went crashing earthwards...[4]

Lieutenant Aubrey Evelyn Horn, 7(N) Squadron RNAS

A new arrival at 14 Squadron in February 1918 was Sergeant Leslie Alexander Dell. Dell had lead an interesting life with aircraft already; before the war he would spend his Sundays with someone who had a biplane in Ealing, helping him try to get it off the ground. The owner and pilot, Temple, did eventually succeed in getting airborne, but died in a crash. At the outbreak of war, he joined the Royal Naval Air Service and ended up serving with the armoured cars. Dell served with the heavy Seabrook armoured lorries, which were armed with Maxim machine guns and a 3-pounder gun that were designed to give mobile light artillery support to the lighter, faster Rolls-Royce and Lanchester armoured cars also in use. While on coastal defence duties in north Norfolk, a Zeppelin flew over one Sunday, low enough that Dell could see the Zeppelin crew walking around inside the gondola cars. Despite having such a clear target, the Seabrook armoured lorries were powerless as they were still awaiting their ammunition to be brought up by train; all the men could do was to give chase in an attempt to at least be seen to be doing something, and so the bulky armoured vehicles drove through Cromer with crowds cheering them on. When the unit was disbanded and given the chance of staying with the Royal Navy or transferring to the British

Army and working with mechanical transport, Dell decided to stay with the senior service and went to Dover as a 1st Class Air Mechanic with the RNAS. He served with 3 Wing at Luxieul on Sopwith 1½ Strutters and then on Airco DH4s before gaining his Royal Aero Club Certificate in January 1918. Despite being a qualified pilot, as a non-commissioned officer he did not fly a Handley Page on operational duties; this could have been due to snobbery, or also perhaps owing to the fact that as he had significant previous experience as an observer, his skills were in high demand.

Further arrivals of aircraft and crews allowed a third Handley Page squadron to be formed at Coudekerque on 10 March, 15 Squadron, becoming the fourth active Handley Page unit in total. The night of 11–12 March saw four Handley Pages on a raid to hit Bruges. Horn was not airborne until 02.08, noting no moon and slight ground mist. *En route* to Bruges an unusual type of enemy fire was seen:

I noticed one particular form of 'Hate' which I'd never noticed before and that was a sort of shrapnel burst high up above the thickness of the other 'gubbins' immediately following the burst a perfect rain of fire of burning sparks fell from it and seems to fall slowly covering a larger area all the while. Whether it was intended to fall on the raiding aircraft from above and set fire to it I don't know.[5]

Lieutenant Aubrey Evelyn Horn, 7(N) Squadron RNAS

Over Bruges they came under heavy anti-aircraft fire and were picked up by searchlights again, so the pilot dived and side-slipped to avoid them as best as possible:

You can almost hear the lights strike the machine! One gets on to us and sticks there immediately every other swings over and you are well caught. They simply sweep across the sky and as it strikes you there is sticks. The 'crump' of the bursting shrapnel is not an amusing noise, and you can feel the concussion. Looking above and around the after cockpit I saw black and white puffs floating by, and the shrapnel bursting with a white flame, while the high explosive leaves a black cloud and bursts with a deep red flame. At least we cleared all this trouble, and now having released the bombs had to take a new line.[6]

Lieutenant Aubrey Evelyn Horn, 7(N) Squadron RNAS

Flying away from Bruges, the aircraft gained height while flying in a wide circle before approaching again. To try and remain undetected, the pilot feathered the engines, gliding towards the target. The remaining bombs were dropped, the engines opened up and headed for the lines, leaving the searchlights and anti-aircraft fire behind them.

The raids on Bruges continued—Horn describes the night of 23–24 March, when loaded with fourteen 112-lb bombs:

> The usual green 'flaming onions', searchlights and shrapnel showed us that the first machine was already over Bruges. Continuing on our course we picked up the Bruges-Ostend canal and skirting the western side of Bruges we caused the fireworks at Bruges to come up again. They were nowhere near us and we crossed the Zeebrugges-Bruges canal at 8,500. Zeebrugge put up lights and Bruges died down again. Turning we picked up the Zeebrugge canal and started down but up came Bruges hate and we steered off, after a while everything was again quiet and turning to the mouth again crossed the canal, more lights and strafe from Bruges. We were picked up by a light but side slipped out, and kept north to gain our height and again Bruges became quiet. After having got height we again got on the canal. Once again lights, and 'hate', but shutting off the engines we glided along the canal. The Huns evidently thought we'd departed and stopped their fire and the lights died out. We still kept on the course undetected and just when the sights got on the submarine shelters I let them go.[7]

Lieutenant Aubrey Evelyn Horn, 7(N) Squadron RNAS

On the way back, the crew tried a neat little trick that had a one in three chance of success:

> When we were well clear of Bruges a searchlight went up so we tried the effect of a Verys light. The Hun colour for the night was also white evidently for the lights went out. Arriving near Ghistelles we fired a red light, to see what would happen, but he immediately swung round to try and pick us up, but there was nothing doing! Mist was not getting thick so we cleared for home.[8]

Lieutenant Aubrey Evelyn Horn, 7(N) Squadron RNAS

Late March saw 16 Squadron move to Villeseneux aerodrome near the Marne. Those not ferrying the aircraft made the journey by motor lorry.

On 1 April, the Royal Flying Corps and Royal Naval Air Service were amalgamated to form the Royal Air Force. The only immediate change for the Handley Page Squadrons was that all Royal Naval Air Service Squadrons now had their numbers increased by 200, whereas Royal Flying Corps Squadrons would keep their original numbers. After the amalgamation, 16 Squadron, now 216 Squadron Royal Air Force, was paraded by Squadron Commander Buss. Buss along with the rest of the Squadron regretted no longer being part of the Royal Navy, but they continued to uphold naval traditions. This was common with all other RNAS units, and likewise RFC squadrons were reluctant to part with their Army ways. Both RFC and RNAS men kept their uniforms for as long as possible, often well into 1919. The first sortie for 216 Squadron (as part of the RAF) was on 12 April, when railway junctions were targeted—two Handley Pages aimed for Amagne Lucquy and one to Juniville, thirty-six 112-lb bombs dropped in total. By now there were just three serviceable Handley Pages; the aircraft moved to Cramailke aerodrome the day following the raid on the 19, and then raided Chaulnes the next night. Meanwhile, Buss visited the RAF Headquarters to try and acquire more aircraft; with just three aircraft airworthy, 216 Squadron would simply have to stop operations if no more were forthcoming. Crew lost had also not been fully replaced either. Fortunately Buss's trip was successful and the Squadron was back up to strength again, and if a replacement was needed in the future, one would automatically be sent down from 3 Aeroplane Supply Depot at Courban.

A bold naval raid to block the U-boats access to the sea via Zeebrugge and Ostend was planned for April. The idea was to sink block ships as close to the lock gates of the canals from Bruges as possible, to bottle up the U-boats. Although they could eventually be moved to other bases, such as the German naval base at Kiel, it would take a lot of time, perhaps long enough for the war to be won on the Western Front. The former RNAS squadrons had been involved in reconnaissance for the planned raid for a while, and would play an important role in helping to try and silence the defences so that the block ships could be manoeuvred and sunk successfully in the correct place. The attack was to take place on the night of 11–12 April, with ten Handley Pages in total to attack the Zeebrugge Mole. From 22.00 to 01.00, the Handley Pages were to bomb Zeebrugge Mole and the nearby coastal batteries, as one machine finished then another started. From 01.00 onwards they would drop parachute flares to help bombing parties on ground attack the Mole. A great flare will be lit on a vessel 20 miles north-west of Ostend to show everything was proceeding satisfactorily at that point.

Corporal William Edward David Wardrop was in one of the Handley Pages:

Our role there wasn't very—how can I put it—a means to do any damage but just to attract the searchlights and force them to put their searchlights up while our Navy tried to get in as close as they possibly could without being found. But as soon as the first shot was fired by the Navy, so all the searchlights went down on the sea and they started bombarding them, of course. So far as we were concerned we were just left alone. We had no more to do so we came home. All we were doing was going round dropping one bomb at a time, coming in and going out again. There were several of us, we were doing that in turn, to keep on making a nuisance of ourselves to force them to put the searchlights up and the guns.[9]

Corporal William Edward David Wardrop, 207 Squadron RAF

Bewsher was flying that night with pilot Flight Commander J. R. Allen DSC, detailed to bomb Zeebrugge Mole from 22.30 to 23.30 and drop flares at 01.00 (Bewsher appears to have been transferred to 214 Squadron by this stage, the crew seemingly being interchangeable between 207 and 214 Squadrons at this point):

Again and again we fly into Zeebrugge. Through the mist the great white beams stagger and wheel and swoop and wait. For once they do not terrify me. In the haze I see the quick flashes of the guns, and shell after shell bursts in a barrage over the Mole. In the ghostly light of the incessant green balls I see the round puffs of the shell-bursts, actually touching each other in a long line, so closely together are they placed as a barrier. We drop two bombs over the Mole at a low height, and, pursued by the malignant searchlights and the rapid ineffectual flashes of the shells, swing out to sea, turn in once more, and drop another bomb.[10]

Captain Paul Bewsher, 214 Squadron RAF

Allan repeatedly did this, Bewsher firing a bright (red or green) light after each attack 'to show my contempt of the defences':

As we move away, we see the shape of another great Handley-Page pass exactly over us as it flies on to attack Zeebrugge Mole for another hour. Our place is taken at once. The attack is being carried out, as arranged, in exact detail.[11]

Captain Paul Bewsher, 214 Squadron RAF

Allan was now to loiter until 01.00 when it would be their turn to light flares, but engine trouble intervened—perhaps hit by anti-aircraft fire:

At once the clamour of the engine ceases, and I look quickly to the radiator on the right, from the top of which is blown backwards a thin streak of white water and steam. As the engine cools through inaction, the ill-boding wisp of spray lessens and died. Slowly the slender white scarf appears again, and grows wider and more evident in the darkness. It is the pale finger of doom…[12]

Captain Paul Bewsher, 214 Squadron RAF

The Handley Page ditched into the water despite attempts by Allan to head towards Nieuport. The Handley Page sank before Bewsher or Lieutenant Purvis the gun layer could retrieve Allen, and if not already dead, he drowned. Bewsher and Purvis were rescued by a Royal Navy motor launch. A bitter blow came for them when they learned that due to the weather, the attack had been called off—unbeknownst to the Handley Pages that were already airborne. Two other Handley Pages were lost, one in a forced landing in Holland resulting in the aircraft and crew being interred, and another when one of two Handley Pages that had to land on the beach at Mardick, owing to poor weather, crashed. The attack ultimately went ahead on 22–23 April without support from the Handley Pages. Although the attack on Zeebrugge was considered a success at the time (the one at Ostend was not, and required another attempt, which again failed in its purpose), any effect on operations at Zeebrugge was very brief indeed.

The night of 25 April saw Horn again in the rear, with Tullis as pilot on his first operational night-bombing mission. They took off at 22.20 in Handley Page 1462, with Terrell as observer and loaded with fourteen 112-lb bombs. Bruges Docks was once again the target, though this time the men were to come in for a very hot reception. After crossing the lines, they became caught in the glare of searchlights near Ghistelles, lighting up the interior of the aircraft 'as though lit by electric lights'. Horn shot at the searchlight using the lower machine gun, which temporarily succeeded in putting the searchlight off target, although it soon returned:

The 'Archies' now began their work and for the first time I actually heard the 'crump, crump' of the exploding shrapnel which could may have been a great distance from us. This rather alarming—to my mind—state of affairs caused a slight upward motion of wind. However, we drew out of range and I was not a bit sorry, for they'd evidently got our height with an uncomfortable degree of accuracy.[13]

Lieutenant Aubrey Evelyn Horn, 207 Squadron RAF

Things were to get worse over Bruges. On arriving near, they skirted along the south side of Bruges, then went up the east side of Bruges to reach the docks from the opposite direction they would be expected to arrive. On reaching the north side of Bruges the searchlights opened up and an anti-aircraft barrage started:

> We managed to get clear of all this, but when we came to the Northern side leading towards the docks—Shades of Methusaleh! The strafe that had died away after passing the southern side began again with uncalled for fury. We were picked up by nine of the searchlights, and the inside of the machine was lit as though arc lights were put in every conceivable place. With more wind up than Beaufort ever dreamed of I got to the lower gun, and could not get it to work, the pan being faulty, another pan also failed me, they were two that had been left in by error. At this, shrapnel began bursting pretty close, and 'crumps' and sharp cracks followed in rapid succession. Suddenly the nose of the machine dived down, and thinking something had happened to Tullis, for a big burst had just gone off, I sprang to the upper deck, assisted by the bump of concussion from a close shrapnel! The lights still held us, and the 'onions' were very close, soaring above us. I couldn't see Tereell and Tullis appeared to have fallen back in his seat.[14]

Lieutenant Aubrey Evelyn Horn, 207 Squadron RAF

Horn was under the impression they were hurtling to their doom, the engines being full on and not being able to see any activity at the front, giving the impression they were either incapacitated or worse. Suddenly the pilot sat up and turned the aircraft to the right, and headed away from Bruges. Horn thought that was it and were heading for home, but upon checking to see if any bombs were hung up, he saw that all were still present—they would have to go through the maelstrom again. They headed over Bruges again at 7,500 feet, dropping the bombs despite enemy attention. Horn was ready with a new drum of ammunition and fired at the searchlights below, but without any apparent effect; a single bomb hung up was forced out by Horn, judging as best he could for it to drop while flying over searchlights. A brief respite was given by clouds below the aircraft, taking them out of searchlight view, and they left for home. For Tullis's first operation as a pilot, it really was a baptism of fire.

In late April, 207 Squadron and 215 Squadron returned to England to equip with the Handley Page O/400s and also train new air and ground crew. This halved the amount of Handley Page Squadrons in France with 216 Squadron as the solitary Handley Page unit in the south with 41st Wing and 214 Squadron at Coudekerque.

In May, 214 Squadron spent most of the month targeting the main U-boat base at Bruges. U-boat *UB-59* was in Bruges after hitting a mine in the English Channel on 4 May, surviving, but severely damaged (indeed, it had sunk twice during the journey back). While in dry dock for repairs, a bomb dropped by a British aircraft exploded in the torpedo room in the bow, causing extensive damage including total destruction of the ballast tanks on the starboard side and a large hole in the pressure hole. Even so, it was estimated it could be repaired in six months, but became one of four U-boats that would be blown up by the retreating Germans in early October. At the start of May, 216 Squadron returned to Ochey and now that they were back up to strength they could really get to grips with their intended tasks. One aircraft raided Thionville on the night of 17 May, then on 20 May an unprecedented seven Handley Pages from 216 raided various locations, dropping a total of sixty-six 112-lb bombs on Coblenz, Thionville, and Metz. At Thionville the railway suffered heavy damage, the railway line broken in many places as well as damage to the passenger and goods stations, and a large engine shed and sidings. Aerial photographs taken in daylight showed evidence of many bursts on the lines; according to a civilian repatriated back to France later on in the war, a German had told them that twenty German officers and sixty men had been killed during the raid of 20–21 May, as well as two fires that were started east of the railway station. Another civilian saw a train containing killed and wounded from the raid. Similar numbers of Handley Pages were put up on five further nights in May—the Soda Fabrik works at Mannheim being hit a number of times (the first time it was hit on the night of 21–22 May a laboratory and workshop were destroyed, killing sixty workers). A Swiss source stated that following the bomber's attentions in the area, 'members of the government and Reichstag are continually bombarded with petitions from the Rhine towns imploring them to come to an immediate arrangement with the Allies for cessation of reprisals'. On 25 May, a Swiss newspaper reported that 'thieves and burglars made good use of the air raid warning at Mannheim. While the inhabitants were in the cellars, light fingers cleared out everything upstairs'.[15]

Independent Force was formed on 6 June 1918, commanded by Major General Hugh Trenchard. Still comprised of the original units from 55, 100, and 216 Squadrons, the 41st Wing formed the major part of the Independent Force; although, two day bomber squadrons (99 and 104 Squadron, both equipped with the Airco DH9) joined the Independent Force the next month, following their time with VIII Brigade. The new force was to take part in the same type of attacks that 41st Wing RFC did, but with more aircraft available in a determined attempt to expand the use of strategic bombing. The Airco DH9 was supposedly an improved version of the DH4—the pilot and observer now sat back-to-back as on the Royal Aircraft Factory RE8 and Bristol F2b Fighters, allowing for better communication between the two, which was hampered on the DH4 by the fuel tank separating the two men. Aside from this it was not as good as the DH4; the Siddeley Puma BHP engine was supposed to be a suitable replacement for the Rolls-Royce Eagle, however, it was unreliable and not as powerful as was hoped. The two new squadrons were based at Azelot, and so 100 and 216 Squadrons continued to operate at Ochey as the only British units. As well as a change of name, supplies started to improve to 216 Squadron as they moved up the priority list. On the night of 5 June, the evening before joining Independent Force, twelve 112-lb bombs were dropped on Thionville and seventy on Metz. The next evening, Independent Force was given a good christening, with sixty 112-lb bombs dropped on Thionville by five Handley Pages. There was then a break of almost three weeks, and then on four nights (up to the end of June) various locations were raided, focusing on Mannheim, Metz, and Saarbrücken. The night of 30 June included one aircraft targeting Mannheim with only one bomb hitting the Badische Works there, but it damaged a distillery on site and killed thirty-five workers. The other bombs damaged houses, burying some people in their cellars, suspending the tramway service, and bursting gas mains, which hampered rescue work.

By coincidence, the German bombers that usually targeted England headed to Coudekerque on the night of 6–7 June, arriving not long after nine Handley Pages from 207 Squadron had left to raid Bruges and St Denis Westrem. Wardrop was on one of the Handley Pages that raided the Gotha aerodrome:

> The landing lights were on. So we obviously attacked it and naturally enough the lights went out. We hovered in the vicinity and presently a red light was fired from the air and two white from the ground. Then all the lights came on again. That was a signal, of course. We took a run from the West to the East and down the southern side of the 'drome. Then a parachute flare was dropped. It enabled us to see the ground like daylight.[16]

Corporal William Edward David Wardrop, 207 Squadron RAF

On the way back, the aircraft crashed at Gravelines burying Wardrop in the sand, but he managed to get himself and the pilot out. The rear gun layer was flown back to England, but sadly succumbed to his injuries. On the night of 15–16 June, while raiding Bruges docks (now with 214 Squadron, although he may have been 'on loan' as other 207 Squadron crew were to 214 Squadron), it seemed as if Wardrop's luck had ran out:

We'd been hit in the propeller, I think the radiator went. The propeller stopped, you see, over Bruges. We had only one engine, so we couldn't fly the other one because with one engine racing away we would have gone round in circles and spiralled down. That was no good so we had to throttle down the other one and make a glider of it. Naturally enough, the searchlights picked us up and carried us over one to the other, not only searchlights, but everything I think possible to fire at us they did. I had almost an idea they were using peashooters at the finish. They threw everything at us, but it didn't bring us down.[17]

Corporal William Edward David Wardrop, 214 Squadron RAF

The pilot managed to glide the aircraft down as far as Nieuport, crash landing the machine in no man's land. Fortunately none of the men were injured, but they were in a very unsafe position. Even with no engines running the sound would surely have been heard on both sides, and they could have been taken prisoner, or worse.

I thought they were Germans at first and I nearly made the mistake of my life. I just pulled my revolver into this man's side and thought he was a German, because he wore white trousers. And luckily enough he wasn't, he was Belgian. He took us to a dug-out and they wouldn't believe that we were British. They insisted we were not British, you see, we couldn't convince them we were British. We showed them our uniform and everything else, but they wouldn't believe it. And neither could they, they said they could speak English, and we could neither speak Flemish which really they were speaking. And none of the three of us were very good linguists anyway, we had just a smattering of French, but they couldn't understand, they kept on saying, and all that sort of thing.

After about two hours they gave us some sandwiches and beer, and we were allowed to smoke, of course, and after about two hours one man said to me, 'Do you come from London?' And I said 'Yes'. And he said 'Do you know the Strand?' And I said, 'Yes', and I then began to think; they said they couldn't speak English, I must be dreaming. You know your mind was in such a confused state by this time, I mean, having been on the raid itself, being brought down from No-Man's-Land, and sitting there for nearly two solid hours not making out they could speak English, full of sandwiches and probably had a couple of beers. I began to wonder what the deuce was going on, you see. And suddenly I said to this man, 'I thought you said you couldn't speak English?' He said 'I couldn't two hours ago'. He said, 'I can now'. He said 'It's got to be verified', he said 'Who you are and where you come from'. 'You see', he said 'Well going back to the Strand. D'you know the Black Hole?' I said, 'Yes, rather. Been down there many times'. He said 'I used to be a waiter there'. I said 'Well, I never'. And he told us then that a car would come for us next day-break from the squadron.[18]

Corporal William Edward David Wardrop, 214 Squadron RAF

When daylight came, the Germans shelled the Handley Page, which simply disintegrated under the firepower. The driver did turn up as promised. The rescued flyers warned the driver not do drive down a certain road as it was a frequent target for German shelling—he ignored this and drove down it, until a German shell flew over them and landed nearby. The driver stopped the car and flung himself into a ditch, but after protestations from the crew he got back in and sped back to Coudekerque as fast as he could. On their arrival back at Coudekerque the men received a dressing down from the armaments officer for the loss of equipment, especially the Lewis guns:

He almost threatened to court martial us because we didn't save the guns. I asked him if he thought I was going to put five Lewis guns up me waistcoat in No-Man's-Land. All I did save was the maps we had and brought back our own revolvers.[19]

Corporal William Edward David Wardrop, 214 Squadron RAF

Raids on Metz through June resulted in more damage to the railway lines; aerial photographs showed two bursts among large numbers of railway vehicles, and direct hits on two goods trains. The railways at Thionville also suffered heavy damage through this month, two bombs hitting the same goods train. Leutnant Fritz Nagel, stationed with an 8.8-cm anti-aircraft battery at Metz, described the atmosphere in June:

Whenever bombers made a raid they always hit something and seeing part of Metz burning was a common sight, exciting no one... June 23 was a lively day. Several bomber squadrons came over and we shot 120 rounds. Later on the sky became cloudy and we hoped for a peaceful night. But from midnight until 3am they came back. The searchlight crews had trouble holding the targets and we seemed to do no good at all. Large fires started burning in Metz. One big Handley Page circled our battery at leisure and Leutnant Braus seemed to have a good time banging away.[20]

Leutnant Fritz Nagel, Heavy Kraftwagen-Flugzeugabwehrkanone
Battery 179, German Army

Tournai was targeted by 207 Squadron towards the end of June. On 29–30 June, ten Handley Pages, each with a full load of sixteen 112-lb bombs, went to this target:

> Arriving near Tournai I got back to my bomb bay and guided old Ladd to the objective at about 5,500 feet. I picked up the railway at a conspicuous bend dropped about half. Turned on another bend and ran in to the bridge which 'piffling' thing was our objective. In my mind and most of our minds it is a sheer waste of good metal and time. The bridge is only a tiny thing, a single track over a canal and even if destroyed could be repaired in no time. However the wiseacres told us to bomb it and try we did, but all missed. When one thinks that the bridge at Etaples has only been hit once in three appearances by the Huns, some of our squadrons have tried one big bridge down south for 1½ and it is still there what chance have we of hitting a tiny French one on the map?
>
> Anyway I unloaded the remainder of our bombs which fell short of the objective and then turned for home. The railway station or one of the big main lines would have been very much more useful to try for.[21]

> Lieutenant Aubrey Evelyn Horn, 207 Squadron RAF

The next night Tournai was targeted again, but with a change of specific objective that pleased Horn:

> Same town, colour of night red, letter O, and our letter A. The objective was changed for a wonder and a bigger bridge was tried for, namely the one on the north-west side of the town where the Lille-Tournai and Mauscheron-Tournai railways junction just before passing over the bridge into Tournai. The visibility was very poor, and misty clouds were already growing from the west quarter and north west, all machines lined up and took straight off.[22]

> Lieutenant Aubrey Evelyn Horn, 207 Squadron RAF

Unfortunately, on the night of 30 June, HP C9648 of 214 Squadron ended up in front of the guns of a German aircraft and was shot down just before midnight, south-east of Wulpen. One of the men, Sergeant R. G. Kimberly, had joined the unit at the same time as Sergeant Dell:

> Well, we didn't know what had happened to him and he and I, we had both got an arrangement that if I had any difficulty he could take my things home and that or if anything happened to him I would go and see his brother. I

took all his personal things and I took the wife when I was home on leave you see and we were made very welcome and all that sort of thing but I don't know. You miss them at the time but you still have to carry on.[23]

Sergeant Leslie Alexander Dell, 214 Squadron RAF

No. 215 Squadron returned to France from Andover on 4 July, this time for longer than its original spell of just over a month, before being sent to Britain for re-equipping on O/400s. They were based at Alquines in the Pas-de-Calais area, and attached to 54 Wing along with 207 Squadron. No. 215 Squadrons O/400s first saw action during a raid on Armentieres on 20 July then again on the night of 24–25 July, focusing on the railways around the town. On the same day 215 Squadron returned, 207 Squadron sent seven aircraft to a new target, much to the satisfaction of the crews:

> This was a new objective, and I don't think about any of us were sorry for the change. It becomes very monotonous to continue bombing one place all the time. The squadron with seven machines set out the previous night and only one machine piloted by Captain Scott reached Courtrai, one bombed through the clouds after returning above them on a time and bearing scheme, while another got near little and seeing no objective returned.[24]

Lieutenant Aubrey Evelyn Horn, 207 Squadron RAF

No. 216 Squadron's Handley Pages were aloft for thirteen nights in July, one aircraft being lost on 19 July when on take-off it struck the church spire at Ochey with a full load of bombs on board. Fortunately they did not explode and no one was particularly hurt. The accident was caused owing to an extra passenger climbing on board at the last minute just as the pilot, Lieutenant Anthony Conning Kilburn, was preparing to take-off, and allowances had not been made for the extra weight and effect the person would have on the centre of gravity of the aircraft. In the first week of July alone, photographic evidence showed further destruction on the railway lines with two trains entirely burnt out. A reliable source also reported that a railway locomotive shed, containing twenty-five locomotives, had been hit; once again, Thionville suffered along with Metz, with the goods station there completely destroyed as well as railway vehicles and buildings associated with the railways in the area. Three aircraft raided Offenburg on the night of 25 July, dropping thirty-eight 112-lb bombs. Two fires were seen to break out at the station, one of them being seen from over 30 miles away. A reliable source stated that the station buffet as well as the Empire Bank and post office were badly damaged.

Offenburg was hit again on the night of 29–30 July by a single Handley Page carrying thirteen 112-lb bombs. This time it was reported that of the eight railway lines running through Offenburg, several were so damaged they were beyond use, and wagons of three trains were badly damaged. The electric power station was hit with the main engine damaged, resulting in a power cut that lasted for two days. As well as three aircraft raiding Stuttgart on the night of 30 July, a single aircraft raided Hagenau, some of the sixteen bombs falling on barracks killing a large number of recently commandeered horses and wounding around twenty soldiers.

HP 3135, piloted by Lieutenant Kilburn, was one of the three that raided Stuttgart that night, reporting heavy mist and heavy anti-aircraft fire and searchlight activity, but the 112-lb bombs dropped caused at least two fires visible to the crew. A letter to a German soldier, dated 4 August, which was subsequently captured stated:

> You will probably have heard of the air raid on Stuttgart-Unterturkheim. We heard the bombs fall on the Electricity Works. This will remind a good many people who are only interested in making a fortune that there is a war on.[25]

Reportedly civilians taking shelter were killed when a bomb fell through the entire house and exploded among them in the cellar. On the way back the crew became lost and eventually ran out of petrol, landing at Maison du Bois, 5,500 feet above sea level and 4 miles from the Swiss border. The aircraft ran on into the river and crashed, pinning the pilot and observer (Sergeant Adkins) in the wreckage, partly underwater. The aircraft caught fire, but the rear gun layer Sergeant G. Mills put it out. The crew in the front were rescued after two and a half hours, but, fortunately, they were not badly hurt. A telegram was received on 31 July congratulating the pilots and their crews for reaching Stuttgart.

Among the twelve flying officers who joined 216 Squadron in July was Lieutenant Hugh Baird Monaghan, fresh from Stonehenge (a large training aerodrome for FE2b and Handley Page night bomber crews, close to the ancient stones).

The continued allegiance to the Royal Navy of 216 Squadron was more than clear when Lieutenant Monaghan arrived:

> The squadron was made up entirely of Royal Naval Air Service personnel in navy blue uniforms and my RFC khaki attire stood out like a sore thumb. To make things worse, I was the only Canadian, and uninvited guest.[26]

Lieutenant Hugh Baird Monaghan, 216 Squadron RAF

Monaghan's flying career was certainly not going as he had hoped; just being on the Handley Pages had originally been a disappointment to him, when his next training assignment had been given to him some time previously:

> He asked me to sit down and said, 'I have decided to send you to Stonehenge for training on Handley Pages'. I broke in with, 'But, Colonel, why me?' He replied, 'A new force called the Independent has been formed and pilots are required for the big night bombers. Your record of take-offs and landings is excellent and I was asked to take this into consideration when making my recommendation. I believe you are specially qualified'. Although terribly disappointed, orders were orders and there was nothing for me to say but thank you. Standing there I thought that after the sweet frivolity of a Pup my joy of flying was over.[27]

> Lieutenant Hugh Baird Monaghan, RAF

Despite being a trained pilot, Monaghan was passed over even for the routine taking-up of new officers as rear gunners on operational sorties to get them accustomed to conditions. After ten days he protested and was taken up, despite officially not being on the strength of the squadron as his papers had been lost.

> We went in on the Sablon Triangle at Metz, a large railroad marshalling yard and it was quite a show. Searchlights criss-crossed the sky, heavy anti-aircraft fire met us and the sharp crack of exploding shells could be heard above the roar of the engines. The air displacement snapped the canvas on the sides of the fuselage in and out and pockets of cordite fumes made us catch our breath. I was busy firing the lower gun down the fingers of light hoping for a hit otherwise we would be temporarily blinded when a powerful ray caught and held us; but the pilot flew steadily on and at 4,000 feet unloaded the sixteen 112 pound bombs. On the return trip I analysed my reactions and found that I had been so busy and so curious that I felt no sense of personal danger, a good omen, an excellent beginning.[28]

> Lieutenant Hugh Baird Monaghan, 216 Squadron RAF

Monaghan went on two other trips in the rear gunner's position, but then fell ill and ended up in hospital for ten days. After being discharged he was sent to 215 Squadron at Xaffévillers (which had become part of Independent Force on 18 August). Despite again being a former RNAS unit, Monaghan received a better reception, possibly because it had only been formed less than a month before the formation of the RAF, but also owing to the presence of four other Canadian officers.

Another new Handley Page pilot, Second Lieutenant Francis Edward Rees, undertook his first sortie on the night of 21 July, a member of 215 Squadron flying HP C9659—his 'bus', which he had trialled as new on the first day of that month. He recorded the flight in his log book: 'first show. Armentieres. Dropped 16 112lb bombs on station and railway, and 10 cooper bombs. 400 rds S.A.A. fired.[29] Three nights later he went up again: 'second show. Same objective. 4 OK's observed. 900 rds S.A.A. fired. Ring post wires on port wing extension cut by A.A. Extension drooping'.[30]

The large amount of bullets being fired by the Lewis guns (SAA—Small Arms Ammunition) shows they were being put to good use, and as no enemy aircraft are described, presumably against targets of opportunity seen on the ground or at searchlights.

The first SN 1,650-lb bomb was dropped on the night of 24–25 July, by one of five Handley Pages from 214 Squadron airborne that night. Handley Page O/400 C9643 armed with the single SN 1,650-lb bomb went to Middelkerke, while the other aircraft targeted Zeebrugge, Bruges, and Ghistelles. In the nose of C9643 was Sergeant Dell, with Lieutenant Ellison as pilot.

Dell's concise report summed up the raid:

We took three runs over the objective before I was able to drop. First run was from NE to SW at 5000ft, had to turn out to sea again owing to being held in the searchlights and Westende battery putting in too good shooting. Hostile aircraft was also about. One machine passing very close to us, but he did not open fire. Second run was also from NE to SW at 4000ft, but we were again held in the lights. Third run was down wind, SW to NE at 6000ft. The bomb was observed to burst on the NE of the town. Visibility—very good. Full moon. Fair amount of AA and very accurate. Landed at Mardick.[31]

Sergeant Leslie Alexander Dell, 214 Squadron RAF

The bomb landed in an open field, and although no damage was caused, Reuters reported an unusual consequence while describing the introduction of the new bomb:

An amusing incident occurred when the first of these was dropped on enemy territory which is much harried by our bombers, and consequently bristles with searchlights and anti-aircraft batteries. So terrifying was the explosion that every searchlight went instantly out, and the airman was furious at thus being deprived of the land-marks on which he had counted to find his way home.[32]

Whether the 'airman' (and as to which one it refers to out of the Handley Page's crew of three, but presumably the pilot) was furious or not, the observer at least didn't mind searchlights some of the time, and in fact would taunt them using the Cooper bombs kept in the fuselage for targets of opportunity:

> You know you couldn't see your target and then we would give them one or two of these you see and that would fetch them up then the searchlights but they were quite simple to get out of. Well, I say simple. One or two yes, but not when you got in a lot. I mean when you got in a lot round your actual target.[33]

> Sergeant Leslie Alexander Dell, 214 Squadron RAF

Although the SN 1,650-lb bomb landed in a field, the fifty-foot diameter crater was a potent sign of what would come when dropped onto something worth hitting. The matter of aiming this weapon particularly intrigued Wardrop at 207 Squadron, who considered that owing to the cylindrical shape of the bomb it would need a different method of aiming than the pear-shaped bombs of various sizes used up until that point:

> Being cylinder shape as against pear shape it took a different angle, it must have done. Anyway, it was doing an awful lot of damage when it did explode wherever it exploded, I mean 1,660-lbs. Of course compared with this was it's not to be compared, but in those days it was quite an outsize bomb, when you think of it. I argued in my way that—it might have been theory—but I said that one bomb sight for two different types of bombs was ridiculous. It had to be re-calibrated, it had to be by trial and error, because the bomb I dropped, the 1,660-lb was right off target. I knew I wasn't such an idiot as to drop miles away from the target after the experience I'd had, both before going to France and while I was in France, I'd dropped enough bombs to know full well I was getting somewhere near a target. But when you drop a bomb and it's five miles away, something's gone wrong somewhere. I said to Commander Brackley, I said, 'It's about some time somebody else had a shot with this bomb', and he wouldn't hear of it. He said, No, Wardrop, I want you to do it'.[34]

> Corporal William Edward David Wardrop, 207 Squadron RAF

Although the effects of the SN bombs could be learnt from agent reports, captured letters, or aerial photographs taken after the raids, it must have been quite a feeling for the Handley Page crews to see first-hand the devastation caused, as L. G. Semple did eight days after the Armistice came into effect:

> Went into Peronne this morning and there I saw the tail fins of one of the 1,650lb bombs we dropped there some time ago. It had absolutely blown everything down in the immediate neighbourhood.[35]

Lieutenant Leslie George Semple, 207 Squadron RAF

It was those on the receiving end that understood the true damage of the bombs dropped by the Handley Pages and other bombers:

> The destructive power of bombs seemed to increase all the time. A British Handley Page bomber used bombs of 1,000 kilos *(presumably referring to the SN 1,650lb, which was closer to 750kgs)*. Bombs of 300 kilos were in daily use. Even the small 50 kilo bombs had a destructive power equal to a 15 cm shell, and anybody who had survived a nearby explosion of a 15 cm shell would testify that such a shell could do fearful damage. All these missiles had to be feared. A 12 ½ kilo bomb dropped on living targets moving on hard ground would burst into 1,400 pieces, each one sizzling parallel to the ground, and could cause very bad wounds.[36]

Leutnant Fritz Nagel, Heavy Kraftwagen-Flugzeugabwehrkanone Battery 179, German Army

A second Handley Page Squadron for Independent Force arrived at Xaffévillers on 8 August. No. 97 Squadron had been in existence since December 1917 as an RFC squadron, but did not receive its first Handley Pages until May 1918. Originally formed at Waddington in Lincolnshire, it moved to Stonehenge where the men were supposed to get the chance to work with Handley Pages before they received any. No. 97 Squadron moved to Netheravon in April, but when the Handley Pages did arrive the training was shown to be lacking—a number of ground crew had to be sent back to Stonehenge to learn how to fold back the wings, then return and instruct the others, not an auspicious start. Their start of operational duties in France did not go too well either, three days after they arrived one of the Handley Pages was taxied into a hangar, the day after that a Handley Page crashed onto a road while landing, the day after that (13 August) two Handley Pages (that were on local flights to get accustomed to the local area and the lighthouses) crashed, killing one pilot and badly injuring the other. Before their first sortie, another one crashed, leaving just five aircraft available for raids. The first raid by 97 Squadron was on the night of 19–20 August when the railway triangle at Metz was hit. Their ex-Royal Flying Corps colleagues at 100 Squadron were called upon to help out:

> Several new squadrons arrived about this time. The enemy was apparently in for a good go and things were going to be hot. 97 Squadron turned up with Handleys, followed by eighteen Camels and a squadron of DH10s. Ours was some busy aerodrome. 97 borrowed some of our observers to show them round the country at night, but the boys weren't too keen as crashes were frequent, some of the pilots being mere novices.[37]

> Lieutenant Alfie Reginald Kingsford, 100 Squadron RAF

While Independent Force was increasing in size, the Handley Pages in northern France were used for an unusual task on the night of 7–8 August. The next day would be the start of the Battle of Amiens, when artillery tactics (finely developed over the course of the war) together with heavy tanks, Medium Mark A 'Whippet' Tanks, designed to exploit breakthroughs by the heavy tanks, armoured cars, and low-flying aircraft used for ground attack would, together with the infantry, take part in a large offensive on the Germans. Since the German spring offensive in March, this was now a chance for the Allies to turn the tide and break the German lines. The Handley Pages task was to fly over the front line areas, the noise hopefully disguising the approach of the tanks as they formed close to the front line, ready to advance as soon as dawn broke, to the surprise of the Germans.

Next day, 207 Squadron raided Peronne, continuing to support the Allied offensive. Lieutenant Semple was on one of the aircraft, which struggled to find his way to Peronne owing to poor weather—although this had the added benefit that the searchlights were unable to find them. Anti-aircraft fire was still active anyway in the hope of hitting them, but Semple and his crew bombed Peronne. Shortly after regaining friendly territory, the port engine cut out, Semple trying to keep the aircraft airborne for as long as possible. They came across an airfield with the landing 'T' switched on, and signalled the emergency code to it in the hope they would let them land as soon as possible; however, their plea for help resulted in the T being switched off. Heavy ground mist meant they could not see the ground at all, and used the Holt wing-tip flare and the Aldis lamp to try and land in a field, judging their height as best as possible while trying to discern if they were landing in a suitable place. Unfortunately they weren't; the aircraft went into the side of a sunken road, and then into the trees:

With a sickening crash we went through it and then, bang into the ground. I jumped from the back seat immediately and extinguished the Holt flare which was burning furiously and might have ignited something. Then I shouted to those in front. Hearing no reply I shouted again and again, gradually worming round to the front of the machine, which I found reduced to matchwood. Both in front were OK but the machine was right over, resting on leading edge of bottom plane. Engines stuck in the ground and generally completely smashed up. We then started walking to the searchlight and were met halfway by some chaps from 102 Squadron who took us into their mess, gave us cocoa and biscuits and then bed.[38]

Lieutenant Leslie George Semple, 207 Squadron RAF

Bruges became the recipient of four SN 1,650-lb bombs on the night of 10–11 August, when five Handley Pages of 214 Squadron set off, all carrying the giant bombs. Four were dropped on the docks, but one was dropped on Ostend under heavy anti-aircraft fire after the aircraft had a problem with the dropping gear:

Once again we visit Bruges, with Lieutenant Ellison. Rather a strong head wind, so we went via the coast, and attacked Bruges from the north east to south west, our objective being the large buildings on the east side of the Eastern Basin. Barrage was very heavy and more searchlights and parachute flares than usual. Visibility—fair. Fuse of Big Bomb (1,660lb bomb) was set for delay action (15 seconds) but burst on impact.[39]

Sergeant Leslie Alexander Dell, 214 Squadron RAF

The next night 214 Squadron sent up four Handley Pages again, three with SN 1,650-lb bombs and one with the normal load of sixteen 112-lb bombs. Two were dropped on the factory belonging to railway equipment manufacturers La Brugeoise et Nicaise et Delcuve, and another landed on the docks. It had not been an easy night for the crew of HP C9643; even before the attack it had taken five attempts to drop their load, partly owing to problems with the dropping gear for the bomb, but also mist and searchlight activity. German scouts were being sent up in response to the Handley Pages and FE2b night raiders. Sergeant Dell described one encounter:

We left the aerodrome and it was just dusk at night and we had passed over the flooded water at Nieuport. That was all flooded area you see.

Then you were in enemy territory of Belgium. I can't tell you off hand where we were making for but I spotted a Hun in the air. I knew it wasn't any of ours because we hadn't got any fighters up at that time and it was over enemy territory and there was only this one on his own and he must have spotted us. He came towards us and Studd got into a spiral and of course, I could follow him round. I didn't give him a chance to get underneath. He could see that we were firing and that I had got two guns and I suppose he didn't like the look of that. He dropped that and left us alone. We went on.[40]

Sergeant Leslie Alexander Dell, 214 Squadron RAF

After their first raid of the month—a solitary Handley Page dropping twelve 112-lb bombs on Buhl aerodrome on 11 August—216 Squadron moved to the American base at Autreville. Like Ochey, Autreville was close to a large wood in which the aircraft and hangars were camouflaged from the air.

On Lieutenant White's raid on Thionville on the night of 13 August, he was loaded with thirteen boxes of Baby Incendiaries. Ten were dropped (which would have meant 2,700 Baby Incendiaries in total), but three were hung up and, despite attempts, could not be released. One box then fell out as the aircraft was returning across the lines, but the other two were not released until the aircraft landed. The remaining 540 Baby incendiaries 'jumped and fizzled in every quarter', but as well as giving a good demonstration to the witnesses of the weapons in action, no one was injured and the aircraft suffered no major damage.

The Baby Incendiaries were put to good use on the night of 17 August when two Handley Pages, with a total of twenty-three boxes of Baby Incendiaries between them as well as petrol tins, took off for the edge of the forest near Offenburg. The petrol tins were used to encourage the flames (which certainly worked, as a French reconnaissance flight two days later reported the forest still on fire). On the same night as the Black Forest fire 216 Squadron dropped its first 1,650-lb bomb during a raid on Forbach.

Back in Britain, an accident resulted in the worst air crash hitherto involving British aircraft. On 19 August, Handley Page O/400 D4593 left Castle Bromwich near Birmingham with two pilots and five passengers on board, the reason for having such a large number of additional men on board is that the pilot wanted to recreate the 'war load' of the aircraft. While in flight, fabric from one wing detached and the pilot lost control, the aircraft crashing into a field and killing all seven men.

A Handley Page of 214 Squadron became the first Handley Page to attack a German warship since the Handley Page Flight at Redcar on

U-boat patrol the previous September, on the night of 22–23 August. The aircraft bombed the airfield at Maria Aalter, reportedly leaving craters on the main runway and also the sheds and hangars. On the way back, the crew saw three German destroyers bombarding the French coast:

> So, I said to Russell, let us have a look at them shall we. He said, right. So, we turned off and came round and it was a beautiful moonlit night. We came round the back of these 4 boats. I think it is 4. I see it in the log. It is either 3 or 4. We came round the back of them there. You see, I was up here in the darkness. They were in the light because the moon was up here. They were still flashing out. Their guns were going. They were in line and shelling the coast. The searchlights on the coast were being attacked by German planes which were diving down and shooting at the searchlights you see trying to keep them off.[41]

> Sergeant Leslie Alexander Dell, 214 Squadron RAF

With enemy aircraft operating in the area it was certainly risky—the last time Handley Pages had attacked German destroyers it resulted in one being shot down with most of the crew killed, and Handley Pages subsequently being banned from daylight operations. But the crew felt they had to do something. Dell could see that the French were firing star shells to try and see where the enemy vessels were so they could fight back, but they were not having any effect:

> Anyway, we came round behind these boats and shut off and glided down. They didn't know we were there until I got in the front. Russell was Captain. He was piloting and we signalled to the rear gunner that we were going to attack. He could see what was happening anyway and as we came down they must have heard us or something. They picked us up because the guns suddenly all stopped at once shooting at the coast. It was then that I opened up spraying the decks you see. Well, then they broke up then. These three or four boats. They separated you see and got further apart and all lights out. There wasn't a light to be seen on the boats anyway and they all made as if making for Zeebrugge or Ostend, into that direction. Well, we sprayed them for a time and then I thought we haven't got a bomb. If only we had a bomb. We had just thrown sixteen 100 weight bombs away on a job you see. That was the unfortunate part we had just been to an aerodrome. Then we thought we had enough of it because the searchlights would probably have known that something was happening. The guns had stopped. So, we decided to come back.

So, I got in front of them or at least I guided Russell round to get round in front of them and as we passed in front of them I dropped three parachute flares right in their path you see. Well, of course they stay up there for about eight minutes these parachute flares. I could see that they spread further apart and then we came home.[42]

Sergeant Leslie Alexander Dell, 214 Squadron RAF

The men put themselves at extreme risk, but pulled it off, and were able to curtail the bombardment—fortunately with no damage or injury to themselves.

Handley Page O/100 1466 from 216 Squadron was lost on this night, following a raid on Frankfurt in which a 550-lb bomb (among others) was dropped; they were returning to Autreville when the port engine started to make a popping noise and then stopped completely. The pilot, Wing Commander Browne, changed course for Ochey instead, which was possible on the remaining engine until that also failed. Browne hoped to land on the edge of a valley so that the aircraft would, in theory, be slowed down enough before hitting trees. He turned the Holt's wing tip flare on to see how far they were from the ground, and had a nasty shock when he realised the aircraft was heading straight for the woods. Fortunately the aircraft was stopped by the trees and all the crew escaped serious injury. What the crew didn't realise was that the engines had failed as anti-aircraft fire had pierced a petrol tank, and the petrol-soaked starboard wing soon caught fire. Browne and his observer got out as quickly as possible (Browne had, until the observer finally managed to make himself noticed and pointed out the situation, been gathering all of his kit; the rear gun layer, Yelverton, was equally nonchalant and appeared to be enjoying the spectacle, getting out just as the fire started to close around the fuselage). The men all got down as low as possible while ammunition started to cook off and explode in the heat.

The night bomber experts 100 Squadron finally received their Handley Pages in August. Second Lieutenant Kingsford, who served with 100 Squadron, described the change from flying the 120-hp Beardmore engine Royal Aircraft Factory FE2b night bomber to the twin Rolls-Royce 375-hp Eagle engine Handley Page O/400 in 1918, which started on 13 August when the first one arrived, even though they had seen them before as they operated alongside them:

No one knew they were coming, they just arrived, and great excitement prevailed. There were more to come, and the Squadron was at once reconstructed as a Handley Page Squadron, with two flights of five machines each. We said 'Good-bye' to the first of our good old friends, the 'Fees,' two being transferred to the depot. The Handley Page pilots stayed a few days, to give us a bit of instruction.

These buses, with two three hundred and seventy-five H.P. Rolls-Royce engines, were a very different proposition to fly, heavy on controls, and it was like driving a motor lorry after a Baby Austin, although we soon became accustomed to them and everyone went solo without any crashes.[43]

Lieutenant Alfie Reginald Kingsford, 100 Squadron RAF

Lieutenant Shillinglaw was one of the FE2b observers who had the unenviable job of being sat right at the front of the FE2b, the very low coaming was the only thing in front of him and the open sky—but at least with the Handley Page the observer got some protection from the elements:

I had the honour of serving in 100 Squadron which were FE2b's—two-seaters—from which we carried out raids on, as far as we could, into Germany, bombing German aerodromes, machines, blast furnaces any trouble we could cause, transport, railway junctions and so on. And then we converted onto the large machine the Handley Page which is a, well, a more serious job from the point of view of finding your way and navigation and so forth. So we should read our orders, find out our targets and the bombs we were going to carry and meteorological reports and then we should work out the course during the afternoon. As it got towards dusk we would go aboard and get into our aircraft, the mechanics would wave us away and we should taxi out to the far side of the aerodrome, turn into wind and then take off.[44]

Lieutenant Roy Shillinglaw, 100 Squadron RAF

The first operational use by 100 Squadron of the Handley Page was planned for the night of 25 August. The men relaxed during the day:

When we got our first Handley Page I was swimming in the river. There was a small river nearby and we used to go and swim there in a pool. A fellow called Boyd was with us. We were having our swim and so on at about three or four o'clock in the afternoon. Boyd was down to go in this Handley-Page as rear gunner that night with Box and Inches. Box was the pilot, and Inches was the observer.[45]

Lieutenant Roy Shillinglaw, 100 Squadron RAF

As he was not yet assigned to a Handley Page, Shillinglaw was to go up in an FE2b, as usual. As they did not yet have a full Squadron of Handley Pages, the raids with the shorter range aircraft would continue:

> I was sitting in a 'Fee' waiting to take off and Hugh Monaghan (of 215 Squadron) was in his Handley Page alongside us and we saw this Handley Page go across us just like that (gesturing). We were sitting waiting for our signal to take off from the control tower. This Handley Page of ours went across that way (indicates to right) to take off, went along and along the ground... rose about ten or fifteen feet from the ground. At the far side there was a row of poplar trees. They went between the poplar trees and the right wing hit a poplar and they peeled over into the ground... hit head on, fired straight away...and a hell of a flame! I said to Middleton, my pal, 'We should get down, there'll be a hell of an explosion when those bombs go off!' So we got down on the ground and these bombs went off. There were these trees behind us and it was a very still night and it blew those trees like a hurricane had hit them—the blast.[46]

> > Lieutenant Roy Shillinglaw, 100 Squadron RAF

Sat close by, Monaghan also witnessed the sickening sight:

> The plane rose to about two hundred feet then slowly banked to the right, crashed in a field near our huts and burst into flames. Five of our chaps rushed over to help the crew and just as they arrived, the plane blew up killing eight of our messmates. It was a cruel blow.[47]

> > Lieutenant Hugh Baird Monaghan, 215 Squadron RAF

Kingsford was also watching:

> They took off over the control tower, while those on the ground gave them a cheer and wished them luck, when suddenly the machine stalled and fell to earth like a stone, bursting into flames. A full load of benzene made it impossible to get near. Bombs exploded and everyone had to scatter, helpless to do anything for those three lads trapped in a blazing inferno.[48]

> > Lieutenant Alfie Reginald Kingsford, 100 Squadron RAF

Lieutenant Robert Kirk Inches DFC died aged twenty years old, and was posthumously awarded the Distinguished Flying Cross in 1919 for conspicuous gallantry. Lieutenant George Holyoake 'Little Box' Box had been awarded the DFC little less than a month previously. He was twenty-three. Lieutenant Harry Boyd from Belfast was nineteen. As well as the eight on the ground that were killed in their attempt to save the men, fifteen more were injured. The explosion was so powerful it blew one engine 250 yards away from the wreckage, and the other 150 yards. Shillinglaw was under the impression that the elevator controls at the rear of the aircraft were strapped down so that they would not move while on the ground and potentially cause damage to the aircraft if moved too much, but that for whatever reason they had not been removed before flight. A visit from Trenchard did not have the morale increasing results he intended:

So the next day Lord Trenchard comes along. We officers got together at the aerodrome...he sat on his stick there. 'Gather round' and he gave us a pep talk—'It's unfortunate, just getting a new machine and this happens' and this, that and the other. 'But nevertheless, there are plenty more pilots, plenty more observers and plenty more machines in the pool. Get cracking! My targets have got to be bombed!' That's all he said and that was that. I heard him say that myself.[49]

Lieutenant Roy Shillinglaw, 100 Squadron RAF

The accident meant there was no flying for 100 Squadron that night, although 215 Squadron still got airborne—three aircraft dropped bombs on Boulay airfield, and two others were to undertake a daring raid on the chemical works at Mannheim. As it was such a heavily defended area, a special method would be used—risky, but worth it if pulled off:

Our machine would go in at 5,000 feet, draw the enemy fire for fifteen minutes until Purvis pulled into range, then we would veer off for four miles, shut off our engines, turn and silently glide toward the target hoping we would not be detected.[50]

Lieutenant Hugh Baird Monaghan, 215 Squadron RAF

Monaghan was in the rear gun laying position of the Handley Page, with Captain W. B. Lawson as pilot:

With everything in readiness and shortly before dark, Lawson pulled the seven tons of Handley over the trees at the end of the aerodrome and we commenced the half hour's climb to 6,000 feet before crossing the line.

As I peered ahead, I felt a sense of satisfaction in knowing that cities such as Strasburg, Saarbrücken, Kaiserslautern, Karlsruhe, Weisbaden, Frankfurt, Stuttgart and others would be on the alert not knowing whether they were in for a clobbering or not. One thing we were sure of, Mannheim had one hundred guns and forty searchlights so we were not on our way to a garden party.

As we approached Mannheim the reception committee was out in full force and a curtain of fire surrounded the city. Lawson, flying superbly, avoided much of this as we waited for Purvis to make his appearance but occasionally a heavy burst rocked the plane.[51]

Lieutenant Hugh Baird Monaghan, 215 Squadron RAF

As well as the anti-aircraft fire and searchlights, the crews also had poor weather to contend with, which further hampered visibility:

Right on time, our partner pulled into range and as the weaving searchlights picked him up we veered away leaving him in his role as decoy. It was not easy to pinpoint a spot exactly four miles from our objective but we estimated as accurately as we could, turned, shut off the engines and commenced our glide. The silence was startling with only the whistle of the flying wires and the soft sound of the wind to break the quiet although we could hear the sharp crack of exploding shells as they pounded away at Purvis.[52]

Lieutenant Hugh Baird Monaghan, 215 Squadron RAF

As the gliding Handley Page arrived at an altitude of 1,000 feet, which should have meant they were now over the factory, the factory was now visible, just under a mile away. They had been warned not to drop bombs below 1,000 feet as the blast would damage the aeroplane, but Lawson continued to glide down to keep the element of surprise for as long as possible:

As we swept over the huge works at 200 feet, the full load of bombs crashed dead centre and exploded with a roar. The plane lurched and reared but held together and with full power on and dropping the nose to pick up speed, we tore ahead. Alerted by the noise of our engines, the searchlights swung down in our direction lighting up the area like day, outlining two high smokestacks and a church steeple directly in our path which Lawson just missed. We were then down below a hundred feet. Meanwhile, I was throwing the Coopers overboard and remember looking down a long street and seeing, with astonishment, a house topple into the roadway. One of the Coopers must have landed beside its foundation. There was no shell fire. Apparently, we were so low that the gun crews situated high on the banks of the Rhine dared not fire down on us for fear of damaging their own buildings.[53]

Lieutenant Hugh Baird Monaghan, 215 Squadron RAF

One possible effect of bombs being dropped at such a low altitude was that they might not explode; however enough did explode, and the chemical plant was knocked out of action for a number of days.

Following the accident that killed three popular officers, the first use of Handley Pages by 100 Squadron was on the night of 30–31 August in conjunction with Handley Pages of 97, 215, and 216 Squadrons. The target was Boulay aerodrome. As the full complement of Handley Pages had not yet been received, only two from 100 Squadron took part, three FE2bs joining them. In all, 10 tons of bombs were dropped on Boulay, the aircraft flying very low (some reporting heights as low as 300 feet) to aid accuracy, the gunners taking the opportunity to shoot up any visible aircraft or buildings. It was to be 100 Squadron's last use of the FE2bs—even though Handley Pages were still arriving, from now on they would only use the new aircraft, even though it meant only small numbers of aircraft could be used on any night. Indeed, the maximum amount of Handley Pages flown by 100 Squadron until the end of the war on any night was four. On their return, a 97 Squadron Handley Page had a lucky escape when on landing a 215 Squadron Handley Page—on an almost identical landing flight path—crashed into the top wing of Lieutenant Hopcroft's aircraft, but fortunately Hopcroft was able to land the (now) monoplane Handley Page safely.

Independent Force gained another Handley Page squadron on 1 September when 115 Squadron arrived at Roville airfield. Like 97 Squadron had been this formed on 1 December 1917 as an RFC squadron. After initially training at Catterick the unit moved to Netheravon in April 1918 and had considerable manpower issues; the vast majority of the ground crew had not worked on a Handley Page before, and most of those working on the engines had not even seen a Rolls-Royce Eagle, let alone work on one. Eventually the deficiencies were overcome, and the unit moved to Castle Bromwich for final working up before heading to the front. The ground crew left on 23 August, the first aircraft following six days later. Another ex-RFC unit was to receive Handley Pages—58 Squadron—who had already been serving on the Western Front flying FE2b night bombers. They were moved to Provin at the end of August to train on Handley Pages.

September started with five aircraft from 207 Squadron raiding Marquion on 1 September in conjunction with an artillery strike on the area at the same time. The incoming artillery shells added to the spectacle and experience of a night raid, as Lieutenant Semple wrote in his diary:

> Very interesting sight at night from above—when a 'strafe' is going on. To see the shells bursting—ammunition dumps blowing up—then when the Hun spots us—searchlights and 'Green flaming onions' and star shells—streams of 'tracer' bullets coming up and going out just in front of one. Then 'bang' an 'archie' on your tail—Zip-Zip-Zip—goes the machine-gun at the nearest searchlight which wavers and goes out. Another spring up and then by throwing the machine about—and shutting off engines—we are out of the searchlights. See them wavering and searching. One comes closer—closer and closer—will she find us—yes-no-yes—it flickers across and then passes on—it has passed right over us and not seen us. On we go—the objective sighted—boom-boom—go the sixteen heavy bombs and around we turn to come home as fast as we can—to run through a similar gauntlet as before
>
> After crossing the lines—we throttle back and come home at our own ease. The dummy aerodrome sighted—we signal our code letter—which is answered—and then the landing T lights up and we land. Another raid over and done. Into the Office to make a report and then to the mess for a hot drink and something to eat. Everybody is discussing the raid and finally after the last machine has returned to its lair, we turn in for a well-deserved rest—next morning—or rather the same morning but some hours later—the batman wakes us with a hot breakfast in bed.[54]

Lieutenant Leslie George Semple, 207 Squadron RAF

The next night some twenty Handley Pages were airborne; No. 97 Squadron and 215 Squadron were both raiding Buhl aerodrome with some of 215 Squadron's aircraft also attacking Ehrang, while two Handley Pages from 100 Squadron attacked Boulay aerodrome along with three Handley Pages from 216 Squadron. Five 216 Squadron Handley Pages raided the Burbach Works at Saarbrücken, dropping a total of sixty-two 112-lb bombs and two 550-lb bombs.

After Lieutenant Monaghan's move to 215 Squadron he was immediately assigned his own Handley Page, O/400 D4566, as he had already had three of the four traditional flights in the rear gunner's position. Monaghan's first raid as pilot was on Buhl aerodrome:

> It was customary to cross the line at about 5,000 feet to lessen the chance of being hit by enemy fire, but it took half an hour to reach that height

and I thought this was a waste of petrol, besides it was monotonous, so I headed over at about 2,000 feet. I had asked to have a Michelin flare attached under one wing. This gave off a powerful glare for five minutes as it dropped under a parachute and helped to pinpoint the objective. A curtain of tracer bullets greeted us as we circled a couple of times but that was to be expected. We could dimly see the long line of hangars and, dropping our flare, approaching from one end at 1,500 feet, Mitch pulled off the bombs. I don't know what we hit but the whole set –up burst into flames and we could still see the fire from thirty miles away. I couldn't contain myself and slapped Mitch on the back, much to his surprise.[55]

Lieutenant Hugh Baird Monaghan, 215 Squadron RAF

Using the lighthouses to navigate back to Xaffévillers, Monaghan came in to land. Xaffévillers was only 12 miles from the front line, and so 215 Squadron was forbidden from using flares to light up the ground, so the pilots had to use all their skill to bring the 'big jobs' safely onto terra firma. Although Monaghan got back to earth safely, one Handley Page crashed into the petrol store at Xaffévillers on landing, killing the twenty-one-year-old pilot Captain Buck MC, DFC. On 3–4 September 97 Squadron, 100 Squadron and 216 Squadron combined forces and attacked enemy airfields at Morhange and Boulay, three Handley Pages from 216 Squadron going to each target, dropping forty 112-lb bombs on each location and a single 550-lb bomb on Morhange. A single 216 Squadron aircraft went to Esch to drop a 550-lb bomb and eight 112-lb bombs too.

Continuing to support the ground campaign, on the night of 6–7 September 207 Squadron attacked St Quintin. Lieutenant Semple had yet another bad experience with trying to land at someone else's aerodrome despite doing everything by the book. After his engines started to overheat, he tried to cool the engines (including by flying lower)—he fired the colour of the night as recognition that he wasn't an enemy aircraft trying to fool them, and also his aircraft's letter. The FE2b night bomber equipped 102 Squadron put on their landing searchlight, but as Semple started to use it as a landing aid, turned it off. Shortly after this, both engines failed, leaving Semple with little control over what happened next. The aircraft crashed onto the side of a steep hill, pinning Semple and his observer Hamilton in the wreckage, although Semple managed to get himself and then Hamilton out. An ambulance and men from nearby 101 Squadron came and helped, and after taking Hamilton to Number 2 Stationary Hospital at Abbeville, went back his unit to report what happened, and then took a crash party to the scene of the accident, near Famechon. It took three days for them to clear the site, making sure they got a few souvenirs—as seemed to be standard practice for pilots and crew at the time.

For over a week 216 Squadron did not raid owing to the weather. Then, Metz was the focus of four Handley Pages on the night of 12–13 September, three Handley Pages returning there the next night whilst others from 216 Squadron hit Courcelles, Saarbrücken and the enemy airfield at Frescaty. One aircraft flown by Lieutenant Heine was shot down on this night, all three crew (including one American, Lieutenant F. F. Jewett of the United States Air Service,) being taken prisoner:

'INDEPENDENTS' HELP.
Independent Force (R.A.F.).—on the night of 12th–13th inst., in conjunction with the attack of the American First Army, the railways at Metz, Sablon and Courcelles were heavily bombed by us with good results. On the 13th inst. Operations were continued against Metz, Sablon, other railway junctions and enemy transport on the battle front. Nearly seven and a half tons of bombs were dropped.

Daily Mirror, 14 September 1918

One of the two Handley Pages from 100 Squadron on the night of 13–14 September was flown by American Second Lieutenant Gower, accompanied by observer Second Lieutenant Shillinglaw and rear gunner Second Lieutenant Warneford. Not long after the aircraft crossed the front line, the port propeller of the Handley Page O/100 was shot away, and the entire engine and fuel tank located behind it were enveloped in flame. Shillinglaw noted that the flames trailed far beyond the tail of the aircraft, and terrifyingly close to the fuselage, especially for Warneford in the rear for whom it must have seemed incineration was imminent. As they were only 15 miles from the front line, the aircraft had not fully gained height yet and were only between 1,000 and 2,000 feet above ground. Gower did his best to side-slip the aircraft and try and get the fire out or just keep it from the fuselage, despite the small amount of height to play with. Shillinglaw used the navigation lights, Morse and even the aircraft's klaxon horn to try and let those on the ground aware of their emergency, but on receiving no response he tried firing lights from the Very pistol as well as using the Aldis lamp. The bomber, loaded with eight 112-lb bombs and six cases of Baby Incendiary canisters, narrowly avoided two hangars and pancaked onto the airfield, writing it off but fortunately with no major injury or explosion. It transpired that the officer in charge of controlling movements that night was new and did not understand why Shillinglaw was using every method available to him to try and get noticed, so ignored them. The other aircraft piloted by Captain Savery in the other 100 Squadron aircraft successfully dropped ten 112-lb bombs on the railway line south-east of Courcelles railway junction.

Two Handley Pages were lost on the night of 14–15 September; the crew of HP C9683 from 207 Squadron were taken prisoner, and at least one crew member from a 215 Squadron machine was killed when one of their aircraft was lost. It had been a busy night for 215 Squadron, one aircraft and crew undertaking three raids. Various targets were hit by 215 Squadron, but they were all railway junctions. Monaghan had been asked to raid Kaiserslautern, describing it as 'medium hot' with around twenty anti-aircraft guns and twelve searchlights:

> But a new menace was rearing its ugly head. Balloons were being put up to 4,000 feet and between their cables, wires were stretched to form an invisible curtain which was fatal if we crashed into it. It was a clever idea because with our elementary bomb sights, above that height a direct hit was plain luck. A spy had reported that balloons were up around Kaiserslautern.[56]

> Lieutenant Hugh Baird Monaghan, 215 Squadron RAF

Something else for the Handley Page crews to bear in mind was the proximity of Alsace-Lorraine to Kaiserslautern. With this former French territory still home to a lot of pro-French civilians, there were strict orders that if in doubt, not to unload their bombs in case they were over Alsace-Lorraine. As Monaghan approached at 5,000 feet, railway lines could be discerned, and although Mitchell, Monaghan's observer, was certain of their location, Monaghan wasn't sure and didn't want to risk the possibility of wasting his load of bombs dropped from this height:

> Finally I called out, 'Set your sights for 1,500 feet I'm going down'. Following the tracks, we slid across the station and according to a spy report received later, badly damaged the place. But I'll never forget my anxiety at the thought of crashing into a curtain of wires.[57]

> Lieutenant Hugh Baird Monaghan, 215 Squadron RAF

On landing, another threat that was not on Monaghan's mind at the time was discovered when his aircraft HP D4566 was inspected:

> Two machine gun bullets had buried themselves in the compartment just back of my head and a third had nicked one of the propeller blades. Evidently, completely unknown to us, there had been a night fighter up.[58]

> Lieutenant Hugh Baird Monaghan, 215 Squadron RAF

The stepping-up of bombing missions by Independent Force was matched by German attempts to shoot them down:

> Several pilots had reported that they were sure the enemy had scouts up at night, one crew even reporting that they had been fired on from above while being held by a searchlight. The presence of mysterious coloured signals from the ground was also noted. Everyone got a bit on edge and wondered what this new stunt was; it was anything but pleasant to be potted at by scouts, and these Handleys presented a target big enough for the average scout not to miss.[59]

Lieutenant Alfie Reginald Kingsford, 100 Squadron RAF

The next night, 97 Squadron lost their third aircraft in action. One Handley Page was brought down during a raid on Cologne carried out at an altitude of just 500 feet owing to heavy anti-aircraft fire. A crowded theatre below the aircraft received the brunt of destruction, killing many and having a terrible effect on the moral of the local population. Lieutenant Semple on 207 Squadron went on two raids to Étreux, after having spent the day helping with experiments on new sound locating instruments. On his return from the first raid to Étreux, which he described as 'very hot— searchlights and AA very active', he found the aircraft had been damaged, the starboard lower wing damaged in around ten places by anti-aircraft fire, with damage to the starboard propeller too. The losses from these few days were a bad omen for the following night, which was to incur the heaviest losses of the 'Bloody Paralysers' throughout the war.

The Worst Night

On the fateful night of 16–17 September 1918, ten Handley Pages were lost. It was to be the worst single night of losses suffered by the Handley Pages throughout the entire war. Nos 97 and 100 Squadron Handley Pages attacked Frescaty and Lorquin airfields, as well as one aircraft from each attacking Frankfurt. One of the 100 Squadron Handley Pages attacked Frescaty twice, dropping a total of twenty-four 112-lb bombs and seven cases of Baby Incendaries on the aerodrome, reportedly setting a Zeppelin hangar on fire. The 100 Squadron Handley Page that attacked Frankfurt was D8302, flown by Lieutenant F. R. Johnson, with Lieutenant R. C. Pitman as rear gunner and Second Lieutenant Frederick Howard Chainey as observer.

The raid had gone fine up until the point Chainey dropped the bombs. The journey to Frankfurt had been without harassment by anti-aircraft fire or searchlights—there was even a location lit-up well enough for him to drop all his bombs in confidence. It was not until Chainey went to the rear to check all the bombs had been dropped that the pilot made him aware something was amiss:

> Johnson tapped me on the shoulder and pointed to one of the propellers, which was stationary. We turned back immediately south, and I at once attempted to start the engine, but all my efforts failed, so we were forced to land near Darmstadt. We made a splendid landing on a ploughed field, and set fire to our machine. Lights were seen approaching, so we made of for a forest close by to make up our plans of escape.[1]

Second Lieutenant Frederick Howard Chainey, 100 Squadron RAF

The crew ditched their flying gear and headed south, hoping to reach the Swiss border, travelling around 9 miles that night. The men hid in another wood during the daytime and they did have some provisions with them—

biscuits, a tin of beef, and a box of chocolates, but had little water. They found that the small rivers in the vicinity were mostly dried up, and so the first movement the next night when they felt safe to move was to try and find a stream, finding a water pump by the roadside instead, then finding another wood to hide in. By this point food was running out and the three men had to live off the land, mostly turnips and beans. The next night they left cover at around 21.30, trying to find a stream but only finding a dry bed, but then found another water pump. The new plan was to find a railway line, and try and climb on a passing railway wagon heading south. When they came to a railway crossing were challenged by the gateman. The men ignored him and headed cross-country, and so again took shelter in a small wood just south of a railway junction near Mannheim. By now the food supplies had been completely exhausted, they were almost spotted by boys picking berries, and deteriorating weather meant the men were wet through. The chances of escaping to a neutral country were by now almost nil, and so the decision was taken to hand themselves in. They went to a small village and instructed the first person they found to take them to a police station; the man brought them some bread, then took them to a police station where they were kept in a cell overnight.

The next day, a British captured soldier who had been put to work in a local factory was brought to them, and he brought the men some food (most of which was later stolen by their German guard), and then put on a train into Mannheim. They were kept at a prisoner of war camp in the morning until put on another train to Karlsruhe, where they were put in an old hotel where prisoners were examined before being sent on again. As per usual, the Germans attempted to get information from the men about which unit they were from and where they were based, but learned nothing. Six long days were spent here, until being moved to a camp just a twenty minute walk away—then after a week transferred to Landshut, then to a camp in Bulgaria in October where news eventually reached them that the Armistice had been signed, finally leaving on 17 December then onwards through Switzerland, France and finally, via Calais, England again. For those left behind at Xaffévillers, and in any unit where men were missing, it left an awful atmosphere, not knowing whether to grieve for dead friends or be comfortable in the knowledge they were at least safe and alive. Lieutenant Kingsford of 100 Squadron was one of those:

> It was a doubtful show night and the weather had looked threatening
> when they left. Johnny had reported scouts and has expressed a dislike
> for them. That bride of his would be worrying her head off, we knew,

so some of us wrote to her, trying to put a hopeful tone on the event. Great was our relief when, some time later, we heard that they were all prisoners.[2]

Lieutenant Alfie Reginald Kingsford, 100 Squadron RAF

The Handley Page that was lost, D8302, was recovered by the Germans more or less complete, despite Chaincy saying it was set on fire, and was roughly re-marked with a black cross on a white background to show the new ownership.

No. 115 Squadron mounted its first raids on this night, eight Handley Pages heading for the vital enemy railway triangle at Metz-Sablon. Three Handley Pages were lost, two of them crashing on friendly territory, petrol systems or inexperience being to fault—the mechanics had had little time to get to know the workings of the Handley Pages, and also the pilots had only flown at night time on several occasions at the very most. The third Handley Page lost came down in Luxembourg, following the crew getting lost and then losing petrol when hit by anti-aircraft fire. The men tried to return to the lines, spending a few days hidden by sympathetic locals, but after being handed over to the authorities were interred and fortunately well treated. No. 207 Squadron got away with no losses, five aircraft raiding Étreux airfield, one of them dropping an SN 1,650-lb bomb, the four others dropping a combined total of sixty-three 112-lb bombs, and between the five aircraft forty 25-lb Cooper bombs contributing to the damage which was visible to the crews. Semple of 207 Squadron had a fortunate escape, which almost resulted in a loss; he found searchlights and anti-aircraft fire very active, and had to fly through several thunder and lightning storms when returning home. On landing it was found his undercarriage was damaged, one part having been knocked away during the flight, no doubt by anti-aircraft fire. The trailing edge of the wing had also been shot through, and the crew were very fortunate not to have added to the losses for the night.

No. 215 Squadron was absolutely mauled and five machines were allotted to attack that night. One had to return shortly after take-off owing to a leaking fuel tank and fortunately landed with no incident, but the other four did not return. HP D9684 flown by Second Lieutenant Lacey with Lieutenant Yelverton and Second Lieutenant Down was the only aircraft not to be sent to Cologne, attempting to raid Mannheim instead via the aerodrome at North Landrau to observe activities there. They were shot down over Saarbrücken and went into captivity. One of the aircraft that had set out to raid Cologne, D4566, was commanded by Canadian Lieutenant Monaghan. The two bridges at Cologne were the objectives of the raid for Monaghan, although looking over maps and photographs of the area before take-off he voiced his fears to the commanding officer after noticing the cathedral directly in line between the two bridges—the course Monaghan was planning to fly to give a good chance of accuracy:

> 'What if we miscalculate and dump our load on it?' He answered, 'Better not come back here. The British government and the world would be horrified and you would probably end up with a court martial. I'd advise you to try Holland or Luxembourg, both neutral, and hope for the best. Can you imagine how Germany would play that up?'[3]

Lieutenant Hugh Baird Monaghan, 215 Squadron RAF

Monaghan's usual gunlayer was unwell on the morning before the raid, and as he was considering a replacement three new officers arrived—one of them an old friend from the Central Flying School, Lieutenant Herbert Ernest Hyde. In peacetime he had already made a name for himself, having written three books on world problems and how to solve them, in his view. He agreed to go along as a gunner on the raid and at 19.46 took off with Monaghan, just clearing the trees with a new 90-gallon petrol tank installed on Monaghan's instructions. It was to be a long trip, as Handley Page raids tended to be. Despite the Sidcot suits being much more comfortable and warm than the previous long leather flying coats, it still was not enough. Heated suits were being installed, but they had not reached 215 Squadron yet. After two hours of heading north, Monaghan was nearing Trèves when two explosions came from the port side, and the engine on that side stopped:

> The plane seemed to stagger and turned to the left under the drive of the starboard engine which was still running full out and when I cut this the left wing dropped. We were at 5,000 feet and I wasn't sure we were finished; so, with height to spare, I let the plane fall off, meanwhile calling to Mitch to release the bombs. We must have dropped 2,000 feet. I tried the controls which appeared to be locked and when I put full pressure on the wheel it spun loose in my hands. I knew then we were done. There was nothing to do but sit and wait for the crash.[4]

Lieutenant Hugh Baird Monaghan, 215 Squadron RAF

The port wing hit the ground first, slightly cushioning the impact as the rest of the aircraft slew round as the nose went into telegraph wires, which slowed it down further. The fuselage hit the ground 'with a tearing of canvas and the sound of splintering wood'. Monaghan was momentarily stuck in the cockpit, owing to being surrounded by wires, until Mitchell climbed through the wreckage and removed the wires, then helping Monaghan onto the ground. Hyde was 'a bit roughed up', but fine not long after. The men decided to make a run for Luxembourg, hoping that the silence they could hear meant they had briefly evaded detection; although the downing of the wires would surely bring investigation as to the reason for lack of service before long. Fortunately the wreckage had not caught light, so Monaghan returned and found a pair of shoes, cigarettes, chocolate and tins of sardines, all kept in the compartment behind him. As was customary the crew set light to the aircraft, Mitchell finding the Very light pistol and firing it towards the leaking petrol tanks while Monaghan and Hyde headed down the road. The Handley Page instantly went up, and by the time Mitchell had reached the other two, the 1,500 rounds of ammunition had started to go off—shortly joined by a large explosion, when the three remaining bombs went up. The men planned to hide in a nearby woods for the day, and move only at night, managing to get a few hours' sleep before awaking again.

At daybreak the men went down to the Moselle River, although they were disappointed not to find a boat to enable them to cross. The other two men were keen to swim, but Monaghan stopped them owing to the width and fast flow of the water—they did however fill their Sidcot suits with stones and dumped them in the river. The trio went back to the woods, with still no sight or sound of a search party or anyone at all, and enjoyed a meal of sardines and chocolate bars. At around 15.00, Monaghan noticed a police dog only 50 yards from where they were, then noticing three parties of four men each heading towards them, all armed. Any chance of escape had gone, and Monaghan crawled into the open then stood up with his hands in the air, hoping one of the men in uniform would stop any trigger-happy or overly patriotic civilians from opening fire:

When the nearest four saw me, there was a shout and all raised my rifles, pointing directly at me, and for a moment my knees wobbled but the soldier snapped an order and they came running up. Pointing to myself, I said, 'Englander, offizier' and the soldier said, 'Ya, offizier?' I answered 'Ya'. Calling the boys out, we were marched along the road past the spot where we cracked up. There was nothing left but part of one engine. We entered a small village and were hustled into a cell-like room attached to the station and locked in.[5]

Lieutenant Hugh Baird Monaghan, 215 Squadron RAF

Monaghan was then interviewed by a German major with a distinct American accent; it transpired he was from Rochester, New York, where his father ran a number of dried apple factories, and became trapped in Germany visiting grandparents at the outbreak of the war. The men were soon put on a train to Saarbrücken, one local woman spitting in Monaghan's face on the way there—it could have been worse, Monaghan was particularly worried about getting caught by locals while on the run as he believed they would pitchfork him and the others. The interrogations took place here, being asked via an interpreter for his squadron number, aerodrome, raid objective and other questions. Apart from declaring himself to be a member of the Royal Air Force he simply answered 'I cannot answer that'. The interpreter, coming under pressure from who Monaghan described as 'a typical Prussian, if I ever saw one', wanted an explanation, to which he was told:

> Tell the officer I am a British officer and I have been instructed by my government to answer only two questions, my name and the branch of service I was attached to. I will answer nothing more.[6]

> Lieutenant Hugh Baird Monaghan, 215 Squadron RAF

Interrogations continued to be conducted despite Monaghan's refusal to answer, and he was well aware that there were microphones embedded all over the building to pick up on anything he or the other prisoners may reveal. A particular favourite trick of the Germans was to embed a fake prisoner to gain the men's trust and again try and find something out—discovered quickly by Monaghan after being told by a supposed French pilot that he was a two-seater pilot based near Verdun, who claimed to have only just crashed his aeroplane. Monaghan was instantly suspicious of a two-seater based near Verdun being able to fly so deep into Germany—not impossible, but certainly very unlikely—and the constant questions from him made it even more obvious to the men. After Monaghan told him that they were all suffering from memory loss and that he was wasting his time, the 'French' pilot suddenly stood up and went out of the room. That was the end of that, and Monaghan and his crew spent the rest of the war as prisoners. Among those back at Xaffévillers, who endured the wait of hearing what had happened to them, was Second Lieutenant Roy Shillinglaw of 100 Squadron who had been working in the control tower that night, set up to organise flying on what was by then a very busy aerodrome:

> I had to go across to the control tower... and we'd got two Handley Page squadrons and our own FE2bs and whatnot, about forty or fifty planes

on the aerodrome. So, I had to flash them off and flash them in, and all this and the other, and we lost six machines that night. 100 Squadron lost one at Frankfurt—Johnson, Chamey and Pitman. 215 Squadron lost several and the other squadron lost one or two. Included in this 215 squadron was my friend Monaghan. I waited up for an hour after sunrise hoping they'd come back, but they never did. He was shot down.[7]

Lieutenant Roy Shillinglaw, 100 Squadron RAF

Six aircraft from 216 Squadron were airborne that night, one machine each attacking Trèves, Merzig, and the aerodromes at Boulay and Frescaty. Two raided Metz, one of them, flown by Lieutenant B. Norcross, being shot down over Metz. Norcross was later reported by the Germans as having died, but the others, Second Lieutenant R. H. Cole and Sergeant G. Hall, were taken prisoner. The other machine that raided Metz successfully dropped a single 550-lb bomb and seven 112-lb bombs over the target, but crashed on its return injuring the observer Lieutenant Cotter.

As well as the seven aircraft lost over enemy territory and three crashed behind Allied lines, two men were killed and a further nineteen taken prisoner, as well as a number of others injured. While men and aeroplanes would be replaced (aeroplanes still taking somewhat longer to arrive than the men to fly them), the hard won experience of the crews now sat in German prisoner of war camps would take time to replace and their loss would have a detrimental effect on further operations, as well as the effect on morale of those left behind.

The End in Sight

Autumn came along and with it the longer nights once more. Each evening at dusk, the usual procedure was gone through and the big aerodrome presented its usual scene of activity, mechanics getting machines out of hangars, while loads of bombs in trolleys were pulled up to the planes, detonators were put in and the bombs placed in their racks. Pilots and observers, with maps, would saunter up to their respective machines and carry out an examination of all the important points. After the preparatory part, we all stood by until orders were given to take the air, or if the weather was 'dud,' the 'wash-out' would be given.[1]

Lieutenant Alfie Reginald Kingsford, 100 Squadron RAF

Despite the losses of 16–17 September and the effect on morale on the squadrons that suffered them, the numbers of Handley Pages in action was ever-growing. This was especially true of the Handley Page squadrons that were part of Independent Force where the use of day bombers meant the industrial areas in the Rhine Valley and important rail centres were more or less continually being harassed. The Independent Force Handley Page squadrons had a few days rest thanks to the weather, no doubt very much appreciated by the men (but 207 Squadron were up on the night of 17–18 September with five of their aircraft dropping a variety of bombs including an SN 1,650-lb bomb on Tupigny aerodrome). The next busy night was to be 20–21 September, when the five Independent Force Handley Page squadrons were 'up' on what was to be up until that point the most effective night in terms of total bomb weight dropped. The poor weather of the past few days caused difficulties at Xaffévillers with aircraft getting stuck in mud, but eventually the aircraft got airborne. Newcomers 115 Squadron attacked Morhange airfield, reporting four aircraft hangars hit, the Lewis guns also taking an effect on taking out a number of searchlights, attacking two trains and shooting down a German aircraft, shot down in flames by Lieutenant E. J. Whyte (who was awarded the Distinguished Flying Cross for his efforts) whilst the German was trying to shoot down the Handley Page. No. 215 Squadron was also partaking in aerodrome raiding, this time at Frescaty which was well defended, the Handley Pages flying low across the airfield to ensure accuracy. One aircraft circled the aerodrome putting the heavy defensive armament of the Handley Page to good use machine-gunning buildings and anti-aircraft guns. One of the 215 Squadron Handley Pages, C9732, was shot down in flames over Metz during the raid. The crew, Second Lieutenant ACG Fowler, Second Lieutenant C. C. Eaves and Second Lieutenant J. S. Ferguson were all killed.

No. 100 Squadron sent two Handley Pages up, attacking Burbach and Mannheim. The 100 Squadron aircraft both appear to have flown two sorties each that night, and put their experience acquired on flying FE2bs on low level raids before converting to Handley Pages to good use by gliding in on the target at Karlsruhe, dropping fourteen 112-lb bombs and observing 'several direct hits on Wharves'. The Handley Page that hit the iron works at Burbach flew over the target on a different course to which he would return on, and so the works were still lit up as he came in for the bombing run—the result was 'three distinct hits on Blast Furnaces'. By this time 100 Squadron were settling in well with the Handley Page:

Well after we'd prepared our course and the direction in which we were going to fly we would then get into our flying clothes which constituted of a pair of flying boots made of sheepskin, a Sidcot flying suit which was a padded monkey suit with a fur collar, a helmet and fur lines gloves. Underneath my own gloves I used to wear a pair of silk gloves for your flying times in very, very cold weather and if you took your gloves off to clear a jam in your gun your hands would get very cold and I used to slate myself against that cold with pure silk, and when I'd cleared the jam I'd put my gloves back and carry on. As we get into the aircraft the pilot would sit on the right hand side and I would sit on the left hand side of him. He would fly the aircraft, get us airborne, my job would then be to give him a course which he'd very conscientiously carry out. I would be watching the temperatures of the engines and a few other instruments, we didn't have very many instruments, and we'd carry on for an hour, two hours perhaps three hours on that particular course and then as we approached the target I should then crawl through a hatch into the front of the machine where we had two machine guns firing on one trigger, our bomb sights and a bomb release. To the rear of us we also carried a rear gunner who had two gunners firing on the port and the starboard and if we were attacked at all from underneath there was a hole in the body of the machine underneath with another gun firing from there, so he the poor chap was running up and down if we ran into any of that sort of trouble. Now we'd go into our target, we'd turn into wind, my job was to find the way, set the course, adjust the course if we had a variation of wind, we were flying at about sixty miles an hour airspeed so that if we had a thirty mile wind we only had a thirty mile ground speed and if the wind moved at all we'd adjust our course. Well, we'd approach our target, I should go through into the front cockpit where we had our bomb sights, machine guns and also the bomb release controls and I would then direct the pilot onto the target—right, or left, or straight ahead by signs with my hands and at the same time I'd have my right hand on the bomb release control and as we got onto our target away would go our bombs. We didn't always drop all our bombs in one go, we'd observe results and come round again and do the same thing again. Then of course we'd try to get home as quickly as we could. Unfortunately we had a prevailing wind against us, generally the wind was to the south west invariably so it took us much longer to come home than going out to the target.

It was of course very cold and the wind of course sometimes was severe and I have known a groundspeed of even five miles an hour where we've been flying for perhaps three hours to get back fifteen to twenty miles from the line but we always managed to make it somehow.[2]

Lieutenant Roy Shillinglaw, 100 Squadron RAF

No. 207 Squadron also took part in the night's activities on 20–21 September, despite very poor weather. Lieutenant Semple was certainly not happy about the situation:

Tonight we were sent on a raid—Wing Orders—under disgraceful conditions. The weather report was as follows. Wind increasing from 40–60 mph with squalls of gale force. Overcast. Very heavy rain squalls. We crossed the lines—dropped our bombs and then turned for home— going against wind. Caught in searchlights and only doing a ground speed of about 10mph. Ran into storms and hail and gales, and finally landed after 3.5 hours of disgusting weather in a storm. Good landing. Part of the time the machine was out of control owing to the extreme bumpiness of the weather. It was a disgusting shame that we were made to raid, and somebody should be made to suffer. My propellers were so damaged by the rain and hail that they had to be changed today.[3]

Lieutenant Leslie George Semple, 207 Squadron RAF

On the same night, 58 Squadron, after three weeks of receiving and training on the Handley Pages (while still flying the FE2bs on night operations), undertook their first raid with the new bombers on this night, with two Handley Pages accompanying four FE2bs to attack Froidmont airfield. At this point there were a total of eight Handley Page squadrons operational on the Western Front. Five were with Independent Force (97 Squadron, 100 Squadron, 115 Squadron, 215 Squadron, and 216 Squadron). The other three were located elsewhere; No. 58 Squadron located close to the Independent Force squadrons, but separate, and 207 Squadron and 214 Squadrons were close to the northern French coast. No more Handley Page O/400 squadrons were sent across to France before the Armistice.

The next night, 21–22, 58 Squadron only had one Handley Page airborne, going with five FE2bs to attack the airfield at St Maur. Seven aircraft from 97 Squadron were aloft targeting Buhl aerodrome, Frescaty aerodrome coming under attack from 100 Squadron. The Handley Pages of 100 Squadron ran into an unwelcome reception, the anti-aircraft fire bursting so close that observer Lieutenant Shillinglaw claimed he could smell the cordite. The aircraft came under attack from a German aircraft, firing and diving past so quickly that Shillinglaw did not get the chance to dive into the nose and let loose with the twin Lewis guns at his disposal, the rear gunner similarly not able to react, the bullets shooting away a strut. The anti-aircraft fire resumed and the fuselage was hit just behind the petrol tank; however, it did not explode—fortunately—and despite damage to the fuselage spar the aircraft remained controllable. The raid still had good effects, nine direct hits on hangars and sheds, as well as four direct hits on buildings west of the sheds and six hits on the railway junction east of Frescaty. Meanwhile, 215 Squadron bombed Hagondinge, despite very heavy anti-aircraft fire aided by searchlights, and finished by machine-gunning trains. No. 207 Squadron was engaged on airfield attacks, six Handley Pages heading to Saultain airfield; one had to drop out towing to the weather and bombed Douai railway station, but the remaining five dropped an SN 1,650-lb bomb, forty-eight 112-lb bombs, and twenty-five 25-lb Cooper bombs. Finally, 216 Squadron raided Rombach with six aircraft, dropping seventy-seven 112-lb bombs and a single 550-lb bomb.

The main objectives for the Handley Page squadrons for the rest of the war became airfields and railways. With the Allied ground offensive making great gains, these would be much more effective and of use to the war effort by disrupting the flow of reinforcements and supplies as well as helping to ensure the allied air superiority continued. The aerodrome raids also helped to make sure German bombers would not do to the Allied armies what the Allied aircraft were doing to the German supply chains.

The shorter distance between the objectives and the aerodromes meant the Handley Pages could return, refuel, rearm, and attack again, keeping up the intensity of the attack and causing more damage—and restless nights for an already exhausted enemy. The naval blockade of Germany meant food shortages were severe in Germany. At least one German pilot had had enough and decided to do something about it, surprising 207 Squadron:

> One morning just as dawn was breaking, a German fighter pilot threw out Very lights to surrender. On landing, the pilot left his plane intact and walked up to myself and other mates and said in broken English, 'I vas hungry and I vas fed up.'[4]

> Air Mechanic Percy Young, 207 Squadron

No. 207 Squadron returned to raid Saultain on 22–23 September, the airfield being the recipient of an SN 1,650-lb bomb again as well as a mix of 112-lb and 25-lb Cooper bombs. Douai was also hit a second night in a row, a load of 112-lb bombs tumbling out of the night sky towards the railway lines there and another SN 1,650-lb bomb from 207 Squadron was dropped on the railway north of Valenciennes. On the next night, 23–24 September, 214 Squadron bombed both the Zeebrugge Mole and Bruges with two aircraft. A third aircraft, D4579, suffered with engine issues and in the forced landing crashed, killing Lieutenant HA McCormick of the United States Naval Air Service. The same night, 58 Squadron sent three Handley Pages to raid St Maur aerodrome. The Independent Force Squadrons spent several days out of action, the weather only just allowing them to conduct operations on 26–27 September, mainly targeting railway lines, and 58 Squadron raided a German aerodrome with a mixture of Handley Pages and FE2bs. The only 215 Squadron Handley Page, which was 'up' that night crashed on the allied side of the landings owing to one engine out of action, injuring Second Lieutenant E. Anderson and Second Lieutenant J. Durie.

The attacks made by the two 214 Squadron aircraft on Bruges and the Zeebrugge Mole appear to have been the last time in the war that the Handley Pages were used against the U-boats. Disabling lock gates on the canals that gave the U-boats access to the sea only ever temporarily disrupted their operations, but together with the increased number of U-boats destroyed by the Royal Navy and the use of convoys and other preventative measures, the U-boats were not able to take Britain out of the war by destruction of merchant shipping, as had been the aim at the start of 1917.

On 27–28 September, both 207 Squadron (with seven aircraft) and 214 Squadron (with eight) attacked railway targets, one of the 215 Squadron

Handley Pages dropping an SN 1,650-lb bomb on Thourout. No. 58 Squadron attacked the railway junction at Inglemunster on the night of 28–29 September with six Handley Pages with no FE2bs being used, four of the aircraft making two sorties and the other two an impressive three sorties, all against the same target. No. 214 Squadron put up eleven aircraft that night, again attacking railways, D4591 with Sergeant Wardrop as observer carrying an SN 1,650-lb bomb:

It was railway siding full of ammunition, and we hit the sidings all right, and I think they saw the fire about forty miles away, a terrific explosion. That's when we woke up over Holland. We were not supposed to come down under I think 4,000 feet, for this bomb, I think it was 2,000 ft and we shouldn't have dropped this bomb. Again we were so determined we were going to do something with the wretched thing that we went down lower than we should and we nearly got concussed. We woke up over Holland. The poor chap at the back I don't know where he woke up he was sick as a toad, of course. But then we found ourselves over Holland. The machine was just flying itself. We were quite safe. We just went out to sea and came home and that was it. Many people saw the fire as well as us.[5]

Sergeant William Edward David Wardrop, 207 Squadron RAF

The weather on the night of 30–31 September meant only five Handley Pages from three squadrons made any attacks.

The coming winter would bring longer nights to cloak the Handley Pages, but also meant worse conditions both in the air and on the ground. The units prepared to make themselves as comfortable as possible, 100 Squadron already having a very popular large brazier in the centre of the mess, open on all four sides to warm as many men as possible. A cinema was also installed by the commanding officer and a band was formed, as well as a concert party. Although that made the men comfortable on the ground, it was a different closer in the air when temperatures dropped even further:

It was of course pretty cold at times particularly as winter came on and we'd be flying in an open cockpit with very, very small windshields.... one had to be careful for frostbite. Some people used grease on their face in order to avoid this. The pilot and the observer would sit side by side, sometimes the pilot would be strapped in but it was not really possible for the Observer to be so because he was moving about—in the event of attack by enemy aircraft he was very busy, moving around, and in the

same way he was dropping his bombs. Furthermore he'd be looking over
the side looking at a drift indicator or spotting something on the ground
so that it was not possible to be strapped in.[6]

Lieutenant Roy Shillinglaw, 100 Squadron RAF

Despite some of the 100 Squadron pilots seeming to prefer the FE2bs,
they became accustomed to the Handley Pages—one new member of the
Squadron certainly liked them:

Joss, a new observer, was in his element with those sixteen bombs
hanging in the engine room, and would pop in about every five minutes
to see if they were O.K. He gloried in destruction, his only growl being
that there wasn't enough. His face always betrayed disgust when the last
one went, and he wasn't satisfied unless he could let go all of his .303. He
would fire a whole drum at one searchlight, and if it didn't switch off, he
would give it another. When everything was gone, he would sit down in
misery for the remainder of the trip.[7]

Lieutenant Alfie Reginald Kingsford, 100 Squadron RAF

Yet another unusual use for the 207 Squadron Handley Pages almost came
about on 1 October; during the day, the aircraft were loaded up with food
and ammunition to be dropped on positions held by American forces,
which had reportedly been cut off by the Germans and running low on
supplies during the Battle of the St Quentin Canal. The men and machines
stood by all day waiting for the order to go, but the news eventually came
in that British troops had managed to reach them.

No. 58 Squadron were brought up to full establishment strength on the first
day of October with the arrival of an additional Handley Page, bringing them
to a total on strength of ten. On the night of 3–4 October they dropped over
10 tons of bombs at the railway junction at Valenciennes with six aircraft, 214
Squadron getting ten aircraft airborne and also raiding railways, delivering
an SN 1,650-lb bomb amongst the load. The SN bomb was dropped by HP
D4591, the only Handley Page on 214 Squadron's strength that had the proper
equipment to carry them. No. 215 Squadron raided Frescaty aerodrome, with
one bomb seeming to directly hit the ammunition store, as the Handley Page
was rocked by the explosion while flying at an altitude of 2,500 feet away
from it. Other squadrons focussed on railways too, and one Handley Page
from 115 Squadron was lost after a forced landing.

In October a new paint scheme was introduced for the Handley Pages. The
'Nivo' finish had been developed to minimise the reflection of the aircraft
when in the beam of a searchlight; this had been standard for Home Defence

aircraft back in Britain since June 1918, but became available for night flying aircraft on the Western Front later. A new bomb sight emerged too, the Wimperis Course Setting Bombsight, which included a compass, designed to be fitted to the nose of the aircraft, but Handley Page crews adopted it to be fitted alongside the negative lens sight in the floor of the aircraft—more preferable in bad weather. To aid precision bombing at low-level lights were sometimes mounted underneath the aircraft (the numbers varied but usually two, three or four) so that the beams would converge when the distance between the aircraft and whatever the lights were shining on was at a certain point. Although the new sights and other aids helped accuracy, there could be no doubting that the raids affected civilians, and the crews were aware of this:

I don't think that anybody deliberately bombed civilian houses or civilian people so far as my colleagues and myself were concerned. We were very, very keen to be on our target but there's no doubt that our raids on German towns, railway stations and factories in those towns must have been demoralising to some of the civilian inhabitants for we used to see the intelligence reports that came through after our raids. Spies on our side would convey this information to our authorities, and we would be told about this in information reports that we got. Furthermore in our night bombing it was difficult to see our results, we would see a fire burning or the explosion in a works or something like that. Next day the day bombers would be over at dawn (and) as they crossed over our targets they'd photograph them and within twenty four hours we should be seeing pictures of our own targets and where we'd perhaps hit the target or whether we'd just missed it or so forth. We were very keen to be on target because our errors were shown up on those photographs, there was no kidding the authorities and I think we were pretty accurate on the whole.[8]

Lieutenant Roy Shillinglaw, 100 Squadron RAF

A similar attitude existed in 207 Squadron:

We were very severely reprimanded if they found we'd even bombed a house, even by mistake or design. But we'd certainly get a reprimand over it. Oh no, we had specific objects like docks, railway stations, ports, of course, all kinds, Zeebrugge lock gates, canals, aerodromes, you see. But where we had a target and they had a hospital, which we could clearly see, of course, the Red Cross, we used to refrain even from going to that particular target. We were told it's not worth the risk.[9]

Sergeant William Edward David Wardrop, 207 Squadron RAF

On 4–5 October 58 Squadron targeted Valenciennes with eight aircraft. One was lost when after take-off an engine caught fire, the just-airborne aircraft not able to continue climbing and hitting the ground nose first and exploding. Amazingly the crew, despite being in shock, physically suffered nothing more than cuts and bruises. The other seven aircraft were able to attack their target successfully, and all made two sorties against the target that night. 'Dud' weather continued to ground the Independent Force Handley Pages, on the night of 5–6 October a raid was mounted by them despite poor visibility, meaning they could not always see the effects of the bombs. One of the four 100 Squadron Handley Pages active that night was however able to see well enough to use the Handley Page as a weapon of opportunity, shooting up targets such as enemy artillery, transport and trenches as they showed themselves. Another 100 Squadron Handley Page found a blast furnace at Burbach fully lit up—soon to be further illuminated by the addition of the Handley Page's full load of bombs. The Handley Page squadrons not part of Independent Force found the weather clearer (as they tended to fairly regularly owing to the Independent Force operating close to mountains which meant cloud and mist was common) and were more active. Even for these squadrons there were nights of no flying, which could mean a long night for the crews:

> If we were likely to go on a raid at night and we were waiting, that was the worst part. You would wait perhaps all night and then at daylight you would get all the clear and you could go to bed or do what you liked. We used to play solo or roulette. All things like that you see to keep you going. To keep your mind off it as much as possible.[10]

Sergeant Leslie Alexander Dell, 214 Squadron RAF

High winds precluded 58 Squadron returning to Valenciennes on the night of 6–7 October which also caused two of the 207 Squadron aircraft to revert to closer targets, although 214 Squadron was able to successfully attack with nine aircraft. Two nights later 58 Squadron successfully raided Valenciennes, the bombs dropped including their first SN 1,650-lb bomb, and elsewhere 214 Squadron also dropped an SN 1,650-lb bomb over Melle, one of nine 214 Squadron aircraft up that night. The next evening, Independent Force Handley Pages were airborne and active, although one of them appeared to have taken off rather too quickly, got itself into the slipstream of the departing aircraft and side-slipped into a field from a height of just 50 feet. Thick mist continued to cause issues on the night of 9–10 October, Independent Force crews having to land through a seventy foot thick bank of mist which obscured the ground.

Heavy mist and cloud the next day did not prevent five Handley Pages from Independent Force doing their best to be of use—they had to use the compass to navigate to the targets, and spent a long time just trying to find gaps in the clouds to position themselves accurately. A sixth Handley Page (from 100 Squadron) was forced to return without attacking and crashed at the aerodrome, killing the pilot Second Lieutenant L. Rattle and injuring Second Lieutenant J. M. Rennie and Sergeant J. H. Donoghue. The weather worsened, and raids were continually laid off.

The Handley Page squadrons further north did not face the same problems. On the night of 13–14 October, sixteen Handley Pages were aloft from three squadrons. One of the eight 214 Squadron aircraft looked as if the engines would fail while over Ghent. After dropping bombs on Melle, the pilot deciding to head to Holland as a preferable alternative to being taken prisoner by the Germans, although was able to get back to allied lines. No. 58 Squadron again kept the pressure up on Valenciennes, although the single aircraft carrying the SN 1,650-lb bomb was unable to release it. The thoughts of landing with it still attached understandably rattled the crew, but they landed safely. The next night 58 Squadron raided Audenarde railway station and the SN 1,650-lb bomb was able to be dropped successfully, as did the loads of the other four aircraft. Two aircraft from 207 Squadron raided Tournai and seven aircraft from 214 Squadron returned to Melle, the starboard engine of one catching fire on the return resulting in a forced landing on the beach at Dunkirk. Although the Rolls-Royce Eagle engines were amongst the best aero engines used in the war, they were still not perfect and it did not need enemy action to ruin the night of a crew:

> There was a reduction gear for the propeller and I suppose that alone would weigh a hundred weight at least and then your propeller on it and that is fixed to the engine by means of a number of little screws all the way around. Probably three dozen, all the way around there. Well, this was on a Rolls engine too. It broke away completely like that, so that you suddenly saw your propeller and it was going ahead of you. Going down and gradually falling—we had a forced landing.[11]

> Sergeant Leslie Alexander Dell, 214 Squadron RAF

A Handley Page from 214 Squadron was used as an aerial sight-seeing vehicle on 18 October—Brackley collected King Albert and Queen Elisabeth of Belgium from St Pol so that they would be able to see the Allies liberate Ostend, Ghent and Ghistelles as the German forces were pushed back towards Germany.

The continued bad weather affecting the Handley Page squadrons of Independent Force continued to interfere with raids. On the night of 18–19 October all five Independent Force Handley Page squadrons had tried to undertake attacks, but just a single aircraft (from 100 Squadron) managed to drop bombs on the railway junction at Sarrebourg, persevering after previously attempting twice to attack the railways around Metz and Sablon. It was not until the night of 21–22 that the Independent Force Handley Pages attacked again, 97 Squadron and 100 Squadron both attacking Kaiserslautern and Mézières. Three SN 1,650-lb bombs were dropped that night, one of the 100 Squadron SN bombs reportedly landing in a field around 50 to 100 yards from houses, but still did extensive damage to a wide area, damage to housing being so severe that some houses were unsafe to live in. The other SN 1,650-lb bomb dropped by 100 Squadron was able to be heard over the roar of the engines as well as felt by the crew of the aircraft that dropped it, which also dropped fourteen boxes of Baby Incendiaries with it. A Handley Page from 97 Squadron dropped an SN 1,650-lb bomb on a munitions works.

The next night a solitary 215 Squadron Handley Page delivered an SN 1,650-lb bomb to Kaiserslautern in poor weather that grounded the rest of the Independent Force Handley Pages. Two attempts were made to drop it over the target but were unable to do so, and on the third attempt the pilot, Lieutenant J. Lorimer left the controls with the aircraft running straight and level whilst he and the observer, Lieutenant R. H. Bruce, used their hands to try and release the bomb. This was successful, and after the giant bomb was dropped a further two 112-lb bombs also carried were dropped, but the weather was too poor to see what damage had been caused by the bombs. Lorimer brought the aircraft down to an altitude of 2,000 feet and the observer and rear gunner between them expended 900 rounds of ammunition in shooting up the town before returning. The weather made visual navigation almost impossible; after seeing lights, which the crew believed to mark the Swiss border, they turned west and then south-west, hoping to see something that would give them an idea of where they were. Eventually, after over five hours of attempting to position themselves, they landed alongside a railway, hoping they were arriving in Allied territory, the aircraft falling into a hole, severely damaging it, but without injury to the crew. The crew then came under fire from Allied troops, who once they had realised the crew were friendly, directed them to an American camp where they were looked after, while a guard was placed on the damaged aircraft.

More and more use of the SN 1,650-lb bombs was being made, four being dropped on the night of 23–24 October, one dropped from a 97 Squadron aircraft killing twelve people and injuring thirty-six after landing on a residential street in Mainz. Four 100 Squadron Handley Pages were airborne, one with an SN 1,650-lb bomb, one with one 550-lb and eight 112-lb bombs, and the other two with sixteen 112-lb bombs each. The SN 1,650-lb, 550-lb, and eight 112-lb bombs were all dropped on Saarbrücken, direct hits being observed on the railway station. The aircraft with the 550-lb and eight 112-lb bombs was attacked by two German aircraft but both were driven off by the Handley Page's defensive fire. Of the other two 100 Squadron aircraft, one attacked the Burbach works causing a large explosion, and the other attacked Metz, but the results were not seen. Two of the five 216 Squadron aircraft airborne that night carried SN 1,650-lb bombs, one left at Saarbrücken and the other at Metz despite anti-aircraft fire.

The Allied advance through northern France and Belgium meant even the night bomber squadrons had the opportunity to move to aerodromes closer to the front line, allowing them to penetrate further into enemy territory. Although the situation did not change enough to warrant any movement of the Independent Force units, the others were moved in late October. Despite preparations to move, 207 Squadron sent three aircraft to Namur, but only one was successful, one aircraft being lost in a crash on landing. On 24 October 214 Squadron flew to Quilen, and six days later to Camphin. No. 58 Squadron had moved to Provin and 207 Squadron from Ligescourt to d'Estrées-en-Chaussée on 26 October. The use of Handley Pages to fly saboteurs to German aerodromes was mooted—they would either parachute in using the new 'Guardian Angel' parachutes, or the aircraft would actually land at the enemy aerodrome and the occupants get out as quickly as possible so the aircraft could rapidly depart again. These operations were planned for the December full moon period.

Poor weather again precluded operations for a number of days until on the night of 28–29 October raids were mounted again. Things started badly for 97 Squadron, who had already had an aircraft written off in a crash during a daytime test flight resulting in four deaths. On take-off, HP D5417 crashed and exploded killing two and seriously injuring a third. No. 100 Squadron HP C9736 crashed at Roville injuring the crew as did HP D4594 injuring two. With the losses, these two squadrons only sent up a single aircraft each, the 97 Squadron aircraft dropping an SN 1,650-lb bomb over Mannheim on a chemical works, the 100 Squadron aircraft dropping a single 550-lb bomb and eight 112-lb bombs on Longuyon railway junction starting a large fire. Three 115 Squadron Handley Pages also bombed Longuyon as well as Thionville, and a single 215 Squadron Handley Page bombed the railway at Écouviez. No. 216 Squadron had two aircraft armed with the SN 1,650-lb bomb operational that night with four others.

At Roville where 97, 115, and 216 Squadrons were based, the evening took a strange, colourful turn. One of the 115 Squadron aircraft had become stuck in the soft ground whilst attempting to take-off, and could not be moved so red lights were placed around it. No. 216 Squadron added to the illuminations:

> When Lieutenant Carroll took off, his starboard tail plane fitting broke at the fuselage causing the lower starboard plane to flap about. He succeeded however, in landing the machine safely but it stuck fast in the mud and red lights were also placed around this machine. When Lieutenant Puncher landed he struck a 1650lb bomb which unknown to us had dropped off a machine belonging to 97 Squadron and was left lying there. His undercarriage was damaged and red lights had to be placed around the machine. Lastly, a machine of 100 Squadron tried to land, stalled, side slipped at twenty feet, and piled up just beside the landing 'L'. Red lights were placed around it. At the end of the night the aerodrome had assumed something of the appearance of a fairy palace, and the bandstand officer was kept very busy with his telephone and megaphone.[12]

Anonymous Officer of 216 Squadron RAF

The deteriorating weather meant few of the Handley Pages were able to take part in operations, but the enthusiastic crews still managed to do what destruction they could. On 29–30 October two 100 Squadron Handley Pages, one armed with a single 500-lb bomb and eight 112-lb bombs and the other with 112-lb bombs unleashed their loads on Offenburg, and eight aircraft from 58 Squadron attacked Louvain and Mons, focusing on the railway stations. One of the 215 Squadron Handley Pages, C9720, was shot down, the last Handley Page shot down during the war.

As Austria-Hungary had surrendered on 3 November this facilitated the possibility of a raid mounted from Britain using the larger Handley Page V/1500 on Berlin and then landing near Prague. Plans were also then made to move Handley Page squadrons already on the Western Front to Prague too, the two hundred mile distance between Prague and Berlin putting it finally in the operational range of the Handley Page O/400. No. 216 Squadron was chosen to be the first to move to Prague owing to their experience to be the first of the Independent Force Handley Page squadrons. Seventy-four men and thirty officers were hand chosen to be part of this expeditionary force, which would take six aircraft. To facilitate their operation, a train was prepared to set up the aerodrome; as well as carrying men, they would take 600 112-lb bombs as well as petrol and oil, three light houses for the bombers to navigate by, rations to last six weeks, and various other pieces of equipment. All the men were trained in rifle drill and they would be armed with revolvers and rifles in case they came up against any opposition. The aircraft would carry supplies with them too, all the spares and tool boxes would be with the aircraft. The aircraft would be kept out in the open as it was not envisioned they would be there for long, simply operating until either petrol or bombs ran out and then returning. The men would be out in the open too, sleeping in tents, so extra clothing, including waterproof clothing and gum boots were taken too. A large amount of money (£4,000) was given to the commanding officer so that he would hopefully be able to procure further supplies and possibly billets while there. When all was prepared, the train was kept ready in a nearby siding, ready to go with just thirty minutes notice, as were the aircraft.

The remaining Handley Pages continued business as usual, although bad weather meant that the only Handley Pages operating on the night of 3–4 November were from 207 Squadron:

Raid carried out tonight. I had a pair of engines on my machine, which were absolutely rotten, also speedometer was broken. Anyway I went across the lines and dropped the bombs at Aulnoye junction—all the time the Port Engine giving trouble and ready to cut out. Reached the aerodrome after a rotten raid.[13]

Lieutenant Leslie George Semple, 207 Squadron RAF

Despite strong winds on 4 November, Lieutenant Semple of 207 Squadron took part in a raid on the railway junction at Namur, and again 207 Squadron were the only Handley Page unit flying that night. Able to set off as early as 17.45 owing to darkness, Semple was back by 21.30 after dropping bombs on target, observing some direct hits. The early return raised the possibility of a second raid that night, but the winds had now built up to a strong gale, and so he was able to enjoy dinner before going to bed.

The nights of 5–6 November saw small numbers of aircraft airborne, attacking enemy aerodromes despite heavy cloud and rain throughout the night. Of seven Handley Pages in total airborne that night, three were wrecked. Out of the two 97 Squadron aircraft airborne, only one was able to drop bombs on Morhange aerodrome, as did a single aircraft from 216 Squadron, dropping a 550-lb bomb and eight 112-lb bombs, as well as one aircraft from 215 Squadron, which crashed on landing at Xafevillers killing pilot Lieutenant J. B. Baldie and injuring the observer and gunner. The 216 Squadron aircraft also crashed on its return, the observer's goggles coming loose and flying into a propeller, shattering it and in the resulting forced landing the aircraft ran into trees, destroying it. No. 100 Squadron dropped fourteen cases of Baby Incendiaries at Lillingen aerodrome. Two 115 Squadron Handley pages were active, one raiding the aerodrome at Frescaty and the other one the one at Dieuze, which crashed on returning. An accident on the ground on 8 November caused further fatalities and damage to aircraft when a number of bombs exploded, killing five, injuring thirteen, and damaging five Handley Pages.

It now looked as if the war was coming to a close, but the pressure had to be kept up. Semple's diary records the atmosphere at 207 Squadron on 9 November:

Great excitement prevailing with regard to armistice. Germans falling back in every direction, ten miles a day. German fleet mutinied and revolution in Germany. Rumours of Kaiser's abdication, also Crown prince. Raid carried out on Liege. About four hours. Very tiring and cold, back about 10pm.[14]

Lieutenant Leslie George Semple, 207 Squadron RAF

The news of the impending armistice had not filtered through to all units: On the evening of the 10 November the Squadron was thrown into a state of excitement by loud cheers and a pyrotechnic display of Very's lights and rockets, which were sent up in great profusion. All asked 'was it the end', but nothing definite could be learned.[15]

Lieutenant Cyril Gordon Burge, 100 Squadron RAF

The last night of the war was a busy one for the Handley Page crews. Thirty-one aircraft in total were airborne that night, representing all eight Handley Page squadrons on the Western Front, although of those twenty-six aircraft actually attacked their target. Five 58 Squadron Handley Pages bombed Louvain railway junction as did seven from 214 Squadron (one of them crewed entirely by Americans), but three aircraft from 97 Squadron all had their raids aborted. Two 100 Squadron Handley Pages were airborne, one with a half load of 112-lb bombs dropped on Lillingen aerodrome with no results seen, and the other solely loaded with twelve boxes of Baby Incendiaries, which were all dropped on Frescaty aerodrome starting a large fire. One of the two Handley Pages from 216 Squadron taking part in raids that night dropped fourteen 112-lb bombs on Frescaty aerodrome too as did a Handley Page from 215 Squadron, the other 216 Squadron aircraft dropping fourteen 112-lb bombs on Metz.

Two other 216 Squadron Handley Pages were airborne, but had to return. No. 207 Squadron had all available crews flying, but this amounted to just six aircraft as all the other pilots were ill or were new and not ready for operational duties yet. The other 215 Squadron Handley Page bombed Morhange. In all, an astounding total weight of 51,011 lbs of bombs were dropped (a single 550-lb, 101 of the hand-dropped Cooper bombs, and the rest 112-lb bombs) and 7,020 individual Baby incendiaries in twenty-six cases.

A number of crews later believed they were the last ones to bomb Germany, including Lieutenant Semple who was told so, although it would be impossible to determine for certain. The last Handley Page to land was a 58 Squadron machine, landing thirty-five minutes before midnight:

Raid on Namur. Owing to dud engines I was late in starting and consequently bombed one and a half hours after everybody else. Very good shooting obtained, but hundreds of flaming onions all around me. Gave my observer, Boshier, control on the way home. He was quite good. Went to bed about 11pm at 1am news came per Wireless that the armistice had been signed and cessation of hostilities from 11am today. Beautiful news. Lighted a tin of petrol and we kicked it all round the camp. This morning we all had a jolly good drink. Sent somebody to Rouen to buy as much as possible. Just recently we have been stunting quite a lot around the mess so went up today and had a jolly good flip. Have discovered that I was the last pilot to drop bombs on enemy territory during this war. Very good. Well we drove into Amiens tonight, and had dinner and lots of champagne. Very nice too, after which we went to a café round the corner—had some more. We had made arrangements to meet at 11pm. Well all except two turned up and so we drove round the town firing Vereys lights, broke into a house where we thought they were and finally discovered. Jolly fine peace celebrations. Arrived back at camp at 2.30am with a few souvenirs.[16]

Lieutenant Leslie George Semple, 207 Squadron RAF

The next day, all squadrons were instructed that, without permission of Brigade Headquarters, they were not to fly, and later news of the Armistice at 11.00 was received too. The plans made for dropping saboteurs on German aerodromes and moving aircraft closer to Prague would not materialise. While many celebrated, some received the news of the Armistice with disappointment, especially those at 166 Squadron based at Bircham Newton back in Britain, who were equipped with a new type of Handley Page: the V/1500.

12

Super Handley Page

I promise you I'll get there, but I doubt whether you'll ever see me again.

Major Cecil Hill Darley, 166 Squadron Royal Air Force, November 1918

In the spring of 1917, the Air Board issued two specifications for new night bombers, with a range of over 500 miles each. The first specification was for a small design, carrying a useful load (including arms and ammunition, not just bombs) of 500 lbs at 115 mph, which resulted in Geoffrey de Havilland creating the Airco DH10 'Amiens' bomber; a single example of this aircraft took part in a daytime raid on 10 November 1918 with 104 Squadron and served post-war on the North West Frontier, including involvement in the Third Anglo-Afghan War. The second designation was for a large aircraft carrying a load of 3,000 lbs and a speed of 100 mph. Progress was almost halted after a meeting of Army members of the Air Board on 23 June 1917, which proposed a ban on new orders of night bombers. This not surprising given as at that point the Handley Pages were all operated by the RNAS and the emphasis for the RFC was daylight aerial operations. This was overturned shortly after by the Controller of the Technical Department of the Air Board, Major J. Buchanan, and supported by Trenchard.

The timing was perfect for Handley Pages as they had already been working on a larger version of the Type Os, designed to be twice as heavy and able to lift twice as much useful weight as the O/400, powered by two Rolls-Royce 600-hp Condor Engines. With the issuing of the specification, Handley Page were granted an order for three prototypes in August 1917. As well as the specifications for a useful weight carrying capacity of 3,000 lbs and a speed of 100 mph, other critieria that had to be matched were room for three crew members and internal bomb racks for twenty-eight 112-lb bombs, a dozen more than that on the O/100 and O/400s. Work started on what was to be known as the Type V in October 1917 at the Harland & Wolff works in Belfast. This unusual choice of sub-contractor, who were more used to building equipment of war designed to float not fly, was chosen as they had better facilities than at Cricklewood, and it also aided in the secrecy around the new design. Rolls-Royce delayed the production of the new Condor engines to focus on the Eagle VIIIs, so the choice was made to use four of these instead—these were mounted back to back in pairs in a single nacelle, so that two engines were tractors and two were pushers. Fortunately, this had been tried with a Handley Page O/100 at Farnborough in October 1917 with four Hispano Suiza 200-hp engines, with the information proving very useful for the Handley Page designers. The aircraft was only slightly longer than the Type Os, but had wider, equal-span wings of 126 feet. The crew positions were mostly the same as on the Type Os, but with the addition of a tail gunner position at the extreme rear of the fuselage, as well as the mid-fuselage open position. The tail gunner position, the first on a British aircraft, was accessed by a narrow walkway inside the fuselage.

Before any of the prototypes were completed, an order was placed for twenty Type Vs on 27 January 1918, followed by twenty more on 13 March. The first batch of twenty was made with Harland & Wolff, but the other batch was with William Beardmore, to be fitted with BHP Atlantic 500-hp engines, both in the hope that the BHP engines would be an improvement on the Rolls-Royce Eagle VIII and in case production was delayed at Harland & Wolff. By the time, the first prototype (B9466) was nearing completion, the design was known as the V/1500 in reference to the total horsepower provided by the four Rolls-Royce Eagle VIII 375-hp engines. The original plan was for the testing to take place in March at 16 Aircraft Acceptance Park at Crumlin (later known as RAF Aldergrove), but the aircraft was instead sent, disassembled, to Cricklewood, all parts arriving by 12 April and the first flight made on 22 May. Captain V. E. G. Busby of RAF Martlesham Heath took the V/1500 to the same height as that achieved by the Wright Brothers' aeroplane on that fateful day in 1903—a mere 10 feet above the ground. More adventurous flights were taken involving more passengers (only one person, by the name of Hathaway, went up on the first flight with Busby) and heavier loads.

As was to be expected, and intended, the flights showed up minor design faults, which could be ironed out and fed back to the production line. Unfortunately, just over two weeks after the first flight on 8 June, Captain Busby took off with four passengers, when all four engines cut out in a catastrophic failure while climbing at 1,000 feet and banking to the port side over Golders Green. The aircraft stalled then spun into the ground, hitting nose first, instantly killing three of those on-board, including Busby. A staff member of Harland & Wolff, G. A. Cooper, was pulled out of the wreckage swiftly, but died from severe head injuries not long after. Colonel Alec Ogilvie was in the tail gunner's position and got away with a broken arm. What was left of the aircraft was destroyed by fire, and the cause of the accident was never discovered. It was HP B9463's thirteenth flight.

Yet the same day a further ten V/1500 aircraft were ordered via the Alliance Aircraft Company, which were eventually built in component form and built by Handley Page at Cricklewood. Five further aircraft (including the two other prototypes) had now been finished in component form at Belfast and shipped to Cricklewood for completion. Following the tragic end to HP B9463, the next V/1500 to fly was the second prototype (HP B9464) that took off from Cricklewood on 3 August, moving to RAF Martlesham Heath for further trials, resulting in some modifications, until it was returned to Cricklewood in September. Following the appearance of issues with the tail, wind tunnel investigations upon its return to Cricklewood meant that important changes had to be made to the design, resulting in a new contractor and renumbering of the remaining prototypes. Of the Scottish-built V/1500s, the first was completed in September, but not delivered until later October, with the engines now Rolls-Royce Eagle VIIIs as standard on all V/1500s. The first delivery of a V/1500 to an RAF Squadron was made in November, when Beardmore-built E8287 was received at RAF Bircham Newton, Norfolk to 166 Squadron, with two others arriving, both built by the Alliance Aircraft Company and completed at Cricklewood on 5 November. No. 166 Squadron was formed on 13 June 1918 at RAF Bircham Newton, to be equipped with what became known as the 'Super Handleys', for long-distance raids into Germany and German-held territory.

The Squadron was part of 27 Group, Royal Air Force, under the command of Lieutenant-Colonel R. H. Mulock that was formed for the specific purpose of the raids 166 Squadron and others were to undertake, later moving to airfields in Europe if possible. The main objectives were large steel-producing areas, but civilian centres were also to be considered for attack. The aircrews were specially chosen, many from FE2b night-bombing squadrons, and after being selected were put on a special course at the School of Navigation in Andover. Initially, FE2bs were used for training before the V/1500s arrived, but when they did the pressure was ramped up by Trenchard to raid Berlin as soon as possible. Lieutenant-Colonel Mulock decided that although the crews picked had already gained night-bombing experience, training them on how to fly and operate the Handley Pages would add further delay, which they could not afford. To this end, Mulock asked two Handley-Page former crew members,

Major F. T. Digby and Major C. H. Darley who were to fly a V/1500 each, to select crews from O/400 Squadrons who they knew. Most of the men came from 214 and 216 Squadron, although one, Sergeant P. J. Adkins DSM DFM, was from 100 Squadron and was part of the same crew (Major Digby's) as Captain S. N. Pike DFC who came from RAF Andover. The V/1500s certainly had the range to reach Berlin, but not to return back to England. The solution was to head for Czechoslovakia or other neutral country and land there in the highly likely case of not having enough fuel to make a return to England or Allied territory a possibility.

The mechanics worked constantly to keep the machines in a high state of readiness, and on 9 November two aircraft were ready to go and loaded with 1,000 lbs of bombs each. The raid was then postponed for forty-eight hours, owing to the bad state of the weather. The opportunity was taken to replace all four engines on each aircraft with new ones. On 11 November the crews were ready and briefed on the raid. Meanwhile, the two V/1500s sat awaiting their crews ready to roll down the runway, lumber into the air, and head to Berlin. Once they left the ground there would be no way for anyone to effectively contact them to stop or change their plans. Fortunately, news of the Armistice came to the men during the briefing and they were stood down. If the news came a little later it could have been too late and the V/1500s could have been *en route* to Berlin and unleashed their deadly cargo down onto the city without knowledge of the surrender. The news of the Armistice was met with disappointment—a great deal of planning had gone into the raid, and the crews remarked upon the perfect moon on the 11 November and the cloudless night sky, which followed for several days. However, the surrender only meant a cessation of hostilities, not the end of the war, which would come about on the signing of the Treaty of Versailles, 28 June 1919. As a result, 166 Squadron continued to be on readiness in case of a return to hostilities, and 27 Group continued to gear up for the original plan to raid Germany with long-range heavy bombers. A second V/1500 unit, 167 Squadron was also created at RAF Bircham Newton on 18 November. The next day, the formerly secret plan for the Super Handley Pages to raid Berlin was announced to the world in the *Daily News*:

WHAT BERLIN MISSED.
British Bombing Squadron Ready For Flight.
Details of the British preparations for the bombing of Berlin, now disclosed, show how narrowly the German capital escaped punishment.

When the German request for an armistice was made preparations for the feat were already complete. A squadron of super-bombing planes was ready at a certain point on the East Coast was awaiting orders to leave. Each machine was loaded with two tons of bombs, and crews of men selected form many keenly competitive volunteers were standing by in readiness. It was to be a purely British attempt from British soil to show what British machines could do.

The crews held themselves in readiness to leave during the 72 hours' grace allowed for the signing of the armistice terms, and had it not been signed the British bombing squadron would have set out that night for Berlin. Aeronautical experts who know what the machines are capable of believe they would have accomplished their object.

Daily News, 19 December 1918

Had the war continued, the plan was for V/1500s to be based near Prague with Berlin as the main objective following the Austrian surrender on 4 November. As it happened, the V/1500 would only be used in action once. In December 1918, V/1500 J1936 set off for India, specially chosen for a flight out there, where it may have been of use on the North-Western Frontier. The pilot, Captain Archibald S. C. MacLaren MC AFC who had risen through the ranks from Air Mechanic upwards, named the aircraft *Old Carthusian*. *Old Carthusian* finally reached Karachi in January 1919, over a month since leaving Martlesham Heath and having to deal with unplanned stops in various countries including getting stuck in a muddy field in Sicily, and severely upsetting a large number of horses taking part in an inspection of cavalry after force landing alongside in Persia. Upon arrival at Karachi the aircraft had new engines fitted, and with the co-pilot Captain Robert Halley DFC stepping up as pilot as MacLaren went home, the planned destination of Delhi was reached on 23 February. It was used for joy rides for various local VIPs then flown to Lahore and dismantled, being of no further use.

At Lahore, Handley Page O/400 C9700 was also in storage, dismantled, until it was re-erected and flown to Risalpur in May for use in a bombing raid on Kabul, following the start of the Third Anglo-Afghan War on 6 May. When C9700 arrived on 13 May, it was not there long until a dust storm overturned and destroyed it, and thoughts turned to the V/1500 *Old Carthusian*. Although a lot bigger than the O/400 originally intended, *Old Carthusian* did not have any bomb racks fitted as they had been removed before leaving England. Four single racks for 112-lb bombs were fitted from BE2c aircraft and fitted to the lower wings, and sixteen 25-lb Cooper bombs were kept in the mid-fuselage cockpit to be dropped by hand, giving it a much smaller bomb load than even the O/400 would have had, let alone what *Old Carthusian* should have had. Despite this, the raid went ahead on 24 May and Kabul was bombed at an altitude of just a few hundred feet before returning to Risalpur. Despite the small weight of bombs, four hit the Amanullah's palace, narrowly missing killing the ruler himself and one of the bombs reportedly demolishing a wall of his personal harem. The six hour raid earned Captain Robert Halley a bar to his DFC and severely impressed the Afghans, resulting in an Armistice on the 3 June and peace signed on the 8 August. *Old Carthusian* was found to have termite damage to the airframe and so grounded, the fuselage becoming an office at Risalpur.

Although 160 production V/1500s had been ordered, after the Armistice 100 of these were cancelled, the other sixty (as well as three prototypes) being completed and delivered—a number of them as complete sets of spare parts.

An order for a further fifty V/1500s, to be powered by four Napier Lion engines, was expected, but changed to the Vickers Vimy, which seemed a more useful type, as well as being more economical. However, a single aircraft was ordered for trials use, to replace the aircraft being used for the attempted trans-Atlantic crossing. The new aircraft was actually built using spare parts at Aldergrove, first flying in September 1919 and, after being ferried to Hawkinge, was used at Martlesham Heath for ten months. However, the trials to push the design to the limit never happened and it was scrapped in June 1921.

The spectacular sight of three V/1500s airborne at once was a treat for attendees at the RAF Tournament at Hendon on 3 July 1920, Miss Sylvia Boden parachuting out of the tail of one of them. On take-off the aircraft flew directly above the Royal Box, causing King George V to complain to Trenchard, who in turn gave Lieutenant Colonel Sholto Douglas, flying at the head of the trio, a thorough telling-off.

HP V/1500 F7139 was sent on a goodwill tour of Spain, leaving Manston on 6 May 1919. Bad weather made the experience unpleasant, disrupting the tour with heavy rain being experienced, which was enough to remove the fabric of the propellers on the starboard side. On another flight a storm was so severe the aircraft could not land at San Sebastian, having to return to Biarritz and land on the beach there. A fortnight was spent at Cuatros Vientos doing local flights based out of there, including for King Alfonso XIII of Spain. On the return flight back to Britain on 29 May, heavy rain damaged the aircraft—not just the propeller blades this time, but the engines themselves. Lieutenant Kilburn was co-pilot on the tour and described what happened:

> Attempted to return to England in non-stop flight. Just got through a pass in the Guadarrama Mountains by about 150 feet below from wingtip to mountain sides. Just as we cleared the pass the exhaust manifold again

came off and hung on by a wire, causing considerable agitation owing to the awful country we were going over. After a length at clearing the Pyrenees we are very tickled, thinking it is all clear sailing for home. When opposite Biarritz over the Bay of Biscay the rear starboard propeller came right off jarring the whole machine terribly and taking two of the engine struts with it also making great gashes in the wings. Machine more or less out of control, landing attempt on the same piece of shore as landed on before but owing to not being able to keep the machine straight it sunk on into the sea. We are taken off by boats. Lost camera and a lot of kit and also all the notes I took on the trip. Major Darley and Lt Murray lost everything. [1]

Lieutenant Anthony Conning Kilburn, 267 Squadron RAF

The aircraft went 30 yards into the sea and the tide broke the aircraft up, but the engines were later saved. Kilburn had had enough of aviation for now; the flight was the final one entered in his log book, and at the end of it he finished with; 'Demobbed. No more flying for this child!!' [2]

After the war, flyers turned their eyes to the *Daily Mail's* £10,000 prize for the first non-stop crossing of the Atlantic by air. Handley Page were loaned, for no charge, V/1500 F7140 by the Air Ministry to take part in the competition (full circle for Handley Page as the Type L was being built as a competitor for this when war broke out in 1914). Originally it was planned to use Lieutenant Colonel Raymond Collishaw, the famous Royal Naval Air Service ace, however, despite expecting to leave the Royal Air Force shortly, he was sent to Russia to fight against the Bolsheviks. Former commanding officer of the Handley Page equipped 214 Squadron Major Herbert Brackley was chosen as replacement, and work started in early April 1919 with Brackley and his team at Cricklewood to modify the V/1500 to give it the best chance of crossing the Atlantic. An enormous 2,000-gallon petrol tank was designed by Volkert and placed in the fuselage, enough for thirty hours of flight, and it was estimated the trans-Atlantic crossing would use 1,700 gallons, so it had plenty of reserve. In case of emergency, three air bags were fitted to the rear of the fuel tank to aid flotation in case the aircraft had to ditch. By 14 April, Brackley was happy with the aircraft and the aircraft was taken apart, put in crates and shipped to St John's, Canada, hot on the heels of the Sopwith Atlantic competitor, a large single-engine biplane that had travelled on the same vessel on the previous voyage. On arrival, the team leased land at Harbour Grace, Newfoundland, and the aircraft was erected and tested, including fitting of the Wireless Transmitter that was so powerful it could contact Handley Page back at Cricklewood. While the aircraft was being erected, the Sopwith Atlantic and its two-man crew had made their attempt on 18 May. Unfortunately for the crew, the engine overheated and it had to ditch on the 19th, fortunately after finding a Danish ship to ditch near and rescue the crew.

The V/1500 first flew on 8 June with a five-hour test flight conducted a week later, but was cut short with engine issues. Fortunately new radiators were already *en route*, arriving shortly after, so that another flight (this time satisfactory) was conducted on the 18 June. Unfortunately it was too late; despite arriving last, the Vickers Vimy team piloted by Jack Alcock (who had been captured by the Turks when his O/100 was shot down in an attempt on Constantinople in 1917) and Arthur Whitten-Brown had left Newfoundland on 14 June and arrived the next day in Ireland. The crew were to fly the aircraft on a non-stop 1,000-mile flight to New York instead with the intention of meeting the British airship R34 that was making the first east to west crossing of the Atlantic by air. Two hours into the flight the engines again had issues with overheating and oil leaking—two members of the crew even climbed along the wings to the engines to try and fix them several times. With the engine power reduced, as day broke Brackley landed the aircraft on a racecourse in Parrsboro, Nova Scotia, but obstacles collapsed one wheel and the aircraft tipped onto its front, crushing the nose. Replacement parts were sent out by ship and then onwards by rail, the aircraft flying again in October, eventually reaching New York on 13 October.

While in New York, the aircraft made a number of local demonstration flights and on 14 November, undertook a joint demonstration with the American Express Company to transport a ton of cargo including newspapers and urgent mail to Chicago. While on the second leg of the journey, a burst water pipe forced a landing in Pennsylvania, resuming the journey the next day, but landing by mistake at a racecourse in Cleveland instead of the Glenn Martin factory that was their intended destination. While taxiing on the ground, the wing tips on both sides were ripped off as the aircraft went between two stands, which resulted in F7140s career ending, the crew returning back home.

Back in Britain, 166 and 167 Squadrons had been disbanded in late May 1919, although a new V/1500 Squadron was formed again at RAF Bircham Newton less than a month later on 15 June, using some aircraft from the previous squadrons and also new ones. The First International Air Transport Exhibition at Amsterdam held in July and August 1919 was attended by a 274 Squadron V/1500, which was lent to Handley Page for the duration. On landing at Amsterdam, the aerodrome was on land reclaimed from the sea, and together with heavy rainfall resulted in a very wet surface. The aircraft sank up to the axles, and after being jacked up, wooden sleepers had to be laid to tow the aircraft to the exhibition hall. The sheer size of the aircraft in the hall, dwarfing anything else there by far, meant one wing had to be folded while on display.

With the coming peace there was little use for the V/1500—the Airco DH10 and Vickers Vimy bombers fulfilled the need for large bombers, so the large and expensive V/1500 had to justify its existence. No. 274 Squadron was tasked with trying to find such a role, with coastal reconnaissance and long-range transport explored as possible uses. It could not prove that it was suitable for these niches in a satisfactory way so was disbanded in January 1920. There were no civilian buyers for the V/1500 either, despite the attendance at the International Air Transport Exhibition. There were hopes in late 1920 that the military would purchase it as the RAF was in the market for a long-range bomber and also a troop carrier, but these contracts were won by the smaller and more economical Vickers Virginia and Vickers Victoria. The V/1500 was just too big to be of use in the post-war world, and civilian aviation was not lucrative enough to justify such a large aeroplane. It was a number of years, and a second global conflict, until the RAF would have a four-engine bomber again.

13

Paralysers in Peacetime

After the celebrations that came with the Armistice, the question of 'what was going to happen now?' was what everyone wanted to know. The men of the eight Handley Page squadrons on the Western Front naturally were most inclined to get home, but demobilisation would take time. Back home, the contracts for aircraft were mostly all cancelled, very few still being built. For the Royal Air Force, it was important now to prove itself, to show that it had a future and was not just a wartime expedient that would be closed down. Together with other RAF bombing aircraft, the Handley Page O/400 could be put to use immediately to transport passengers and mail rapidly, especially desirable across the English Channel. The 86th Communication Wing was set up at Hendon in December 1918 for London to Paris flights for officials who were involved in the Treaty of Versailles. Eight O/400s were allocated to the unit, two or three of them finished in aluminium-coloured dope and given the prefix HMAL (His Majesty's Air Liner).

HMAL *Great Britain* was fairly Spartan with eight leather seats facing the port side of the aircraft from the inside (although there were small square windows to see out of), and four on the other side. HMAL *Silver Star* had a relatively luxurious cabin with six seats surrounding a round table in the centre, with large windows in the side with curtains. The third 'possible' silver Handley Page interior is not described, but was likely the same as HMAL *Great Britain*, as were the other Handley Pages of 86th Wing, which retained the late-war Nivo finish. The 86th Wing was split into 1 (Communication) Squadron at Kenley and 2 (Communication) Squadron in Paris in May 1919—the Handley Pages going to 2 (Communication) Squadron. The units were disbanded in October 1919 after a decline in use following the signing of the Treaty.

In Britain, the Handley Pages found use as aerial test beds and a number used at Biggin Hill and Andover were fitted with various different types of wireless equipment. One Andover-based Handley Page O/400, F3570, was painted with 'LAST DAYS' in bold white letters on the fuselage, running behind the main planes and towards the tail. The Handley Page and crew conducted a tour of Britain in April 1919, heading to the coast via Waddington then flying anti-clockwise around the country via Aberdeen, Inverness, Mull of Kintyre and Belfast (although had to land on the Harland & Wolff shipyard's wharf as fog covered Aldergrove), then to Dublin, Pembroke (where they rested the night), Bodmin, Plymouth, Bournemouth, and then back to Andover, covering 1,600 miles in thirty hours of flight time across four days.

The Royal Aircraft Establishment at Farnborough also used Handley Pages for research purposes, and small numbers of them could be found at RAF bases around the country, mostly for carrying passengers and cargo. As late as July 1922, despite the availability of more modern types, two were fitted with eight 9-lb practice bombs, which were dropped on the old pre-dreadnought HMS *Agamemnon* that had been converted into a radio-controlled target vessel and was located in the Firth of Forth. Just one of the eight bombs hit the target.

No. 216 Squadron found themselves ordered to move to Quilen aerodrome just two days after the Armistice, leaving on the 15 November by road and the aircraft departing the next day. Although this placed them closer to other RAF units there was very little to do, and the aerodrome found no favour with the squadron, commenting that 'the mud [was] worse, if possible, than that experienced at Ochey'. A use was found for two Handley Pages, which were sent to Rely aerodrome and used to return German pilots who had delivered aeroplanes to the British under the terms of the Armistice. On 12 December, 216 Squadron moved to Marquise aerodrome close to Boulogne, and the aircraft used to transport mail to Cologne, Valenciennes, and Namur. Again, life was uncomfortable for the men staying there and it would take some time until a decent standard of living could be attained. Soft ground resulted in aircraft becoming stuck in the mud, the proximity of a quarry threw stones in the original camp every time blasting was done, and lack of buildings meant the motor transport had to be left outside, tents and huts having to be scrounged. For the mail work, the bomb cells of the Handley Pages were removed from the aircraft and fitted with dropping gear for general post office baskets, fitted with parachutes, the release gear fitted in the rear cockpit. Messenger pigeons were used to communicate to the squadron from Cologne, but not with any particular success—blamed on the number of hawks in the area. Aerial hostilities were clearly not confined to men and their machines.

Bad weather towards the end of the year gave the men plenty of time to dwell on demobilisation. Unsurprisingly, the men soon became fed up of this and rued the fact that they were now aerial postmen—a song written towards the end of the year showing their frustration, one verse in particular showing how they almost seemed to miss the war:

> *The boys are often thinking of when they were Naval 'A'*
> *It seems so remote when the liberty boat*
> *Went every week as a matter of rote*
> *But that was long ago, Boys, before hostilities ceased*
> *When men were kept fit for doing their bit*
> *To enable the Pilots to get in a hit,*
> *Oh! When shall we be released?*[1]

Other squadrons were used for similar work, as well as aiding the Army of Occupation in Germany. No. 97 Squadron ceased to be a Handley Page Squadron when it handed them in for Airco DH10 bombers in April 1919, taking them to India. Nos 115 and 215 Squadrons were disbanded in October 1919. No. 207 Squadron diminished in size, until it was little more than a name, the aircraft and equipment going to 100 Squadron, which itself was disbanded eleven days after 207 Squadron—on 20 January and 31 January 1920 respectively.

The three remaining Handley Page squadrons—58, 214 and 216—received orders in the spring of 1919 to move to Egypt. Despite the success of Colonel T. E. Lawrence in turning the Arabs against the Turks, promises made to the Arabs had not been kept, threatening to turn into a large-scale war. While smaller aircraft from squadrons also being sent to Egypt were simply packed in crates and shipped, the decision was made to fly the Handley Pages there on grounds of difficulty of packing them and (surprisingly, given what happened) cost. The lengthy journey did not go well at all; eighteen Handley Pages were lost through crashes, etc., and eight men were killed. One of the four 58 Squadron Handley Pages wrecked on the journey was carrying Colonel T. E. Lawrence. While landing at Centocelle aerodrome near Rome, the pilot Lieutenant Prince found he did not have enough runway to stop and so opened up the throttles to take off again, but at just 20 feet above the ground the starboard wing hit a tree, turning the aircraft onto its back and crashing. Lieutenant Prince was killed, co-pilot Lieutenant Spratt dying a few hours later. Lawrence suffered broken ribs and collar bone, which resulted in several weeks of hospitalisation. Two air mechanics had just slight injuries. Fifty-one Handley Pages in total were sent, and this includes a number that were replacements for those crashed. The ones that did arrive needed a lot of work on arrival before they could be used again. The availability of the new Vickers Vimy resulted in 58 Squadron being the first squadron to receive this, renumbering as 70 Squadron on 1 February 1920 and being fully equipped with them by April. No. 214 Squadron was disbanded in February 1920, the aircraft going to 216 Squadron, which when 70 Squadron received the full complement of Vimys resulted in 216 Squadron being the only Handley Page O/400 squadron in the RAF. The work done by 216 Squadron was not much different to that done immediately after the war—transporting mail and cargo around the Middle East—but brief duties of escorting trains and used as a show of force livened things up occasionally. A few times smoke bombs were dropped over riots, which soon broke them up. A crash in April 1920 killed four men when O/400 F302 flipped onto its back, killing all on board. Airco DH10s started to replace the Handley Page O/400s of 216 Squadron from August 1920, the O/400s still finding use in a demonstration to the Army in September 1920 when a 2.75-inch mountain gun, together with its crew and ninety-eight rounds of ammunition, were transported by two Handley Pages to prove the use of transport aircraft to the army. No. 216 Squadron finally stopped using the O/400 in October 1921, the squadron now fully equipped with the Airco DH10.

Despite the large size of the Handley Page bombers, they were just too large for the peacetime RAF and were not kept on for home-based squadrons either. The last surviving Handley Page O/400 was most likely F5431. This was one of the aircraft used by the Royal Aircraft Establishment and had crashed in 1923 during tests, but was repaired and last mentioned as at RAF Spittlegate in May 1925. It was not to be the end of Handley Page bombers in RAF service though. Whilst the last of the Handley Page O/400s were in the Middle East, development back at Handley Page Limited in Cricklewood was taking place on a new bomber based on the civilian Handley Page W8. The Handley Page Hyderabad, a large twin-engine bomber, was produced to replace the disappointing single-engine Avro Aldershot, which equipped 99 Squadron post-war. Fitted with two Napier Lion engines, the Hyderabad like the Type Os and Vs had a Scarff ring in the nose and a ventral gun position, and also had a Scarff ring for the mid-upper gun position. It was a popular aircraft and after the initial order of fifteen, eight more were ordered for 99 Squadron in June 1927, as were eleven to equip the new 10 Squadron, these nineteen newer aircraft to be a new variant called the Hinaidi. Another batch of Hinaidis was ordered a year later, and a transport version the Handley Page Clive was also ordered. The Handley Page Heyford—again a large twin-engine bomber, but with modern features and a fuselage that was joined to the upper wing—appeared in the 1930s, and the Handley Page Hampden and Hereford monoplane bombers entered service before the Second World War broke out. The Hampden became the first Handley Page bomber to drop bombs on Berlin, on the night of 25–26 August 1940, some twenty-eight years after Frederick Handley Page had originally built an aircraft to do so. The four-engine Handley Page Halifax entered service during the war and gave excellent service, and after the war came the biggest Handley Page bomber of all, the jet powered swept-wing Victor. Together with the Avro Vulcan and Vickers Valiant, the Handley Page Victor was one of the three 'V bombers' providing Britain's main nuclear deterrent until Polaris nuclear missiles, launched from submarines, took over this role in 1969. Thankfully the chance to use the deterrent never came about, and the Victor never saw active service as a bomber, although came close (albeit using conventional bombs) during the Borneo conflict in the 1960s. The Victor continued on in a new role as an in-flight refuelling aircraft, enabling the Avro Vulcan bombers to fly vast distances across water to bomb the Argentinian invaders of the Falkland Islands in 1982 and then again supporting RAF strike aircraft during the Gulf War following the invasion of Kuwait by Iraq in 1991.

14

From Bombs to Passengers

While the war was still raging, George Holt Thomas of Airco at Hendon was considering the post-war world and registered a subsidiary company, Aircraft Transport & Travel Limited. Although they did not plan to operate in the immediate future (particularly as they could not even if desired—the Defence of the Realm Act banned flying for civilian organisations such as AT&T) it was a clear sign to other companies that if they wanted to continue after the end of the war (as government contracts could certainly not expect to keep them going in peacetime, especially with a surplus of aircraft) they would have to hit the ground running and be ready to adapt to the new market in whatever form it would take. The Civil Aerial Transport Committee was set up in 1917 to discuss what the needs of civil aviation would be when the situation allowed.

At the time it was set up in May 1917, it was estimated the war would last at least another two years, so when the Armistice was signed in November 1918 it rather took them by surprise and the plans had not been fully set up. Frederick Handley Page saw an opportunity to convert the roomy box fuselage of the Handley Pages into an airline—Aircraft Transport & Travel Limited had already declared they would use smaller, single-engine aircraft with room for just a few passengers. In the event these were derivatives of the Airco DH4 and DH9s, fitted with a 'hump' for the passengers as otherwise they would be in the open air, so Handley Page would either have to find another potential customer, or start his own airline. Fortunately for Handley Page, the end of the war meant that he didn't even have to scour the surplus fleet of aircraft; there were already a number of Handley Page O/400s at Cricklewood that had not been delivered, but had been paid for.

The government was more than happy for Handley Page Limited to buy them back off the government (at a reduced price) and they set to converting them into being useable for passenger transport. Handley

Page's eye for publicity ensured his giant aircraft, a favourite of the papers, were kept in the public eye even before a civilian air transport company was permitted to operate:

> On November 15th, 1918, a world's record was created for the largest number of passengers ever carried in an aeroplane, when Clifford B. Prodger, an American pilot, took a Handley Page four-engine super giant biplane with 40 passengers on board (in addition to himself) for a cruise over London at a height of 6,500 ft. In addition to this load, petrol was carried for a six hours' flight so that these 40 passengers could easily have been carried across the Channel to Paris had circumstances permitted.
>
> *Flight Magazine*, 21 November 1918

It was a misty day, and it was already getting dark as the Handley Page V/1500 F7136 (which had only been completed that very afternoon and not yet flown) took off, which meant that flares had to be lit on the aerodrome to help the pilot get down again safely, but as a stunt to show the intentions of Handley Page it worked:

> This flight, as Mr. Handley Page observes, marks a new era in aviation, as it is the first trip made with such a large number of people on board and sufficient petrol for a continuous flight. A large number of passengers will reduce the cost of aeroplane transport to a point where the average traveller desirous of saving time will pay the aerial omnibus fare when he might have objected to paying the cost of a special car.
>
> *Flight Magazine*, 21 November 1918

After the formation of the Department of Civil Aviation on 12 February 1919, the Air Navigation Act was given royal assent later that month and civil flying could start again on 1 May 1919. Frederick Handley Page wasted no time in displaying the fuselage of an O/400 fitted out with lounge chairs for sixteen passengers, uncovered on one side, in Selfridge's department store on Oxford Street, London. Not long later, the formation of Handley Page Transport who would use civilianised O/400s, such as that displayed for transporting passengers, mail, and cargo, was announced at a special luncheon given by Handley Page. Handley Page Transport would start with flying from London to Paris, but as it became more popular it would then go on to fly further—Marseilles, Turin, Rome, and as far as Brindisi, from where passengers and urgent mail and cargo could meet sea liners that would take them on to Port Said, and then via the Suez Canal to India. Plans were even made for a seaplane version of the O/400, but this came to nothing. As good as the O/400 was in terms of suitability for a new role in carrying passengers and cargo, it could be improved. Work on a new type, the O/700, started after Handley Page gained a contract for six twin engine aircraft able to carry ten passengers and 1,800 lbs of cargo for the Chinese government, who aimed to use aircraft to improve transportation and commerce between distant areas, as well as use the new aircraft to move large wireless equipment for planned ground stations to aid communication.

The internal wire bracing of the fuselage was replaced with tubular struts that ran from the upper longerons of the fuselage to the centre of the floor inside the fuselage—not perfect, but it did make it possible for people to move inside the cabin. The height of the fuselage behind the cockpit was raised up so that it was the same height as the cabin towards the rear, rather than sloping downwards. At the front of the aircraft, the former gunner's position had a raised coaming, which protected the occupant from the slipstream and also aided in making the aircraft look less war-like. The fuel tanks were removed from the fuselage too, and placed behind the engines in a longer nacelle, similar to the arrangement of the O/100. The passengers sat in five rows of wicker seats, one on each side of the narrow aisle, with the entrance door at the rear and cellon panels as windows.

Together with Major Thomas Orde-Lees (who, after surviving the failed 'Endurance' Antarctic expedition 1914–16 led by Ernest Shackleton, had spent the rest of the war working on parachute designs), Handley Page converted four O/400s to carry newspapers between London and other British cities, the sixteen bomb cells designed for 112-lb bombs changed to six larger cells, the idea being that they could be dropped out of the aircraft using the Guardian Angel static line parachute system, the work completed by April 1919. This work was no doubt inspired by 216 Squadron's dropping of mail in Europe in the post-war period some months previously. The four converted Handley Page O/400s could not fly scheduled services until May and so were used to give thirty-minute joy rides to members of the public in late April, flying 800 passengers over four days, and were given the first Certificates of Airworthiness on 1 May (although, they were not allotted the now-familiar registrations of four letters with a G- prefix to designate Great Britain and so used their military serial numbers). On the same day, O/400 D8350 flew eleven passengers from Cricklewood to Manchester as the first British civilian post-war passenger flight, the flight taking three hours and forty minutes owing to headwinds. Similar flights to British cities were conducted, mostly subsidised by the newspapers they were delivering. Handley Page Limited's chief pilot, Lieutenant Colonel William Sholto Douglas MC described one such flight on 5 May 1919:

The *Daily Mail* people—who have always been staunch supporters of new ventures in the air—asked us to fly bundles of their newspaper from Manchester to Dundee and Aberdeen. It was a newspaper stunt, but it was an imaginative one, and we dropped the bundles on to local golf courses. The expert responsible for the use of the parachutes came along with me on our first trip, bringing with him his secretary, a young woman. On our arrival over Aberdeen he dropped by parachute on to the golf course, intending to visit some friends, and we watched with delight the comical spectacle he presented as he floated down to earth with a small suitcase in one hand and an umbrella in the other.

It had been planned that we should indulge in yet another publicity stunt when we arrived back over Manchester, and that the secretary should make an exhibition jump with a parachute over Alexandra Park. At the last moment the poor girl got cold feet, and she hesitated about jumping. While the arguments were going on behind me I had to circle around, but eventually she was helped to make up her own mind by what has been described as a wink from me to her helpers, and down she went.[1]

Lieutenant Colonel W. S. Douglas

The 'expert' was Major Orde-Lees and his secretary Miss Sylvia Boyden, who got over her nerves and became a regular parachutist, making a number of drops from Handley Pages. The first accident to occur to a Handley Page Transport Limited aircraft happened on 12 May, when an aircraft piloted by Major W. Shakespeare force landed near Carlisle while *en route* from Glasgow to Didsbury, between which the aircraft had been delivering newspapers for over a week. The engine trouble that caused the force landing was fixed before long; however, the field it landed on was too small and the aircraft crashed on take-off, injuring Shakespeare and Miss Boden who had several teeth knocked out and, with Shakespeare, spent several days in hospital—there was no injury to Orde Lees or the fitter and rigger in the rear of the aircraft. The aircraft was so badly damaged that Handley Page Limited only recovered the rear fuselage and tail, which formed the basis of a newly built Handley Page two months later

On Monday 25 August 1919, international civil flying could begin. Aircraft Transport & Travel Limited were first to depart in Airco DH4A G-EAJC at 09.10 for Paris Le Bourget, piloted by Lieutenant Bill Lawford and carrying a single passenger, George Stevenson-Reece of the *Evening Standard* together with newspapers, leather, grouse for the British Embassy, and tubs of Devonshire cream. Handley Page O/400 G-EAAE was next to leave at 09.30, after arriving from Cricklewood earlier to undergo customs clearance. Piloted by Major Leslie Foot whose passengers included a number of journalists, a mechanic, and a rigger. The next flight was not until the afternoon, when Captain Shakespeare returned from the continent in Handley Page O/700 G-EAAF, which was then flown by Lieutenant Colonel Sholto Douglas to Paris. The fourth and final passenger flight was in an Aircraft Transport & Travel Limited Airco DH16, which was the first scheduled daily international flight in the world. The second was Handley Page Transport's Cricklewood to Le Bourget service via Hounslow, which was inaugurated on 2 September. The larger aircraft operated by Handley Page Transport meant that they would offer a return from Cricklewood to Paris for £15 and 15s, compared to £21 for the faster service offered by Aircraft Transport & Travel; although, both were a lot more expensive than the £5 and 5s first-class return fare offered by the railways, which included the ferry.

The first Handley Page Transport service to Paris took off with seven passengers and 300 lbs of freight at 12.50 on 2 September, offering departures at midday from Hounslow on Tuesdays, Thursdays, and Saturdays with the return flights on Mondays, Wednesdays, and Fridays. With the hoped for popularity of this service, and others Handley Page Transport planned to implement, a further twelve O/400s in storage at Castle Bromwich were purchased from the Aircraft Disposals Board. A service to Brussels Everre was started on 23 September, and just six days later the route gained an added bonus of being used to carry mail following a railway strike that started the previous day. The strike ended after a week, but was able to keep this valuable traffic, and for a brief period helped Aircraft Transport & Travel Limited move a large backlog of mail for Paris. As well as moving passengers and mail, cargo had become just as important. The Handley Page Transport earned a reputation for safe carriage of awkward goods, such as antiques, and one particularly lucrative contract was the import of the latest Parisian fashion for Harrods of London.

The awkward necessity of having to fly via Hounslow was removed in January 1920 when it was agreed to provide customs facilities at Cricklewood (although this did not come into effect until February), and in the same month season tickets offering twelve single flights to/from Paris for £120 were offered. Still, more aircraft were required and Frederick Handley Page managed to acquire the entire stock of the Aircraft Disposals Board in March for just a tenth of their original cost, acquiring thirteen more O/400s for the fleet. Services to Amsterdam started in October. Despite the presence of other airlines on the same routes, by December 1920 over 4,000 passengers had been carried.

Handley Page Transport operated in a highly competitive arena. Aircraft Transport & Travel Limited operated Airco aircraft designed by Geoffrey de Havilland, all modified bomber aircraft to a greater or lesser extent.

Some of them still had open cockpits, the observer's position was simply enlarged to take two passengers. A slight improvement were the Airco DH4As that at least had a cabin, the passengers facing each other and with a hinged canopy above them. The larger Airco DH16 was able to carry four passengers and the similar in appearance, but larger (and with the pilot positioned to the rear of the passenger cabin) Airco DH18 could carry eight passengers and was the first non-military Airco aircraft. Two Airco DH10 bombers were used by Aircraft Transport & Travel Limited too, but only during the railway strikes for mail carrying. Instone Air Line started as a private airline for ferrying staff and mail for the Instone shipping company until deciding to offer the flights for passengers and cargo too. They used Airco DH4A and DH18 aircraft, but also the larger Airco DH34 single-engine aircraft and Vickers Vimy Commercial (which used a much larger fuselage than the bomber). The Daimler Air Way took over Aircraft Transport & Travel Limited when they closed, but operated new aircraft, mostly Airco DH34s with a single Airco DH18. These were just the major British airlines; French, Dutch, and Belgian airlines were all in competition too, and, in the form of the Farman Goliath, had an aircraft that could offer as many passenger seats as the Handley Page.

The first and only fatal accident to Handley Page Transport occurred on 14 December 1920. G-EAMA was taking off from Cricklewood to Paris, but the aircraft hit a tree and crashed into a residential back garden in Childs Hill. The pilot, mechanic, and two passengers, who were in the front cabin, were all killed. The three passengers towards the rear were able to escape, but the body of Eric Studd, who was in the nose cockpit, could not be found. It was assumed his body had been destroyed in the ensuing fire, but he was found alive in Paris the next day. He had been thrown clear of the aircraft in the crash, but lost consciousness; when he came to, and before help had arrived, all he could remember was that he had to go to Paris urgently and so travelled by train and ferry to his destination, also forgetting how he got there.

The French government were paying their airlines large subsidies, meaning they could undercut the competition, and it severely affected the British airlines. The Handley Page Transport service to Amsterdam ceased in October and the Paris passenger service was reduced down to three flights a week in November. By the end of 1920, Aircraft Transport & Travel stopped operating, Instone were operating a much-reduced service and in February 1921 Handley Page Transport were to stop too—signalling the end of all British commercial air travel on 28 February 1921. The British Government got involved as it became a matter of national pride, and so the Hambling Committee was set up by the Secretary of State for Air that would, temporarily, subsidise the airlines to the extent that they would make a guaranteed 10 per cent profit on the London to Paris route. Handley Page Transport started to fly this route again from 19 March 1921, offering the same fare as the French were. Instone started to fly to Paris on the 21st at the same rate, but the passenger numbers did not increase as quickly as hoped, and a number of Handley Page O/11s were scrapped and two O/10s shipped to India.

In May 1921, after a request from the Air Ministry, operations moved from Cricklewood to Croydon, which was to become London's main airport for most of the inter-war years. Operations continued with modified bombers, and it wasn't until September when the W8 was able to move to Croydon after flying again with a new pair of Napier Lions the previous month. After arrival at Croydon, where it was flown by a number of pilots who voiced their approval, it was approved to carry passengers by the Air Ministry's Civil Aviation department. Unfortunately, the approval was only for a maximum of twelve passengers, despite being originally fitted out for sixteen, but the W8 went into service from Croydon to Paris. The end of the year saw Handley Page O/10 G-EATM wrecked at Berck, France, on 30 December and written off. Another O/10 was lost on 22 January 1922 when G-EATN was flying from Croydon to Paris Le Bourget, and although the pilot believed, owing to an erroneous forecast, that the cloud would break as he descended to land, it did not, and the fog went all the way to the ground. There was no answer from the radio operator's attempts to contact the ground either, and the aircraft crashed at Senlis. The pilot was knocked out and trapped, but fortunately the two passengers were only shaken—although the radio operator had three broken ribs. The three others managed to get the pilot, McIntosh, out of the cockpit, but he was unable to walk for several months. Services to Amsterdam finally returned in May 1922

A few Handley Page Type O conversions could be found elsewhere. Including those sold to China, one operated in South America and one O/700 worked in South Africa, with adverts for Commando Brandy on the underside of wings and alongside the fuselage, later being shipped to India. A number of other Handley Pages were used in India for civilian use, including one bizarre-looking example for the Thakur Saheb of Morvi as a replacement for a previous Handley Page of his that crashed. This replacement was painted overall pink (apart from blue engine nacelles), with pink silk completely throughout the interior, and was nicknamed the *Pink Elephant.*

The use of an adapted bomber design was only ever going to be a temporary solution to providing an aircraft for civilian use, no matter how good the conversions from the original designs were. Development had started in February 1919 of the Handley Page Type W, a large airliner using the experience and designs of the Handley Page bombers, but for passenger use. The nose gunners' position was deleted and the pilot's cockpit moved lower down. The fuselage did not have any internal bracing and was longer and deeper than that of the converted bombers, and could carry sixteen passengers. The prototype first flew on 2 December 1919 and just two days later flew to Le Bourget, Paris, from Hounslow for the *VI-ème Exposition Internationale de Locomotion Aérienne*. Owing to the new Napier Lion radial engines, despite taking off forty minutes behind a Type O on the same route, it overtook it and landed ten minutes before it. The enormous W8 only had the Farman F60 Goliath for competition size-wise, and the W8 was much admired, not just for the size and stunning white finish, but the interior that boasted carpets, a toilet compartment, and opening windows for every passenger. Lack of available Napier Lions meant Handley Page had to continue to borrow the existing pair from the Air Ministry, and as such had to ask permission from them to fly it. When they did become available for sale, Handley Page Transport could not afford the price as it came when the effect of the French Government subsidies to their airlines was being felt by the British competition and a new version using Rolls-Royce Eagle VIII engines was designed, the Type W8b, and three of these were ordered. The three W8bs entered service in May 1922 and an order from the Belgian national airline SABENA came for two more, as well as the rights to build them in Belgium. In August 1923 a new service operating three times a week was inaugurated from London to Zurich, stopping at Paris and Basle *en route*—it was subsidised by the British and the Swiss Governments.

The Hambling Committee made a report in February 1922, which showed that despite the subsidies, British airlines were still losing money, and giving government subsidies to competing companies was not an ideal situation. The committee recommended a new, subsidised single airline bringing the existing major airlines together. After being agreed in December 1923, on 1 April 1924 Imperial Airways Limited came into existence, taking over Handley Page Transport, Instone, The Daimler Airway, and British Marine Air Navigation (formed in March 1923, BMAN operated Supermarine Sea Eagle flying boats from September 1923 between Southampton and St Peter Port, Guernsey). Like the Type O and Type V bombers, the experience working on these enormous aircraft and their use post-war gave Handley Page Limited a good foot forward in large aircraft design, despite the difficult atmosphere and limited market that aviation had in the immediate years following the First World War. The W8 was just the start of a number of purpose-built Handley Page airliners, perhaps the best known being the Handley Page HP42 and HP45 four-engine biplane airliners, introduced in 1931 by Imperial Airways, the HP45 for routes from London to Europe and the HP45 for long distance flights.

Epilogue

The story of the design, construction, and operational use of the Handley Page bombers in the First World War is a fascinating one. When design work and construction started in early 1915 no aircraft like it had been seen in Britain, and there was only one aircraft in the world to compare that was in operational use, and that was in Russia. The difficulty of the task that Frederick Handley Page and his staff had ahead of them cannot be underestimated, for such a small aircraft manufacturer to take on such a large job was a bold risk, but ultimately one that paid off. After a shaky start, including the German capture of one of the O/100s before they had even attempted their first raid (although this was in no way the fault of the aircraft) and a feeling of not being sure what to do with the type, it found itself at home on night-bombing raids on targets such as U-boat bases, aerodromes, and industrial targets. The Handley Page O/100 and the refined O/400 suffered as all British aircraft did at the time from the problems of an inadequate supply of suitable engines. The relatively small losses of aircrew—compared with the day bomber equivalents—meant that shortages of trained pilots and observers was not as major an issue as it could have been, and again it was experienced with other British flying units, but still affected operations to some extent.

Increased production of the O/400 in 1918 and the arrival of more squadrons on the Western Front meant the effectiveness of the Handley Page bombers increased as the war went on. Not only were targets hit more frequently and by larger numbers of aircraft, but the experience of the crews meant new tactics were developed to deal with certain types of target, be more accurate with the dropping of bombs, and be able to get themselves out of trouble, whether it presented itself in the form of anti-aircraft fire, enemy aircraft, or simply the weather conditions. The creation of 41st Wing and later Independent Force, bringing day and night bomber squadrons together to operate in the same area, gave the Handley Pages and their crews the chance to show the type to its full potential.

With the German 'Kaiserschlacht' spring offensive of 1918 eventually coming to a halt and then being turned back, and the 100 days advance following the Battle of Amiens on 8 August 1918, the switch was made to prioritising attacks on enemy railways and aerodromes closer behind the lines. This not only had a more immediate effect on the fighting, but also meant that individual aircraft and their crews could take part in two or even three sorties a night owing to the closer proximity of targets than before, whereas previously it would only be possible to do one trip a night on targets that were further behind the enemy lines.

As the numbers of Handley Pages operating over the Western Front increased, so too did the numbers of men killed operating them, either directly due to enemy action or accidents that were an all too common occurrence in aviation at the time, particularly at night time and in poor visibility, which became more common as 1918 stretched into autumn and then winter. The night of 16–17 September saw ten Handley Pages lost, seven due to enemy action. Fortunately this was a freak occurrence and the numbers lost on a single night came nowhere close to that number again, nor had it previously. As the weather worsened in late 1918, opportunities to use the Handley Pages were hampered, but it did not deter crews from trying when possible. The SN 1,650-lb bomb and Baby Incendiaries were used in greater numbers, as was the large 550-lb bomb. The Allies continued to advance on the ground, enabling Handley Page squadrons to move further forward following the advance where suitable. Back in Britain the new Handley Page Type V, even larger still, was created to conduct even longer range raids than the Type O was able to, specifically with Berlin in mind. This would be a reprisal raid on the enemy's capital rather than one with strategic targets in mind—since 1915 London had been attacked by] airships and then aeroplane, the Gotha and Zeppelin-Staaken R Type 'Giant' aeroplanes causing much damage, destruction, and loss of civilian life in London and the south-east in 1917 and 1918. As the war came to an end, the O/400 Squadrons on the Western Front prepared to bomb Berlin too, 216 Squadron being selected as the first to move to Prague following the Austrian surrender in early November 1918, from where they would be within operational reach of Berlin. The German signing of the Armistice on 11 November put a stop to these plans, as well as the imminent launching of the V/1500s of 166 Squadron at RAF Bircham Newton in Norfolk.

The effectiveness of the Handley Pages on the Western Front is difficult, if not impossible, to measure. The Handley Pages were mainly used against targets that would directly affect the war effort—U-boat bases, enemy aerodromes, railways (particularly junctions and bridges where damage had a larger effect than just damaging a single railway line), blast furnaces, and other industrial sites, and munitions works, as well as chemical factories producing gas for chemical warfare. The German airship and aeroplane raids on Britain did not, largely, seem to have these targets in mind, mainly focusing on civilians rather than specific factories or other targets; though there were exceptions, such as Liverpool Street Station in London suffering damage in 1917, it was nowhere near like the sole attention given to railways by Handley Page crews. As well as the difficulty of doing so, it is also perhaps inappropriate to try and judge the effectiveness of the Handley Page bombers on their own. It would be more appropriate to look at them in conjunction with the other RFC, RNAS, and RAF bomber crews they worked with—the crews of the Sopwith 1½ Strutters, Short Bombers, Airco DH4s, Airco DH9s, Airco DH9As, Royal Aircraft Factory FE2bs, and other types used to attack the enemy's industrial targets and munitions factories as well as their supply routes. By the formation of the Royal Air Force in April 1918, even scout aircraft, which previously were used predominantly for attacking enemy aircraft, were now being used as ground-attack aircraft, dropping light bombs and machine-gunning enemy targets at and behind the front line. Together with the shortage of raw materials caused by the naval blockade of Germany (which was also crippling the production of munitions and other items), when the Allies turned the tide in August 1918, aerial attacks on the Germans by day and night increased in ferocity until the Armistice.

From the women who helped build the aircraft through to the air mechanics who worked tirelessly to keep them operational in muddy fields on the Western Front, and the pilots and observers who flew long, uncomfortable, and dangerous missions to unleash their yellow 'pills' onto enemy targets, they all played their part in the victory of 1918 on the Western Front. The Handley Page had proved itself in other areas too. In 1917 a Handley Page O/100 made an incredible journey to the Aegean from where it was able to bomb Constantinople. The actual effects of the raid were minimal, but the propaganda value was immense. A single Handley Page that served with 1 Squadron Australian Flying Corps in the Middle East boosted Colonel T. E. Lawrence's presence there, greatly impressing the Arabs and finding use as a strategic bomber on Turkish targets.

After the war, Handley Page Limited found itself better off than other manufacturers who had built smaller aircraft. Although orders for military machines were cancelled and the type was too large for post-war service in the RAF, the size and carrying capacity made it highly suitable for conversion for civilian uses. The development of the Type O into a civilian airliner was easily within the grasp of Handley Page Limited, and laid the foundations of what would be a long tradition of successful large aircraft designs. Handley Page Limited ceased to exist when it went into voluntary liquidation in 1970, eight years after Frederick Handley Page died. The name of Handley Page is still synonymous with large aircraft, a number of which are preserved in museums. Sadly there are no complete original First World War Handley Page aircraft surviving, but what does survive is photos, film, and the testimonies of those who used them in action to keep alive the memory of the Bloody Paralysers and their crews.

Endnotes

Introduction

1. Murray Sueter, quoted by Chaz Boywer *Handley Page Bombers of the First World War* (Aston Publications, 1992) p.9
2. Charles Rumney Samson, quoted by C. H. Barnes, *Handley Page Aircraft since 1907* (Putnam, 1976) p.18

Chapter Two

1. Liddle Collection, University of Leeds, AIR 059, H. A. Buss
2. *Ibid.*
3. Paul Bewsher, *Green Balls: The Adventures of a Night-Bomber* (William Blackwood & Sons, 1919)

Chapter Three

1. *Handley Page Bomber, Type O/400, Descriptive Handbook* (Ministry of Munitions, 1918)
2. *Ibid.*
3. Liddle Collection, University of Leeds, AIR 096, L. A. Dell
4. Paul Bewsher, *Green Balls: The Adventures of a Night-Bomber* (William Blackwood & Sons, 1919)
5. *Details of Aerial Bombs* (Air Ministry, 1918)
6. *Ibid.*
7. *Ibid.*
8. *Ibid.*
9. *Ibid.*
10. *Ibid.*

11. *Ibid.*
12. Roy Shillinglaw, Interviews by Patrick Wilson—www.patrickwilson. com/RFC.html
13. *The Official History of the Ministry of Munitions, Volume XII—The Supply of Munitions*, (His Majesty's Stationery Office, 1919)
14. *Ibid.* Roy Shillinglaw
15. *Ibid.* Liddle Collection

Chapter Four

1. Paul Bewsher, *Green Balls: The Adventures of a Night-Bomber* (William Blackwood & Sons, 1919)
2. *Ibid.*
3. *Ibid.*
4. W. L. Wade, *The Flying Book, 1917* (Longmans Green & Co, 1917)
5. *Ibid.* Paul Bewsher
6. *Ibid.*
7. *Ibid.*
8. *Ibid.*
9. IWM Documents Collection, 4517, L. G. Semple
10. D. H. Montgomery, *Down the Flare Path* (J. Hamilton Ltd, 1937)
11. Liddle Collection, University of Leeds, AIR 096, L. A. Dell
12. H. B. Monaghan, *The Big Bombers of World War I* (JaaRE Publishing Inc, 1985)
13. *Ibid.*
14. Paul Bewsher, *The Daily Mail* 30th December 1918
15. Fritz Nagel, *Fritz—The World War I Memoir of a German Lieutenant* (Der Angriff Publications, 1981)

Chapter Five

1. Liddle Collection, University of Leeds, POW 109, H. A. Buss
2. Werner Fürbringer, *Fips—Legendary U-boat Commander, 1915-1918*, Werner Fürbringer, translated by Geoffrey Brooks (Pen & Sword Books translated edition, 1999)
3. *Ibid.* Liddle Collection
4. IWM Document Collection, 3754, H. A. Buss
5. *Ibid.*
6. IWM Sound Collection, 29, W. E. D. Wardrop
7. *Ibid.*

8. *Ibid.*
9. *Ibid.*
10. *Details of Aerial Bombs* (Air Ministry, 1918)
11. Paul Bewsher, *Green Balls: The Adventures of a Night-Bomber* (William Blackwood & Sons, 1919)
12. *Ibid.*
13. *Ibid.*
14. *Ibid.*
15. *Ibid.* IWM Sound Collection, 29
16. H. B. Monaghan, *The Big Bombers of World War I* (JaaRE Publishing Inc., 1985)
17. IWM Document Collection, 4137, A. E. Horn

Chapter Six

1. *A History of Number 16 Squadron, Royal Naval Air Service, renamed No 216 Squadron, Royal Air Force*
2. Trenchard, quoted by Neville Jones in *The Origins of Strategic Bombing—A Study of the Development of British Air Strategic Thought and Practice up to 1918* (William Kimber, 1973)
3. A. R. Kingsford, *Night Raiders of the Air* (John Hamilton, 1930)
4. *A History of Number 16 Squadron, Royal Naval Air Service, renamed No 216 Squadron, Royal Air Force*
5. *Ibid. A History of Number 16 Squadron, Royal Naval Air Service, renamed No 216 Squadron, Royal Air Force*
6. *Ibid.*
7. Liddle Collection, University of Leeds, AIR 258A, W. G. Hall
8. C. G. Burge, *The Annals of 100 Squadron—A Record of the War Activities of the Pioneer Night Bombing Squadron in France, March 1917 to November 1918* (Herbert Reiach Ltd, 1919)

Chapter Eight

1. Colonel T. E. Lawrence, *Seven Pillars of Wisdom*
2. *Ibid. Seven Pillars of Wisdom*

Chapter Nine

1. A. R. Kingsford, *Night Raiders of the Air* (John Hamilton, 1930)
2. IWM Document Collection, 4137, A. E. Horn
3. *Ibid.*
4. *Ibid.*

5. *Ibid.*
6. *Ibid.*
7. *Ibid.*
8. *Ibid.*
9. *Ibid.*
10. Paul Bewsher, *Green Balls: The Adventures of a Night-Bomber* (William Blackwood & Sons, 1919)
11. *Ibid.*
12. *Ibid.*
13. *Ibid.* IWM Document Collection, 4137
14. *Ibid.*
15. Quoted in *Results of Raids on Germany carried out by British Aircraft, 1ˢᵗ January to 30ᵗʰ September 1918*
16. IWM Sound Collection, 29, W. E. D. Wardrop
17. *Ibid.*
18. *Ibid.*
19. *Ibid.*
20. Fritz Nagel, *Fritz—The World War I Memoir of a German Lieutenant* (Der Angriff Publications, 1981)
21. *Ibid.* IWM Document Collection, 4137
22. *Ibid.*
23. Liddle Collection, University of Leeds, AIR 096, L. A. Dell
24. *Ibid.* IWM Document Collection, 4137
25. *Ibid. Results of Raids on Germany carried out by British Aircraft, 1ˢᵗ January to 30ᵗʰ September 1918*
26. H. B. Monaghan, *The Big Bombers of World War I* (JaaRE Publishing Inc, 1985)
27. *Ibid.*
28. *Ibid.*
29. IWM Document Collection, 10538, F. E. Rees
30. *Ibid.*
31. *Ibid.* Liddle Collection
32. Newspaper clipping in Liddle Collection, University of Leeds, AIR 096, L. A. Dell
33. *Ibid.* Liddle Collection
34. *Ibid.* IWM Sound Collection, 29
35. IWM Document Collection, 4517, L. G. Semple
36. *Ibid.* Fritz Nagel
37. *Ibid.* A. R. Kingsford
38. *Ibid.* IWM Document Collection, 4517
39. *Ibid.* Liddle Collection
40. *Ibid.*

41. *Ibid.*
42. *Ibid.*
43. *Ibid.* A. R. Kingsford
44. IWM Sound Collection, 4224, R. Shillinglaw
45. Roy Shillinglaw, Interviews by Patrick Wilson—www.patrickwilson. com/RFC.html
46. *Ibid.*
47. *Ibid.* H. B. Monaghan
48. *Ibid.* A. R. Kingsford
49. *Ibid.* Roy Shillinglawl
50. *Ibid.* H. B. Monaghan
51. *Ibid.*
52. *Ibid.*
53. *Ibid.*
54. IWM Document Collection, 4517
55. *Ibid.* H. B. Monaghan
56. *Ibid.*
57. *Ibid.*
58. *Ibid.*
59. *Ibid.* A. R. Kingsford

Chapter Ten

1. F. H. Chainey, *The Annals of 100 Squadron—A Record of the War Activities of the Pioneer Night Bombing Squadron in France, March 1917 to November 1918* (Herbert Reiach Ltd, 1919)
2. A. R. Kingsford, *Night Raiders of the Air* (John Hamilton, 1930)
3. H. B. Monaghan, *The Big Bombers of World War I* (JaaRE Publishing Inc, 1985)
4. *Ibid.*
5. *Ibid.*
6. *Ibid.*
7. Roy Shillinglaw, Interviews by Patrick Wilson—www.patrickwilson. com/RFC.html

Chapter Eleven

1. A. R. Kingsford, *Night Raiders of the Air* (John Hamilton, 1930)
2. IWM Sound Collection, 4224, R. Shillinglaw
3. IWM Document Collection, 4517, L. G. Semple

4. Liddle Collection, University of Leeds, AIR 258A, P. Young
5. IWM Sound Collection, 29, W. E. D. Wardrop
6. *Ibid.* IWM Sound Collection, 4224
7. *Ibid.* A. R. Kingsford
8. *Ibid.* IWM Sound Collection, 4224
9. *Ibid.* IWM Sound Collection, 29
10. *Ibid.* Liddle Collection
11. *Ibid.*
12. *A History of Number 16 Squadron, Royal Naval Air Service, renamed No 216 Squadron, Royal Air Force*
13. *Ibid.* IWM Document Collection, 4517
14. *Ibid.* IWM Document Collection, 4517
15. C. G. Burge, *The Annals of 100 Squadron—A Record of the War Activities of the Pioneer Night Bombing Squadron in France, March 1917 to November 1918* (Herbert Reiach Ltd, 1919)
16. *Ibid.* IWM Document Collection, 4517

Chapter Twelve

1. IWM Document Collection, 245, A. C. Kilburn
2. *Ibid.*

Chapter Thirteen

1. *A History of Number 16 Squadron, Royal Naval Air Service, renamed No 216 Squadron, Royal Air Force*

Chapter Fourteen

1. William Sholto Douglas, *Years of Combat* (The Quality Book Club, 1963)

Bibliography

Barker, R., *The Royal Flying Corps in France: From Mons to the Somme*, (Constable, 1995)

Barnes, C. H., *Handley Page Aircraft since 1907*, (Putnam, 1976)

Bartlett, C. P. O., *Bomber Pilot, 1916–1918*, (Littlehampton Book Services, 1974)

Bewsher, P., *Green Balls: The Adventures of a Night-Bomber*, (William Blackwood & Sons, 1919)

Bowyer, C., *Airmen of World War One—Men of the British and Empire Air Forces in Old Photographs*, (Arms & Armour, 1975)

Bowyer, C., *Handley Page Bombers of the First World War*, (Aston Publications, 1992)

Burge OBE, Maj. C. G., *The Annals of 100 Squadron—A Record of the War Activities of the Pioneer Night Bombing Squadron in France, March 1917 to November 1918*, (Herbert Reiach Ltd, 1919)

Cheesman, E. F., and Cole, C., *The Air Defence of Britain 1914-1918*, (Putnam, 1984)

Clark, A., *Aces High—War in the Air over the Western Front 1914–1918*, (Harper Collins, 1974)

Cormack, A. and Cormack, P., *British air Forces 1914–1918, Volume 2*, (Osprey Publishing, 2001)

Davies, R. E. G., *British Airways—an Airline and its Aircraft, Volume 1: 1919–1939, the Imperial Years*, (Paladwr Press, 2005)

Davis, M., *AIRCO—The Aircraft Manufacturing Company*, (Corwood Press, 2001)

Details of Aerial Bombs, (Air Ministry, 1918)

Easdiwb, M., and Genth, T., *A Glint in the Sky—German Air Attacks on Folkestone, Dover, Ramsgate, Margate and other Kentish Towns*, (Leo Cooper, 2004)

Ed. Harding, E. D., revised Chapman, P., *A History of Number 16 Squadron, Royal Air Service, renamed 216 Squadron, Royal Air Force*, (2009)

Fegan, T., *The 'Baby Killers'—German Air Raids on Britain in the First World War*, (Leo Cooper, 2002)

Fredette, R. H., *The Sky on Fire—The First Battle of Britain 1917–1918*, (Smithsonian Institution Press, 1976)

Fürbringer, W., *Fips—Legendary U-boat Commander, 1915–1918*, transl. Brooks, G., (Pen & Sword Books, 1999)

Gibson, R. H., and Prendergast, M., *The German Submarine War 1914–1918*, (Naval & Military Press, 2003)

Gray, E., *The U-boat War, 1914–1918*, (Pen & Sword Books, 2004)

Gustin, Dr E., and Williams, A. G., *Flying Guns World War I*, (Airlife Publishing, 2004)

Handley Page Bomber, Type O/400, Descriptive Handbook, (1918)

Hanson, N., *First Blitz—The Secret German Plan to Raze London to the Ground in 1918*, (Doubleday, 2008)

Hart, P., *1918—A Very British Victory*, (Weidenfeld & Nicholson, 2009)

Hart, P., *Aces Falling—War Above the Trenches, 1918*, (Weidenfeld & Nicholson, 2007)

Hart, P., and Steel, N., *Passchendaele—The Sacrificial Ground*, (Weidenfeld & Nicholson, 2001)

Hart, P., *Bloody April—Slaughter in the Skies over Arras, 1917*, (Weidenfeld & Nicholson, 2006)

Hart, P., *Gallipoli*, (Profile Books, 2011)

Hart, P., *Somme Success—The Royal Flying Corps and the Battle of the Somme, 1916*, (Leo Cooper, 2001)

Harvey, W. J., *Rovers of the Night Sky*, (Greenhill Books, 1920)—pseudonym 'Night Hawk' MC

Jackson, A. J., *British Civil Aircraft 1919–59 Volume 2*, (Putnam, 1960)

Jager, H., *German Artillery of World War One*, (Crowood Press, 2001)

Jefford, C. G., *Observers and Navigators, and other Non-Pilot Aircrew in the RFC, RNAS and RAF*, (Crowood, 2001)

Jones, N., *The Origins of Strategic Bombing—A Study of the Development of British Air Strategic Thought and Practice up to 1918*, (William Kimber, 1973)

Kingsford, A. R., *Night Raiders of the Air*, (John Hamilton, 1930)

Lawrence, Col. T. E., *Seven Pillars of Wisdom*, (1926)

Lewis, C., *Farewell to Wings*, (Temple Press, 1964)

Messimer, D. R., *Find and Destroy—Antisubmarine Warfare in World War I*, (Naval Institute Press, 2003)

Messimer, D. R., *Verschollen—World War I U-boat Losses*, (Naval Institute Press, 2002)

Millar, L., *The Chronicles of 55 Squadron RFC and RAF*, (Unwin Brother, 1919)

Monaghan, Lt H. B., *The Big Bombers of World War I*, (JaaRE Publishing Inc., 1985)

Montgomery, D. H., *Down the Flare Path*, (J. Hamilton Ltd, 1937)

Morris, A., *First of the Many—The Story of Independent Force, RAF*, (Jarrolds, 1969)

Nagel, F., *Fritz—The World War I Memoir of a German Lieutenant*, (Der Angriff Publications, 1981)

Pitt, B., *Zeebrugge—Eleven VC's Before Breakfast*, (Phoenix, 2003)

Robertson, B., *Bombing Colours: British Bomber Camouflage and Markings, 1914–37*, (Patrick Stephens, 1972)

Samson, C. R., *Fights and Flights—A Memoir of the Royal Naval Air Service in World War I*, (Ernest Benn, 1930)

Semple, C., *Diary of a Night Bomber Pilot in World War I*, (Spellmount, 2008)

Sherwood, T., *Coming In to Land—A Short History of Hounslow, Hanworth, and Heston Aerodromes 1911–1946*, (Heritage Publications, 1999)

The Official History of the Ministry of Munitions, Volume XII: The Supply of Munitions, (1919)

Watson, J. H., *Aces High at Redcar—the History of Redcar Royal Naval Air Station 1915 to 1919*, (2014)

Sources

Interviews by Patrick Wilson with Roy Shillinglaw—www.patrickwilson.com/RFC.html

Liddle Collection

AIR 096—Dell, Leslie Alexander
AIR 106—Ellison, H. R. W.
AIR 286—Shillinglaw, Roy
AIR 351—Wilkings, Thomas Oliver
POW 109—Buss, H. A.
AIR 127—Fry, Hubert Owen
AIR 355—Wilson, Hugh Brian
AIR 258A—Box, C.
AIR 258A—Castle, G.
AIR 258A—Hall, W. G.
AIR 258A—Young, P.

Imperial War Museum Documents Archive

1495—Private papers of E. C. Carpenter
245—Private papers of A. C. Kilburn
501—Private papers of E. Q. Cockcroft
4014—Private papers of J. B. Lacy
3754—Private papers of H. A. Buss
4137—Private papers of A. E. Horn
4517—Private papers of L. G. Semple
4807—Private papers of D. R. Goudie
10538—Private papers of F. E. Rees
11505—Private papers of C. E. Wilkins

Imperial War Museum Sound Archive

29—Wardrop, W. E. D.
4224—Shillinglaw, R.
9469—Morton, F. A.